# WHO LOVES
# DIES WELL

## On the Brink

## of Buddha's Pure Land

# D. J. Brazier

First published by O Books, 2007
O Books is an imprint of John Hunt Publishing Ltd.,
The Bothy, Deershot Lodge, Park Lane, Ropley, Hants, SO24 0BE, UK
office1@o-books.net
www.o-books.net

Distribution in:

UK and Europe
Orca Book Services
orders@orcabookservices.co.uk
Tel: 01202 665432 Fax: 01202 666219 Int. code (44)

USA and Canada
NBN
custserv@nbnbooks.com
Tel: 1 800 462 6420 Fax: 1 800 338 4550

Australia and New Zealand
Brumby Books
sales@brumbybooks.com.au
Tel: 61 3 9761 5535 Fax: 61 3 9761 7095

Far East (offices in Singapore, Thailand, Hong Kong, Taiwan)
Pansing Distribution Pte Ltd
kemal@pansing.com
Tel: 65 6319 9939 Fax: 65 6462 5761

South Africa
Alternative Books
altbook@peterhyde.co.za
Tel: 021 447 5300 Fax: 021 447 1430

Text copyright David Brazier 2007

.

Design: Stuart Davies

ISBN 978 1 84694 045 3

Printed in the US by Maple Vail

# WHO LOVES
# DIES WELL

On the Brink

of Buddha's Pure Land

## D. J. Brazier

BOOKS

Winchester, UK
Washington, USA

**Author of**

*A Guide to Psychodrama*

*Beyond Carl Rogers: Toward a Psychotherapy for the 21$^{st}$ Century*

*Zen Therapy*

*The Feeling Buddha*

*The New Buddhism*

# CONTENTS

ONE

# INTRODUCTION TO A SIMPLE FAITH

**Starting the Journey**

**Say the name** of Amida Buddha: "Namo Amida Bu", and you
will go to heaven and partake of the eternal life of the Buddha instead
of the eternal deadness of karmic existence. What an absurd idea, you
might think. Yet, this is the belief of millions of Buddhists. In this book,
we will be exploring this approach to spirituality that is, in one sense,
completely alien to what many people are used to, and yet, as we
penetrate it, turns out to answer so many of our fundamental questions
about the meaning of life.

This, then, is a book about Amidism. Amidism, which is also called
Pureland, is a form of Buddhism. It claims to be the original spiritual
core of the religion of enlightenment discovered by Gautama
Shakyamuni in India 2500 years ago. Buddhism is Buddha's teaching,
but even more importantly, it is a relationship with Buddha and the most
fundamental act of any relationship is to turn toward the other, to call
out to them and to be open to their call to you.

To truly call to the other, however, one must know them in a certain
way. To know someone is not to encounter cells and hormones, nor is it
to be taken in by surface appearance; it is to penetrate the meaning of
their being in a sensitive, intuitive way – a multidimensional way that
can only with utmost difficulty be reduced to the linear flow of words.
To know the Buddha is not so much to have met the man who lived
in India and died a long time ago as to meet and be touched by the
spirit of spiritual exuberance that animated that man and that seems to
inhabit our world too. It is the ecstasy of those whose lives are touched
by eternity. That spirit that is the universal fount of mystical religion is

Nyorai Amida.

This is a tale of faith, love, grace and death. It is both personal and of universal implication. The Amidist believes that Amida calls to everyone, yet specifically calls to each of us, singularly – and that that call is the most important thing that there is to life. Pureland is the kind of religion that is almost impossible to talk about without personal reference. To do so would be like describing one's closest friend by giving an account of the disposition of her bones. Theory is not enough – except in that original sense of the word theory when, back in ancient Greece, it meant reflection upon theos – holy things – and, even then, we have to acknowledge right at the outset that Amidism is a religion of the heart before it is of the head. To convey it to you, therefore, I must have recourse to real life, and real life we must also concede is nothing without a consideration of the reality of death.

**Why tell this tale?** At a time when the world is spiritually adrift there is surely a need for reflection upon the great existential issues. Why are we here? What does living a good life mean in the circumstance we find ourselves in? Do words like noble mean anything anymore? Is secularism enough? Does it satisfy? Can we consume our way to happiness? What do we make of our life when we look at it soberly? What is death? Why be good? Humans ask such questions. To do so is as much part of what we are as having hands and feet. This book, therefore, is both an account of some very personal matters and also a musing upon themes that are vital to us: how to live and how to die well.

Amidism has philosophy. Many of its great sages were deeply learned. But learning was not what they valued most, nor even rationality or wisdom. They tried to answer life's problems in a different, more intuitive way first. They answered and they still answer by a direct appeal to the heart and the reestablishment of faith at the centre of our lives. Only thus is rationality grounded in experience. This book, therefore, is a defence and vindication of the life of faith. In one sense, it is absurd. Amidism is unquestionably a way for fools. The philosophy of Amidism is not a search for wise answers. It is rather a reflection upon our foolish nature. The word Buddha means one who wakes up. Amidism would have us wake up to the fact that we are, in a rather particular sense, complete fools.

One way in which we are fools is that we are dependent. We come into this world in a state of extreme vulnerability and dependency. Buddhism calls this our dependent origination. We do not generate ourselves. We come from other causes. We then grow up and try to convince ourselves that we are independent beings. However, it is never true. I do not mean this in some grand mystical sense – just in the ordinary sense that we depend on others – other people, other creatures, other forces of nature – for everything. In particular, when we are little, we depend on mother. Mother is not always one's biological mother, though usually it is. Mother keeps us alive. She feeds and shelters us. She puts up with our noise, our smells, our mess, our incessant demands. Not only does she put up with it, but she cherishes us. Sometimes she loses her patience with us, but these times are vastly out numbered by the times when she benefits us. We intrude on her life plans in a major way and she responds. Yet, do we feel grateful? What do we do to repay this debt? When we soberly reflect upon life, we may come to see that we are and have endlessly been fools, completely failing to appreciate the nature of the situation in which we live, which is one in which we are upheld by others at every turn. We are the beneficiaries of near miracles and great beneficence day in day out – yet we feel burdened and oppressed much of the time due to our foolish sense of self-entitlement that is so precious to us. Locked up in conceit, the average person finds it very difficult to really call out to the grace that surrounds and ever holds us. In Buddhism, there are many words for that grace. The name of the religion itself, Dharma, means that which holds. It is identified with reality itself and with the teachings of Buddhas. Buddhas appear in the world merely to point it out. Most people are, however, too locked up in the vortex of self-concern to listen or look. This obstinacy is called *avidya* – "not looking". When we look – *vidya* – we feel the overwhelmingly powerful urge to cry out. Then ages of tension built into our being fall away. Whatever language we use, we call out to the grace. that holds us, always held us, always will hold us. We feel ashamed, relieved, liberated, and motivated. This cathartic experience, which Amidists call *shinjin*, seems to me to be not just the root of one religion, but the root of them all.

**My own mother**, Irene Brazier, was very English. She was born in Northampton, in the centre of England, of a family that had lived in the same town for as many generations as anybody could remember. She was brought up in a nominally Christian faith. She imbibed a sense of humane values as much from poetry as from church or schooling. Such poets as Kipling, Tennyson, Keats, Coleridge, de la Mare, Rupert Brooke and others, not to mention Shakespeare, filled her life with imagery and quotations for all occasions. Given that she was the daughter of publicans who had hardly a book in the house, this was rather remarkable. I never found out when poetry had first obtained its hold on her life, but I benefited. My mother was very English: practical, down to earth, a lover of gardens and of nature, and of England, having a high regard for the culture of her native land. She was brought up in a lower middle class social ambiance. She passed her exams and went to grammar school. When she was 17 war broke out. She joined the women's air force and became a radar operative. She fell in love and married a pilot. I was born as part of "the bulge" – the post war surge in the birth rate that followed demobilisation. My mother believed that "god helps those who help themselves," but also that "it is better to be safe than sorry." Her religion was otherwise non-doctrinal. Later in life she developed an interest in yoga and vegetarianism. In her old age she came to live with her son and, finally, was buried by the rites of Pureland Buddhism. Slightly eccentric, but very English, one might still say.

I, myself, steeped in the values she gave me, have also, like many of my generation, turned my eyes to the East and slowly, as life has unfolded, found my place in the Far Eastern faith; only gradually, in my own English way, discovering what it really means to do so, what it is to trust Nyorai completely. In her later years Mother joined me and we shared this important journey together. I will say more about this later. In particular, in the core of this book, I will share with you what I passed through with her in her final days and hours and I hope that through sharing these things I will be able to convey to you the sense of faith that can only be obtained from lived example. Perhaps in this way I can pass on something of what this faith now means to me, and how it has slowly but surely come to pervade life, death and everything.

**This book attempts several things**. It is, to some extent, a book written on demand. Friends have been urging me for some time to write something they can understand about Amidism. Whether I have succeeded, they must judge. Secondly, it is a book written out of personal need: a kind of therapy for myself. Thirdly, I would like to offer something to counter, at least to some degree, a popular tendency to view Buddhism as a kind of secular practice that has nothing to do with faith or religion. Buddhism has become in a small way established in the West, but I feel a small correction of course is needed if it is not just to become another item of conspicuous consumption in the spiritual supermarket. What you will read here, like it or not, is a thoroughly religious approach. Fourthly, and somewhat by the same token, I hope to make this a small contribution to thought about religion in general, given that we now live in a multi-faith world. And finally, but by no means least, I wish to say some things about death and the relation between faith and enlightenment in this life, whatever religious frame they may be couched in, and how faith and enlightenment bear upon that ultimate and unavoidable challenge: how to die well.

In some respects, therefore, the book is an introduction. I hope it conveys the spirit and general tenor of Amidist thought and feeling. It is not comprehensive. One cannot do justice to a tradition of two and a half millennia distributed across half of Asia and now entering the Western world in a single book. In particular, I do not here attempt to cover the distinctions within the tradition between different denominations, nor do I cover the stories and doctrines specific to the major Pureland Sutras. Perhaps there may be time to deal with those matters in subsequent volumes at a later date.

Each faith community has its jargon. If you want to enjoy this book, I am afraid that you will have to get used to mine, though I hope not to make it too burdensome. As we continue here you should acquire the rudiments of what Amidism is about and acquire, as it were, a map and a vocabulary. To assist, there is a glossary at the back.

Each religious denomination is rather like a language. The things that Amidists say are not necessarily any different from what followers of other creeds say, but we say them in our language. Translation, as any linguist will tell you, has many pitfalls. There is nothing quite like reading something in the original, so it is better for me to write in my language and try to help you to understand it. I hope you will bear with me and that you will enjoy the process. If I lose you, I'm sorry.

At the same time, as the main writing for this work was done a mere six months after my mother passed on, and as Amidism is much concerned with the life-death boundary, I am here reflecting on her departure in a particularly raw way. This is a very personal matter for me, but I will try to share with you as openly as I can what happened at that time and what it meant to me.

The Buddhism that you encounter in this book is not a set of self-improvement techniques, nor an intellectual pursuit – though it can satisfy the intellect if you wish – but is, more particularly, a faith to live and die by. It is not something that is designed to make one grand and famous, nor a method of avoiding the dilemmas and responsibilities that come our way. It is more like a mirror that shows us the very depths of our being, but does so, not by introspection, but by examining our encounters – our awareness of all that is not self. This then is a spirituality oriented toward otherness.

**Life is encounter**. There is no escape. Wherever we go we continue to encounter otherness and the power of what we encounter is massively greater than our own potency. Buddhism begins with a reflection upon our origins in dependency. Whence comes this body? Whence our food? The air we breathe? Our good or bad fortune? The things upon which our survival depends? We are dependent in a million ways. The feelings elicited by contemplation of this situation of the totally dependent origins of everything we think of as ours – and, indeed, of everything else we meet in this world – are so strong that we may spend much of our life keeping them at bay. We like to think that what matters about our life is ourselves, but the actual experience of life is of otherness. Buddhism talks of *shunyata* – the state of realizing that otherness is all there is. You and I think that we exist, but it is impossible to find anything in us that does not have its origin elsewhere. All our form, feelings, ideas, mentality, – everything we call self – derives from elsewhere. One incidental consequence is that we are ephemeral. Everything is impermanent, because everything depends on other things. We live in a universe characterised by decay. This is the human spiritual predicament – our deepest intuitions and our observations and reason conflict.

Amidism is a faith that juxtaposes the eternal and the ephemeral and finds in the irresolvable tension between them the springs of grace and love, acceptance and fortitude, a good life and a good death.

## Faith and Faiths

**Amidism is a denomination of Buddhism** among other denominations. This book is written from the perspective of Amida Pureland Buddhism. Pureland is not well-known in Western countries. There are Pureland Buddhists of the Jodoshin School in North America. The majority of them are descendants of Japanese immigrants. There are also some practitioners of Pureland who derive from Chinese or Vietnamese traditions. The forms of Buddhism that have gained large numbers of converts among Caucasian North Americans and Europeans have, however, generally been of a rather different flavour. For many Westerners, Buddhism is virtually synonymous with meditation practice and with a rather secularised and philosophical approach to life centred on such concepts as non-duality and Buddha nature. This book is somewhat different in perspective.

Pureland originated in India, grew up in China and flowered all over the orient, in China, Japan, Korea and Vietnam. Pureland is more than simply a denomination. It is more of a movement with many shades of interpretation. It is the devotional or faith oriented tendency within Buddhism. Specifically Pureland denominations occur in Japan, China and Vietnam but the devotional tendency that it represents is widespread through many others areas also. Pureland, in one form or another, is currently, and has been through much of history, the most popular form of Buddhist spirituality in the Far East. Its arrival in the West is, therefore, in one sense, overdue.

In the Far East, Pureland is the most widespread form of practised Buddhism. Its branches are the largest denominations in Japan and Pureland, either as a separate denomination or as a dominant or co-dominant tendency within other schools and is at the heart of what it means to be Buddhist in the Chinese-speaking world as in Mongolia, Tibet and Vietnam. Most Tibetan monastics pray every day to be reborn in the Pure Land of Amida ("Amitabha") Nyorai. Even in the southern

Buddhist countries where the form of Buddhism is called Theravada, the essential Amidist features of devotionalism, modest gratitude, and reliance upon faith and grace are far more significant features of religion as practised by the mass of people than most Westerners realize.

**Buddhism is one faith among other faiths**. We now, most of us, realize that we live in a multi-faith world and those who are serious about their faith must either adopt a very closed minded position, something I find hardly tenable, or must seek to fathom the significance of this diversity, or can seek to avoid the whole issue by sinking into the kind of relativism that just assumes that "one is as good as another". Religious diversity must tell us something about the human condition. Why are humans religious? We can wonder at the fact that religion seems to be part of human society everywhere. Even officially atheistic societies have not been able to do without ceremonial forms and rites of passage and, in fact, such societies have often been even more dependent upon orthodoxy of belief systems than many of their neighbours.

We can seek to find common ground by examining what many faiths have in common. We can appreciate that creativity plays a part in religion as in all human activities and this inevitably brings diversity in its train. We can also reflect upon the questions that faith addresses. This book is not a work on comparative religion, but the questions posed by such comparison are never far away and they, therefore, form one sub-plot of this story.

There are those who think that faith is now redundant. Faith is thought of as somehow in opposition to fact or science or realism. However, a review of facts does not, of itself, yield meanings. Knowing what one's life consists of does not, in itself, tell one how to live well. Know-how does not yield wisdom. There is more to life than an inventory of its components could ever reveal. Somehow each of us has to assemble those components in a meaningful manner and must do so without prior guarantees. To do so is an act – or a whole series of acts – of faith. In this sense, and it is a very important sense as far as this book is concerned, faith is an essential part of every life, even of the life of those who reject the idea of faith in principle. Even their rejection is simply their way of conducting their experiment with their life – it is a chance they take and they place their faith in that.

The investigation that I make here into my own faith is offered less in the spirit of assertion of a preferred course – though I do believe in its particular excellences – and more in that of an offering of my faith as one of the species of faiths in general. A concrete example helps us to reflect on the important questions. What do faiths as a whole signify? What truth or reality about life do they reflect? What is the nature of faith *per se*? In this sense, I hope the book can be a contribution to inter-faith understanding and also to the elucidation of the importance of faith to those who are not particularly affiliated to a single creed, yet have some feeling for the spiritual need that pervades human life.

## Personal and Universal

**Life comes to life at its limit.** In order to convey the spirit rather than merely the outline of this faith, I shall attempt the task through a particularly personal approach. This approach is to invite you to share in my reflections upon the last week of my mother's life. The ending of life is, perhaps, the time when one's faith is most clearly tried, and the end of the life of one's nearest and dearest is similarly testing. That week was an irreplaceable time, an eternal time, a time when the eternal touched all of us who were involved. As death became real, life became more real – much more real – than it usually is. This is an experience that many readers will be able to relate to. I shall, here, therefore, invite you to accompany me as I revisit these events and through them we can muse together what it is that matters in this existence twixt birth and death and hereafter. What should we do? How should we be, such that, when our time comes, we shall not look back down the years past with eyes of regret, but with settled peace in our heart?

To do this I will have to take you into my confidence and share things that are intimate and personally moving. Obviously I have made some judgments about how far to go in this respect. What is presented would, I am confident, meet with my mother's approval. I have not departed from the facts. I am aided by the circumstance that I kept a journal during that time. None of the events or occurrences mentioned are fiction. All the characters are real. Of course, my own perception enters in and insofar as there is error it is entirely of my own inadvertent construction.

**Death is universal** for living beings and because this is so, the world around us is both beautiful and terrible, often the same phenomenon appearing in both guises simultaneously. Autumn leaves are beautiful tokens of death; they stir both awe and melancholy. Need one speak of sunsets? Or of the cheetah springing upon the buck, magnificent and deadly? Such is life in this world. Religion heightens such sensibility. Yet, religion is still something made in this imperfect world by these imperfect beings. It may be inspired by the beyond, but it is transmitted on this side with the imperfection that that necessarily implies.

Religion I take to be the human attempt to reach out toward that which is more perfect than this life in which we find ourselves. We, as the existentialists say, find ourselves as if thrown here into an existence that seems hardly of our choosing where many things are amiss. There is war and strife, there are carnal and carnivorous passions. There is greed and folly. There are limitations. We do not live a thousand years. We are rarely completely free from discomfort and some live lives of unremitting pain. We do not get all we wish for and we get much we might wish to be free of. Even the functioning of our very minds and feelings seems to defy control. Somehow, in the midst of this we face the challenge of living a life noble and true, of touching or being touched by beauty, love, and peace, by infinity and eternity. In the very midst of finite things, religion orientates us to measurelessness, to eternal and transcendent verity, and, in doing so, throws into sharp relief the way that actuality differs from the ideal.

## Taking Imperfection as Foundation

**Mortals are limited and imperfect**. It is a central part of the metaphysic of Amidism to acknowledge fully the less than perfect status of the person and of this world. In modern Western culture there is a widespread tendency toward that kind of humanism that lauds humanity as the pinnacle of creation. We call ourselves *homo sapiens*, "wise men", and think that arranging everything to suit human convenience will bring paradise in its wake. Such a policy has, however, brought us to the threshold of ecological disaster. Lauding ourselves we have got out of joint with the larger scheme of things of which we are, if we would but acknowledge it, merely one tiny parasitic part. Surely we need to step back from this self over-valuation and be willing to recognize ourselves as less than omniscient, less than all-important; in fact, as continually prone to err.

In Pureland, the key term here is a word from Japanese, *bombu*. Bombu indicates a foolish being of wayward passion. This is what we are. Amidism, though it points out perfection, is not perfectionist. It recognizes that we are weak, vulnerable, fallible, prey to a million karmic obstacles, and liable to make mistakes at almost every turn. To those who, like myself, have previously attempted to practice more exacting recipes for the spiritual path, Pureland may come as a blessed relief, a breath of realism. Taking on fully the limitation inherent in mortal nature, however, by direct implication, also suggests the possibility, in principle at least, of another kind of world, quite unlike this one, a world where all is well. That other world is called the Pure Land. We write Pureland as one word when indicating the doctrine, as two words when referring to that posited realm of bliss: the heaven we long for.

**Religions are also bombu.** If this ordinary existence is, as Amidism asserts, a world populated by bombu, then must it not follow that the religions made by humans are likewise bombu, similarly limited, vulnerable and fallible? It seems to me that this perspective – what we might call the bombu paradigm – is of immense importance in the liberation of humankind. We are foolish beings and we naturally reach out for something more. Spirituality thus plays a crucial part in our lives. But our spirituality is inevitably the spirituality of foolish beings. We live in a universe of imperfect faiths: bombu religions and bombu cultures. The world has suffered hugely from both of the extremes that arise from denying this evident reality. At one extreme there are those that assert that such and such a faith is perfect, complete, final and divine. This drives them to arrogance immediately and iniquity soon after. At the other extreme are those who reject faith because the faiths they find are imperfect – and thereby deprive themselves of the deepest satisfactions known and cut themselves off from the core wisdom that humankind has distilled through its encounter with the beyond over innumerable generations. In the train of this amputation comes cynicism, and the mean mindedness that is cultivated under the rubric of a certain kind of supposed "realism".

Modern people seem to have become somehow trapped between these options of arrogance or amputation. So, let me invite you, rather, to believe that there are many worthwhile religions in this world, none perfect, none final, each worthy attempts on the part of folk like you and I to satisfy that intuition of glory that illumines our hearts and sometimes succeeds in lifting us to heights of rapture and deeds of true altruism and devotion. I suggest that the religions are the finest achievements of the human spirit, surpassing even art, science, literature and every other aspect of high culture, yet they are none of them perfect, any more than art, science or literature are ever perfect. They have character. My own religion is no exception to this rule. It points out the perfect, as do they all, like so many fingers indicating the moon in the sky, but the finger is not the moon itself.

I appreciate that this doctrine of religious fallibility, so fundamental to Amidism, may be difficult for those in certain theistic religions who believe in a perfect or final revelation. However, even if God spoke directly to this or that prophet or son of god, still whatever it was that God said to him has been transmitted to us by beings and measures that are not God. Transmission is imperfect – always bombu. Even if the words remain pristine, they do not mean today exactly what they meant when the god spoke them. Even if Allah spoke directly to Mahomet, he had to do so in Arabic and Arabic, like any language, is a human artefact and one that undergoes evolution over time as culture changes. Associations of particular words thus shift. Who is, therefore, to know exactly what Allah meant – only Allah could know. All actual religions are, therefore, bombu. This does not invalidate them. Quite the converse. It is the attempt to claim for them something that cannot be true – infallibility – that brings them into disrepute.

**Spiritually we are all equal**. We are now into an age in the history of the world where it behoves us to recognize that there are many faiths and cultures and that each is more or less as noble and as foolish as the others. To recognize the more or less equal dignity of each would be a major step toward cultural maturity and could help us avoid untold bloodshed and tears. To recognize that each faith is no more and no less than a fallible human attempt would be a similarly large stride toward sanity, providing the spiritual life with a legitimate place at the same time as avoiding the hubris that has too often brought the purveyors of religion and even the idea of religion itself into such disrepute; something that has, as it were, poisoned the spiritual water supply and left modern people desiccated at heart.

Amidism is *bombu shin gyo*. Shin means faith. Gyo means practice or practical life. So Pureland is faith and practice for foolish beings. It is a religion tailored to ordinary people. It is not something that requires extensive academic education. A simple faith may, indeed, come more naturally to the uneducated. Even if you are wise, skilled and learned, just set it aside and realize that beneath this veneer you are an ordinary being like anybody else.

**Life has a vertical and a horizontal dimension**. The vertical is the dimension of worldly thinking. When we think in worldly terms there is some hierarchy involved. This is worth more than that. This is more beautiful, more desirable, better paid, higher status, more popular, or whatever, than that. The way of the world is comparison, judgement, status seeking. It is a race with winners and losers, high and low, good and bad. Everything is measured on a vertical scale. Consequently there are hordes of unwanted people, those who are at or near the bottom of the vertical dimension – at least as it has been established by the rich and powerful. Verticalism leads to exclusionism and it is one of the plagues of the contemporary world. The spiritual way is horizontalism. This is the Amidist way of thinking. In the spirit we are all the same. We are born, we die; we have a capacity for religious awe; we are fallible. We are all similarly loved by Nyorai.

To Westerners, brought up in a different tradition, it is quite natural to think of the human as the horizontal and the religious as the vertical. Even Stephen Batchelor in his book *Alone with Others: An existential approach to Buddhism* [1] does so. Yet, from an Amidist perspective it is clear that it is the Dharma that is horizontal[2]. It is bombu humans who create vertical structures and who are constantly judging and ranking everything – even to the extent of judging people according to how judgmental they are. Only the Dharma is horizontal, always equal, and unconditional. Only a Buddha does not condemn. The idea of a religion that does not condemn may be quite difficult for some people to accommodate, but it is the key to understanding Pureland. We are up-held by grace whatever our merit. Religious transformation comes through insight into this encompassing reality. We do not rectify our lives because a God judges us. We do so precisely because nobody judges us but ourselves.

**The horizontal dimension is the plane of spirituality**. In the eyes of Amida Nyorai we are equal. Whatever we may be in the world, kings or slaves, saints or villains, paupers or millionaires, we are loved by Buddha in just the same way. The vision, or samadhi, to use a Buddhist word, of spirituality is the samadhi of equality. To be spiritually advanced does not mean to be higher than anybody. The real sages of whatever religion are those who saw through such social pretension and learned to see themselves and everybody else just as Buddha sees us – every one special and unique yet all equal. Spirituality means horizontalization.

This also means that real religion is about grace rather than achievement. It is a free gift. It is not a matter of accomplishment. When we receive something as a grace, it means that we did not do anything to deserve it. It was simply given. The spirit of unconditional giving is very close to the core of what religion is really about. We do not earn the air we breathe. We do not earn our life. All manner of things happen to us. We live in an ocean of grace. Those who belong to theistic religions think of this grace as God's gift. In Buddhism we think that we are part of something much bigger than ourselves. The grace that surrounds us is just part of the great unfolding of causes and conditions. Yet, very important amongst these conditions is the fact that myriads of beings throughout time and space have, at one time or another, been touched by this samadhi of grace and equality. Being touched, their lives have been transformed. Their actions springing from this awakening have sewn this world thick with gracious conditions that continue to bless us. They remain present for us in spirit, or, to put it more Buddhistically, in enjoyment. The enjoyment body of Buddha is a constant presence that never fails. We fail. We fail to appreciate it. But it does not. It waits for us.

Amidism thus encompasses the mystery of life without flying in the face of what humans have learnt through science and it inspires a loving and gracious way of life without setting up the carrot of a hierarchy of spiritual achievements nor the stick of divine judgement hanging over all. Whether we do good or harm is up to us. Buddha advises, but does not punish. Eternity beckons but does not coerce. Buddha smiles on all. Sometimes it is a wistful smile for only he completely sees how much trouble we bring upon ourselves.

## Life in Community

**For the last eight years of her life**, my mother lived with my wife and Me and Buddhist friends in a small religious community that was initially sited in Newcastle upon Tyne and then, in 2001, relocated to the village of Narborough in Leicestershire. Mother loved the new house, especially for its garden and it is a matter of lasting satisfaction to me that we made this move while she was still active enough to enjoy it. Gardens are, of course, Pure Lands in miniature. The duty of a Purelander is to create miniature, even if imperfect, replicas of heaven wherever one dwells to the best of one's limited ability, and in this task mother was particularly gifted.

The miniature Pure Lands that one makes may be gardens or they may be a room welcoming to guests or an office or workplace aesthetically pleasing while also well adapted to its purpose. Even a single object that by its symbolism or its innate quality brings one to an unburdened state of mind fulfils this intention. A Buddhist shrine is a focus for worship, and it is also a miniature Pure Land. For Amidists, heaven is near to the centre of attention; a celebration of life's fecundity and a preparation for its end.

The faith practised in our little community has come to be called Amida-shu, or the Amida School. We believe that the things set in motion by Buddhas during their lifetimes do not cease with their death, but in some mysterious way continue to work on the world or, rather that the things that they do in their lifetimes are echoes of the other world that only they see clearly but of which many of us have intuitions and evidential glimpses from time to time. Nyorai Amida is a figure of mythology, the hero of tales told by Shakyamuni Buddha. Shakyamuni lived in this world 2500 years ago in India. He was the founder of Buddhism. He told his disciples about many Buddhas other than himself, and especially about Amida. Amida made a Pure Land in the West. Amida-shu is inspired by such a vision.

The practices of Amida-shu derive particularly from the Japanese tradition of Pureland and from the initiative of a religious reformer called Honen Shonin (1133-1212) who in 1175 descended from the holy Mount Hiei in Japan and began to spread the simple truth of Pureland to the mass of the general population, liberating Buddhism from its former status as an upper class preserve. Honen brought the Nyorai out of the monasteries, mansions and palaces into the world and popularised the practice of everyday devotion through the use of the single line prayer "Namo Amida Bu", which is a condensation of "I, a foolish ordinary being, cry out to Amida, the Nyorai of limitless grace." Nyorai's light of grace shines on all alike, not just on the rich, not just on the powerful, not just on the clever, not just on the good.

**This simple prayer**, "Namo Amida Bu", is called the *nembutsu*, which literally means "remembering Nyorai". It is a very easy practice that does not require years of training or special intelligence. It invites reflection and, through regular use, becomes a way of transforming everything one does into spiritual life, because, whatever one does, one calls the Buddha to assist. One's life thus becomes a witness to the sacred. Whether it is going or coming, standing or sitting, living or dying, "Namo Amida Bu," and Nyorai is there.

So this simple faith and practice is the foundation of our community. As with everything else, we do not think that our community is the ultimate community or the one and only spiritual way. It is not perfect in any sense. It dwells and functions within the bombu paradigm. The effect of this paradigm, however, is to generate a sense of fellow-feeling. It liberates us. We are not liberated by working hard at this or that practice. We work hard at our spiritual practice and have fun together because this Amida-bombu spiritual paradigm has liberated us already and, therefore, naturally enough, in various ways, we want to celebrate.

## Being Religious

**Religion in not limited to one form**. The sociologist Emile Durkheim established as his working definition that religion exists where people distinguish between the mundane and the sacred. They distinguish them in order to explore the relationship between them. Religion is sacred relationship. Pureland Buddhism is the sacred relationship between each devotee and Nyorai. Buddhism is all the culture that has grown up from and in order to support that relationship.

If religion is concerned with sacred relations then it will offer language and methods for facilitating these relations. It will be concerned with crossings over from one shore to the other. It will have a terminology that distinguishes between the mundane realm (*samsara*) and the sacred one (*nirvana*). It will offer ways of thinking about the structure of this shore and the other shore. It will offer methods for crossing over or for getting a glimpse of the other side and speak of the ways that the influence of the spiritual realm is felt in the worldly one: how Buddhas come to us. Anybody familiar with Buddhism must see that this is precisely what Buddhism does. The structure of thought of Shakyamuni, the historical Buddha, is entirely within this kind of framework.

Some people are attracted to Buddhism because they see that it is concerned with peace in the world and with healing the mind. They are attracted by its highly developed and nuanced systems of ethics. They see it doing good in the world. They see that Buddhists are often calm and cheerful where other folk might not be. These features are genuine. They spring out of Buddhism's fundamental concern with the sacred situation of humankind. The foundation is a religious vision. The good physical outcomes spring from this sound metaphysical root. To seek the superstructure without foundations is to court disaster. Buddhism is not a package of good secular causes. It has consequence in the secular world because it has a firm spiritual root. Without that inspiration of spirit, there would be no basis for resisting war, rejecting consumerism, protecting animals, building exemplary communities, founding new civilizations or any of the other rather splendid things that Buddhism has proved to be so good at over the centuries.

**Amidism is a simple approach to spirituality**. It just has three elements: Nyorai, ourselves and the relation between the two. Religions view the human being in relation to the sacred. In classical Buddhism, the sacred is called nirvana or tathata (literally "thusness") and the enlightened one is either Buddha, meaning one who is awake to nirvana or Tathagata (Japanese *Nyorai*), meaning one who comes from tathata. In Pureland, the sacred realm is the vision of Nyorai in the Pure Land. The mundane world is designated by the bombu paradigm discussed above. The relation between the two is what matters. In Amidism this relation is expressed in the practice of nembutsu: calling out to Nyorai. Amida in the Pure Land, the bombu paradigm, and the practice of nembutsu are thus the three pillars of Amidism. Through their application individuals may come to a transformed conception of their place in the universe. They may experience the bliss and anguish that comes from being identified with such a vision in the midst of a troubled world. All this will be explained further in subsequent sections, but the basics are very simple: Amida's Pure Land, the bombu paradigm, and the nembutsu – that is all there is to it. And of these, the nembutsu, being the bridge between the other two, is central. Nembutsu is what links the bombu with Amida. In its simplest formulation, therefore, Amidism is just one thing, the practice of calling the Buddha prayer.

Amidism accepts all Buddhist scriptures, but it is shaped primarily by a small selection of them called the Pureland Sutras. It is a religion that rejects racism, sexism, ageism and other similar forms of prejudicial discrimination, since it is founded upon equality in the eyes of Amida. It is a religion respectful of its history and tradition stretching back at least to the time of the founder, Shakyamuni Buddha, yet it is also a religion of inspiration capable of change and adaptation to the times and cultures it finds itself in. It is ethical, grounding its ethics in faith and fellow-feeling. It recognizes the fallible nature of all who inhabit the mundane world. It is a religion of our relations with the other shore. It is, in a nutshell, nembutsu: the calling out of we vulnerable ephemeral beings toward the eternal source of refuge beyond.

The simplicity of Amidism is appropriate to the death time. Death is also very simple. At that time our frailty is most evident. The beyond beckons. There is only one thing to do which is to meet it. Those who have lived their life meeting Nyorai have no qualms meeting him at that time. Those who practice this faith in simple sincerity may, therefore, meet their death in a changed way.

Archeologists know that religion goes a very long way back into human prehistory because of the care that humans take over funeral rites. Few other species do anything of this kind. The fact that humans are an animal that is in certain respects wise (*sapiens*) is much less a distinguishing characteristic of our species than the fact that we are religious. Religion is something very deep in the human make-up and this shows in how we meet death and treat the dying. We do not leave corpses lying around to be eaten by ants and beetles the way other species do. Sometimes, for short periods of history, people may start to regard funerals as simply a form of waste disposal to be got over with as quickly as possible without "fuss" but this sort of fashion never lasts long, even in the most secularised society. The "fuss" is vitally important to us.

# TWO

# SHOCK

## Thus Began One of the Most Intensive Weeks of Our Life

We were visiting mother in hospital. It was the 9th May, Sunday evening, almost at the end of visiting time; in fact, we had overstayed a little. The lights were dimmed. Most patients were asleep. Mother, too, was starting to doze and between times telling us that it must be time for us to go. The doctor, a registrar, approached us. I did not recognize him, only his role. Since mother had been admitted to hospital we had seldom seen the same doctor more than once. She had had four changes of ward in six days. He had a pleasant, serious manner.

"I wonder if I could have a word with you and your wife in private. I would like to tell you what we know about your mother's condition."

His accent was English, but his skin spoke of origins somewhere on the Indian sub-continent. Most of the doctors we had encountered were either from India or from Scotland. One notices and speculates rather idly on such details in the long hours passing to and fro. Hospital visiting is a bit like warfare with long hours when nothing happens during which one must keep anxiety on the back burner just in case urgent action is needed, interspersed with moments of intense animation when weighty decisions must be made on inadequate information, or painful procedures witnessed as one wonders whether it might possibly be this one that will effect the desired change.

**Mother had suffered** from rheumatoid arthritis for many years. Most days she was in pain. She bore it with fortitude. She was a purposeful woman who did not readily tolerate physical infirmity getting in her way. Nonetheless, since she turned eighty a couple of years before, she had been getting weaker and, from time to time, had had falls, some of which had occasioned brief hospital admissions. On this occasion she had been admitted three weeks earlier, on the 16$^{th}$ April, during a period when my wife Caroline and I were away visiting members of our congregation in Belgium. Heike, a family friend, had been with her at the time. We visited Mother as soon as we got back to UK and, after some inconclusive tests and medical observation she had been discharged on the 26$^{th}$. By the end of those ten days we had noticed that she had lost weight and that her abdomen was swollen but the hospital seemed unconcerned. The general consensus seemed to be that recent changes in her medication had upset her system and the name of the game was now to find a combination of drugs that would suit her and keep the pain at bay.

During the following week she seemed to have made slight progress each day, but she remained weak, spent most of her time in bed and had no appetite. Then she had another incident of being unable to reach her bed in the night while returning after visiting the toilet. The fall itself was not serious. I noticed that she now had a swelling on her back, but this disappeared again after twelve hours. The following day, 4$^{th}$ May, we called out a local doctor. It was Tuesday morning. We watched as she conducted her examination and heard Mother reluctantly indicate that she had a pain in her side. It was not the side onto which she had fallen, but the right side where the swelling had been. "This might be nothing, but I should get it checked," the doctor explained.

Mother, in a gruffly good humoured way, accompanied by a little smile that was quite characteristic of her, said, "You're going to send me into hospital again, aren't you? Well, I'm not going back to that last one. They didn't do anything useful." Mother had been to all three city hospitals by now and had well developed opinions about them which she would willingly inform you of. Brief negotiations produced, "Well, if I must, I'll go to Glenfield". The accommodating doctor there and then used her mobile phone to arrange a bed in Glenfield Hospital, the most modern of the three infirmaries. No, we did not need an ambulance. We took Mother ourselves, that afternoon. She was admitted at 2.45pm. I stayed with her until she was given an initial examination by a doctor at 9.20pm that night. The working diagnosis was still that she was reacting badly to her arthritis medication and that this was causing swelling of the liver. This was not an unreasonable conclusion given that her local doctor had been trying out some new stronger drugs to see if he could reduce her daily suffering.

The following day she had a variety of tests and I spoke to a consultant, a specialist in intestinal problems. He talked to me about liver function and the side effects of various drugs and I felt broadly reassured. They would keep her in hospital until they had found a medication regime that worked for her. Over the next few days Caroline, Heike and I had spent many hours sitting in the hospital keeping Mother company and seeing to her needs. Now, the doctor wanted to bring us up to date.

We entered a small side office on the ward, sat down, and the doctor put his file of notes on his knee.

"We think that your mother has a cancer in the liver and in the bowel and perhaps elsewhere. We are fairly sure this is the correct diagnosis and so it is important that you are in the picture. There is no treatment for this condition, but we can ensure that she experiences very little pain."

As his grave words unfolded a shudder seemed to pass through my whole being, as if the end of the world had just been announced, which, in a sense, it had. I felt rather as I imagine it would be to drink, like Socrates, the draught of Hemlock. I struggled against the mounting paralysis of shock, sadness and sympathy, something in me still aware, nonetheless, that this was a time when I must gather vital information.

"How long will she live?"

"There is no way of knowing, but, you understand, her condition is very serious. Perhaps when we have done further tests we may be able to give you a better idea."

He gave us some more details which I no longer recall, but my own interpretation of them suggested that Mother was certainly not going to live until Christmas, but might have a few more months with us.

"Can we take her home?"

"There are some further things we can do in hospital so that we are quite sure of the diagnosis, and, of course, in hospital she has the advantage of continuous nursing care."

"She lives with us in a Buddhist community. We would be able ourselves to offer round the clock care.

"I will talk to the consultant, but, in principle, she would not need to be in hospital if suitable palliative care can be arranged in her home."

We talked about what medical services were available and who we should contact to arrange them. It was clear that the main medical effort would now be directed to pain control and nursing care. There is no cure.

It was an effort to keep a rein on my feelings and I could see from his face that the doctor himself was affected by the gravity of what he was saying and by the emotion that he felt radiating from me. Caroline, who tends to be at her best at moments like this, was solid and supportive. Thus began one of the most intensive weeks of our life.

## We Have Been the Lucky Ones

This book is personal because it is a window upon the spiritual life. What you read here is no more and no less than my experience and my perspective on what is important. One's mother only dies once in a lifetime and at such a time one's faith is on trial. In the ordinary run of life, one can be preoccupied with this and that and worried about many things that are ultimately of little significance, but it does not have to be so, and it is at the times when the fabric of the "business as usual" world is torn apart that more fundamental questions come to the fore. I sense that our world is in need of witnesses who can speak out for something more profound than the anaesthesia of consumerism or the mindlessness of fighting over, and even dying for, things that do not actually matter. If I am right, then people who follow a spiritual life must learn to communicate with each other and with society at large, and not just stay isolated in their own group. So here I am writing about how my love of Mother and my love of Nyorai interwove and supported one another through the days of great intensity. I hope this speaks to anybody who is concerned about the place of faith in their life, whatever their creed.

**Buddhism begins with recognition of our limitations**. We are vulnerable; we are fallible; we are dependent; we are mortal; and we suffer. Furthermore, we do not like these facts. We flee from them. We hide them. We try to live as though they were not true. We want to look masterful, wise, independent and to act as though our actions will go on forever. The approach of death cuts through all that. It offends our most cherished fantasies. It is a shock. How we respond to such a rupture of the fabric of our ordinary attitude is an indication of our faith. Most people in my experience really know very little about their faith. Some even think they have no such thing. When we are tested, however, we find our ground somewhere and it is then that what our faith really is revealed. Such reality testing may show that actual faith and overt affiliation are not always aligned. Very few of us is a perfect example of what the church to which we are affiliated holds up as ideal. In this book I cannot put myself forward as an example of what an Amidist Buddhist should be like. I can only share with you what happened and what I think about it. I can share the vision that allows me to make sense of this spiritual crisis and that may be useful for you. Like it or not, we are each conducting our own experiment with faith.

We live in a world torn by strife yet my mother believed that she lived in the best time there had ever been in history. There had never been a better time nor would there be again. "I feel sorry for future generations," she would say, "My generation have been the lucky ones," and that, notwithstanding that she lived through the Second World War, the invention of the atom bomb, and any number of other horrors. "There have always been wars, dear, and in war time people do terrible things. It has always been so. No, we have been the lucky ones." Such was her conviction.

When she said things like this, it did not express some kind of scientific weighing of pros and cons, such as might be made by a god or a visitor from outer space. It expressed her spirit, or, you could say, the spirit that was upon her. She wore that spirit and it was a uniform that suited her well. Inside it, however, there lived a woman of many parts: a generous spirited young girl, a young woman who had enjoyed the teamwork of being a WRAF[3] in the War, a woman who had become a director of amateur dramatics, a guide captain, a maker of gardens and, recently, a much valued friend to many people much younger than herself. Among these she herself had been surprised to find a younger German woman, Heike. She was not blind to the ironies of life – that her friend in old age should have been a German when her formative years had been spent in the crucible of war against that land.

**Mother's spirit was made of resolute goodwill**. In this, she was my first and best teacher. In the Buddhist religious life we also have a uniform. It is the robe. When we have a daunting responsibility to fulfil, we say, "Let the robe do it," and thus know that even a foolish being like oneself can, in the right conditions, play the right part. When one sees somebody do such a thing, one might think, "There is somebody of great self-confidence," but, the truth is, as likely as not, that that person is just as soft on the inside as anybody else. Mother's robe was not made of cloth, but it did its job just the same. "We have been the lucky ones," was an important element of her faith – it was her experience of grace. When we put on the clothes of faith, we should, of course, choose carefully, but we should also trouble ourselves to wear them well, with appropriate dignity, gaiety and zest.

Some praise self-expression. Some demand uniforms. There is, however, a middle path that acknowledges both the personal and the universal. We are each unique, but we each must face the same existential facts. To focus upon uniqueness alone will not suffice to make life meaningful nor give it weight. Many things are common. We live, we love and we die. The essay that one makes of one's life is also an experiment and, indeed, an assertion, on behalf of everyone who walks this earth. We are alone, but we are also, always and inescapably, an instance of everybody, in communion with everybody.

What we do has consequences and is, itself, a consequence. It is a consequence of conditions established by others in former times. It is part of a stream that has its source well prior to this short life span and that finds its denouement well beyond it. The meaning of one's life may lie more in the future than the past. Such is the dilemma of life. One life only makes sense in the context of a greater time and nobody can, from within his or her life, perceive that greater perspective more than vaguely. They cannot see the detail of it, but they can get the feel for it. They can wear a certain spirit and, if they wear it well, the good of it will live on. If they express the grace they experience, that grace will be somehow amplified for others.

## Be At Home in Any Temple

We all have faith. To live without faith would be like trying to live without skin. In fact, nobody does so. Though modern people often have difficulty labelling their faith satisfactorily, every life displays its inhabitant's implicit faith. The conclusion I have reached is that modern life does not suffer from a loss of faith, but from a confusion of faiths. It is not that people do not believe anything any more, it is that they believe too many things – so many that it becomes an incoherent jumble. If one were asked: "How should one begin upon the spiritual path?" a wise answer might be, "Simplify your faith."

At the admission interview, when Mother went into Glenfield Hospital, she recorded herself as Buddhist and Church of England. Did this indicate confusion? In one sense it reflected the confusion of our contemporary world, where one must honour many gods. But, in herself, she was clear. She could as readily participate in a Buddhist service as a Christian one, and, if she had understood the conventions, could have found herself equally at home in the temples of several other religions, just as well. I remember that when I was a child and our family lived in the Middle East, there was a Sufi teke quite close by and in me the memory is tinged with a sense of intriguing mystery. My parents did not instil fear in me. I think that was one of their great gifts.

Mother, born in the English Midlands, had been brought up Church of England. Her parents were not devout. They ran a public house, as I mentioned. She learnt to be hospitable and sociable, but not particularly religious in any formal sense. However, she did impart to me a respect for faith in general and for goodness. One can never hope to completely lay bare the intricate skein of early influences in one's own life, but I acquired a feeling that religion reflects something universal in the human condition.

It has always seemed to me a great folly that different religions quarrel with one another. Such conflicts often become particularly embittered, just as conflicts within a family can do. I am sure this is in part because everybody involved must at some level realize that religions should not quarrel and that by doing so, whatever the merits of the issue in contention, the quarrel itself is evidence enough of bad faith.

Religions are not all the same and some are no doubt better than others in some respects, but most exist to ennoble the human spirit, not to debase it, and when they betray their basic purpose the consequence is necessarily bitter.

**So that was the sense that my mother gave me**: think for yourself and make your own choices, be willing to be at home in any temple without losing thereby the ability to discriminate wisely, and yet, do not allow such liberalism to go so far that you cannot make a clear decision, act upon it and stay committed to the course you have chosen. To put it very simply, her religion was kindness and when she saw religion associated with cruelty, as, for instance, when animals are sacrificed, she simply assumed that that religion had made a mistake in that respect – a mistake that one should be wise enough to eschew.

So it had not been difficult for her to adapt to life in a Buddhist house. She liked, in particular, to come to the Sunday service, and would do so even when it cost her a good deal of pain as she became more and more limited in mobility. Even when she really did have to remain in bed, she enjoyed hearing the sound of chanting rising through the house to her room.

She had come to play a very important part in the life of our community. Her faith transcended particular forms and, in that respect, she embodied the Buddhist ideal better than many who had adopted the faith in a more self-conscious way.

## Making Sense

**I have been a Buddhist** for forty years. It could have been Christianity, or Islam, or Taoism, but I became a Buddhist. Buddhism has been the system that I have worked with in my struggles to make sense of love, life and death, of elation and depression, and of the dramas, poignant or boring, dignified or not, that one enjoys and suffers in the ups and downs of this world. Buddhism has oriented me as I have sought to love life, face loss and my own near-death and fulfil my existence. In this book, I am trying to share some of this with you and to say things that are important to me and to convey my sense, not always orthodox, of the core meaning of Buddhism.

**Writing books is a kind of therapy** – certainly so for me at least. Things that ripen inside me seem to need putting out from time to time or they fester. Writing a book becomes a kind of catharsis – an inner cleansing. So with this mixture of motives I set out to write this book. That it sprung from a spontaneous need is evidenced by the fact that the core of it was completed in a week. Since then I have done some revision and refinement, but the basic story remains.

The story of death is very personal and unique, but it is also the most completely universal story. By writing one externalises what is most personal and, in the process, allows it to become something universal that is both oneself and something other than oneself. As one's personal story becomes the universal story so the personal pain becomes the pain of all beings. So beyond being a personal therapy, writing also becomes a spiritual exercise.

**Death equalises**. From the perspective of the world, people occupy many ranks and grades, social, moral, economic, and political. We are judged for our looks, clothes, jobs, friends and so on. However, a death is a death, whoever it is, and, from the perspective of death we are all equal. So I want to say here something about equality, which is what, to me, lies at the core of religion. Religion as I understand it is about equality in the profoundest sense of that term. We can say, spiritual equality. Death, religion and equality are very closely connected and from this connection spring a host of things, not least of which is love.

We die. That is what is fundamentally equal about us. It is what we most resist facing and it is religion's job to help us face it. Equality implies not measuring. Measurement is inequality. There is a domain of things where measurement is completely proper and useful. It is the realm of science and material life. To make a garment one must measure the cloth. To see a true person, however, one must discard measurement. Each of us is an unmeasurable person, a true being, who lives through time that is not divisible into measurable units. That true being is like a jewel with many facets, but many of the facets are not particularly jewel-like. It makes symphonies sometimes, for sure, but more often it makes wind and phlegm. It does great and good deeds, but it also engages in folly and rudeness. So the unmeasurable person is also an ordinary person – a bag of skin and bone. Nowhere does this become more apparent than on one's deathbed.

## Equality

**We are equal in the gaze of enlightenment**. Pureland is that form of Buddhism where one practises the love of Amida. We therefore face a number of questions immediately. What is Amida? What is the Pure Land? What is love? What is practice? None of these terms are simple. Defining them only leads to a cascade of further questions as the terms in which they are defined then come under scrutiny. I will try to suggest their meanings to you as we go along, but I want to establish first that religion is not a matter of finding watertight definitions or the best or only right vocabulary in which to speak of spiritual phenomena. Religion is, first and foremost a shift of perspective, and then, after that, it is a culture, a community, and the lived life of its adherents. Religions exist to help us to live well and die well: to live in relation to heaven in a world that is not heaven. If they do that, then they succeed in their own terms. They do not need to meet the criteria of science or academia or political correctness, unless those things are making claims to be religions themselves. On the other hand, religion fails when it leads to destructive lives and meaningless deaths.

So let me plunge in and start to hint at one key definition. What is Amida? Amida is the unmeasurable person. This is what the word means. *Mida* means measurement. It is probably related to the English word metre. *A-mida* means without measurement. The Greek would be *ametros*. This does not mean that a person cannot be measured: manifestly people are being measured on all sorts of criteria all the time. The world of measurement, however, is the dead world, the world of things rather than of spirited beings. It is the vertical dimension. In Buddhist terminology, it is the domain of *Mara*, Death. In the world of non-life, measurement is quite appropriate and sometimes we must even treat ourselves as dead things, but religion has the task of waking us up to the world of life, which is where Nyorai comes into it.

**Amidism is thus dualistic** in structure, as is the whole of Buddhism insofar as it applies to ordinary people. At the basic level, Buddhism is about delusion and enlightenment, samsara and nirvana, and so on. There is the dead world and the life world, *marana* and *jivana*. The life world encompasses physical death. Often people are more alive when they are dying than they have ever been. As death approaches we tend to jettison much of the (dead) baggage that has hindered our steps through life. We put our affairs in order in a way we never troubled to do before. The spiritual path, therefore, often requires one to live as if dying. I'm sure that many people who put their affairs in order in later life think, "I should have done this years ago – I should have simplified." The spiritually adept lives a minimalist life, jettisoning attachments as if death were imminent. The presence of death is a great teacher, and not just to those on their deathbed. Mara can just be Amida in disguise.

The most significant measurements that we make of people are moral ones. It follows directly that moral judgement belongs to the dead world. You can probably immediately sense that this produces interesting questions about what the proper relationship between religion and morality may be.

If I may state it boldly, what seems to have gone wrong is that religion has got so involved in moral measurement that it has relegated itself to a place in the dead world and so lost its primary function.

Religion has lost its way by becoming either a punitive judge or a seller of indulgences. Measuring people has become its business and, although that business sometimes flourishes in the worldly sense, it is the abdication of religion's true function and *raison d'etre*. The punitive judge is blind to the unmeasurable person. However, irreligion does not satisfactorily fill the vacuum; it merely makes self-opinion the measuring stick – as though a measure could be a measure of itself – which is an even worse position. Consequently, many people feel adrift.

**There are two ways of having a land that is pure**. One way is to assess who is pure and who is not and to restrict access to those who pass the test. However, none do. The other way is to be so pure that one does not notice who passes the test and who does not so everybody is welcome. Nyorai is like that. Amida's Pure Land is for all because Amida does not measure. If Amida measured, Amida would be less than Amida. Amidism is called Amidism because all are welcome and there is no condemnation. This is real equality. It also means that Amidism is a religion of absolute grace. Of course, the fact that all are welcome does not mean that all enter. Many exclude themselves. Nyorai is not omnipotent.

### The Spirit of Pureland is Bitter-sweet

**Principles are useful**. There is nothing so useful as a good theory. Buddhism has its definitions and therefore dogmas just as every system does – a life philosophy without any fundamentals would be like a body without bones. We have just encountered a Pureland dogma: true religion does not condemn. However, dogma relates to the ideal rather than the real. In practice, we all judge. Only Nyorai does not do so.

Dogmas have their place, but it is just as important that religion be practical. Its central concern is with experience and a change of perspective, an awakening, rather than metaphysical propositions as such. It is more important to confront existential reality and scrabble to give some account of it with whatever half-suitable word-craft one has, than to cling over-tenaciously to a securely dead structure of ideas and concepts, however ideal.

There is, however, also a pitfall in the opposite direction. A great deal of what is professed as Buddhism today is what I would call secular Buddhism. Buddhism has become the religion for people who do not want to be religious. This attempt to have one's cake and eat it too – albeit a dead cake – has many unfortunate consequences. It is another attempt to move religion into the dead realm and it prevents people from really getting to grips with what the Buddha is and what spiritual teachers are trying to do. Many people believe that Buddhism is not really a religion. They prefer to see it as a set of techniques or a rational philosophy. Techniques and rationality, however, are about measurement and they are secondary. Technique can get you somewhere if you know where you want to get, but it cannot help you decide. I worry that secular Buddhists might want to eliminate all meaningful ceremonial and limit the scope so narrowly that Buddhism is rendered powerless to effect the kind of life transformation that it was created for. What can secular rationalism offer to the dying? What can it say about love? Not much.

**Dying is important**. Throughout history, Buddhism has been known most particularly for its skills in managing the life-death boundary. In the Far East, many Buddhist temples are focussed almost exclusively upon funeral rites. Westerners tend to view this situation askance and say that it is a degeneration of the Buddha's noble teaching. Is this because they want that teaching to be rational and secular? Is it because they fear death? In the rational secular world, death is an unwelcome intruder – something that upsets the taken for granted scheme of things. Buddhism, however, is about dying. It is about dying at the death time and about dying in the midst of life. It is about the problem of being as if dead already, about Mara who accompanies us everywhere we go and

to whom we attempt to close our eyes: the Mara that is both our persecutor and our route to salvation. It is through death that we find eternal
limitless life. This kind of death is not part of the dead world. It is a
death that is alive.

Here, of course, terminology becomes confusing. Religion is about
finding unmeasured life and that includes dying and whatever lies
beyond it. Physical life and physical death take place. They happen.
They continue to happen whether a person is awake to the unmeasurable or not. To avoid some of this confusion, therefore, Buddhism calls
the dead world *samsara*, the realm of meaningless circling, and the life
world is called the Pure Land.

Now, however, a further paradox arises. We are equal. We are equal
in that we all die. We are also equal in that, within this life, none of us
is in the Pure Land. We can intuit the unmeasurable person, but we are
not being it. We make judgements. We treat others in a measured way.
We are often selfish, arrogant, biassed, self-pitying and so forth in fluc-
tuating degrees. Pureland, therefore, does not instruct us to be what we
are not. It tells us to recognize what we are. In doing so we become
aware of something that we can intuit, but that we know we can never
in this life actually fulfil. The spirit of Amidism is, therefore, bitter-
sweet. That very bitter-sweetness makes us more alive. We feel everything more acutely. We learn, we live, we love, we grieve, and we die
more intensely. That is what listening to Nyorai does for us.

## You Never Know What Life Has Round the Corner

**After hearing the doctor's definitive words** that Sunday night, back
home, unable to sleep much, I went and sat in Mother's room and
thought about her life. She lived in two rooms on the first floor at the
front of the house. The house in question is The Buddhist House, a
small community of religious in the village of Narborough in
Leicestershire in the heart of England. She came to the community to

live with me. It had been a great success.

I reflected on the day fourteen years before when I had sat with her in a café in Ripon in Yorkshire and discussed the future. We were, at that juncture, each in a similar position. My marriage had broken up and, unexpectedly, so had hers. My father had moved to Devon and my mother continued to live in what had been their house. It was a nicely appointed bungalow with a large garden. In many practical ways it was a suitable situation for her. My parents had bought the house with a view to their old age. It was all on the flat. It was easy to manage. When they bought it they had had the sensible plan that it would suit them well into their later years. Although Mother then already had a small degree of arthritis, she was fit and healthy. The garden was one of her great joys. Now she lived there unexpectedly alone. She was not rich, but "I have enough".

I was living in Newcastle upon Tyne. I had my own house and although I worked from home, it was more space than I needed just for myself. What was on my mind was the possibility of her coming to live with me in Newcastle. I saw some advantages and disadvantages at the practical level for each of us, but my prime concern was that she was in danger of becoming isolated and lonely. Father's departure had been a great shock and I knew that she felt it bitterly.

I had tentatively turned over the idea of Mother joining me in Newcastle with several friends who, without exception, were of the opinion that it would be folly. There was a general consensus that "Nobody would want to live with his mother," coupled with a not too subtle suggestion that I was probably regressing in some kind of patho-logical way in even contemplating the idea. Many of my friends at that time were persuaded by a then current theory that our psychological problems can mostly be explained by regarding ourselves as innocent victims of our parents' misdeeds, though I had never found that creed particularly convincing myself.

Mother sipped her coffee and listened to my proposal. She sounded me out with a few questions to test whether I had reflected long or whether this was just an impulsive remark. "It would be a big step for both of us," she acknowledged. I had worked out how she could be semi-independent in two rooms of the Newcastle house and I could offer her the choice of ground floor or first floor. This was clearly a major change from having a whole house to oneself. Even worse, the Newcastle house had almost no garden.

Nonetheless, I could feel she was warming to the idea. We both knew that it was a proposal that ran against the spirit of the times in which families increasingly fragment and household units become smaller and smaller.

"I shall need a little time to think about it, dear," she said, but I could sense that she would probably say yes.

Over the next week she spoke to friends, who were either as negative as mine had been or were, understandably, cautious. "You will be giving up your house – what will you do if it does not work out?" Mother did not have so much capital that it would be an easy step to undo. But the reckless element was also an attraction.

**She made plans**. Given that she would have less than half the amount of space she was accustomed to, these had to include some fairly ruthless decisions about what to take and what to dispose of. She was, as always, practical, but not at the expense of sensitivity. She, who had moved so many times in her past, was designing a new life once again. She was excited. "You never know what life has round the corner".

Well, that was certainly true. Life continues to unfold in its unpredictable way. By the time Mother was ready to move, I was involved in a new relationship. Caroline and Mother both moved into my house in the same week. Each brought their own furniture and possessions into my already furnished house: on the face of it, a recipe for disaster at both the practical and emotional levels. However, it worked.

I was charmed and amused to see the way that the two women in my life teamed up, sometimes in mild opposition to myself. They would cook up plans together to redecorate or reorganize rooms and then confront me with a united front that was difficult to resist, or even, sometimes, with a *fait accompli* achieved in my absence.

The house was also my workplace and Caroline was joining me in that work. We ran psychotherapy courses and Buddhist events and gradually over the succeeding years these two strands became more and more integrated until in 1996, with a group of friends, we founded a new organisation called Amida Trust and then, in 2001 moved to Leicestershire – but more of those developments later. Sitting there, on Mother's empty bed, that Sunday night, I reflected upon how she had had the courage to start again so many times in her life, and with what relish.

## Unless We Are Loved

**Faith and recklessness are not far apart**. The word reck has been lost from our language, but it meant care. Reckless, does not mean careless in the sense of negligent, but in a more wilful way. "I reck not what they think" was the spirit in which I invited my mother, in the face of advice to the contrary and it was the same spirit in which she accepted. It was an act of faith in each other and in life. To have faith in another to a degree that enables you to stand together against the tide is very close to what we mean by love.

Edith Piaf wrote a Hymn to Love that became a very popular song:

Le ciel bleu
Sur nous peut se fondrer
Et le terre
Peut bien s'écrouler
Peu m'importe, si tu m'aimes
Je m'en fou du monde entière

In translation, this reads:

> The blue sky above us may fall
> And the earth may as well crumble away
> Little does it matter to me, so long as you love me,
> I reck not what the entire world (may do, think or say).

The song catches the spirit of love. Love overcomes the fear that one otherwise has of stepping out of line. It gives one the courage to take hold of one's life and turn it over and begin again.

This always involves risks. Piaf, herself, wrote this song for her lover Marcel Cerdan. She met him in 1947 in America. In October 1949 he was killed in an air crash. She grieved terribly for him and this grief left an indelible mark upon the remainder of her life.

Of course, one can evade such grief by never taking the risk of loving, or one can trivialise life by taking risks so carelessly that they cease to be meaningful any more. There are people who think that the aim of spirituality is to bring us to a state in which we will never run the risk of grieving, in which we will be beyond suffering. I find it hard to believe that that would be a worthwhile goal.

**Mother and I each knew that we were taking a risk**. Whenever you depend upon somebody else, you take a risk. The person you depend upon is mortal. They are prone to sickness, accident, financial disaster, moral failing, madness and death. These things can befall anybody. Yet, if we do not place any dependence upon anybody, what sort of lonely life do we have? I think I can say that I rescued my mother from the fate of living a safe life in which she would have died lonely and bored. And in the process she and I contributed to my own rescue too. But then, none of the great sages, to my knowledge, lived safe, boring lives.

If we take risks with our lives, consciously committing ourselves to a path that is enveloped in a spirit of love, then we will surely suffer sooner or later, but we will also survive and be strengthened. If, on the other hand, we live independently, unhelped and unhelping, we will only shrivel up into an existence that can hardly be called a life.

**Independence is a modern kind of purity**, but it is largely illusory. Modern people would rather be independent than happy and so they try to arrange their circumstances in ways that seem self-sufficient even if this means working long hours at alienating jobs and being dependent upon all kinds of less than totally reliable technology. Independence has its place, but the kind of independence that matters is not really a function of circumstance. Circumstantially we are all dependent, however much we may wish to believe otherwise. Perhaps there are a few people left who grow their own food, but even they depend upon the natural elements and, through doing so, generally develop an acute and healthy sense of their dependence upon forces much bigger than themselves. The independence that matters is the ability to make a sober decision and take initiative without trying to wiggle out of the responsibility that comes with doing so.

The Buddha, in one sense, made his followers independent, by having them live a minimalist life in which their needs were reduced to the absolute basics. At the same time, he brought home to them their dependence upon others by having them beg for their food. Everyday the Buddhist friar, the *bhikshu*, went into a village and stood waiting to see if anybody would give him food or not. His life depended upon the generosity of others. If people did not provide the requisites, he could not live in that place. Bhikshus, therefore, lived in other people's land, dependent upon others, and did so in full consciousness of that reality. Circumstantially they were dependent. Spiritually they were free. Spiritual liberation lies in the willingness to take responsibility for one's life – a life one did not choose. To do so is a voluntary act. That kind of liberation does not negate circumstantial dependency. It simply means that in some circumstances one will be willing to die.

Because we are circumstantially dependent, the ability of a community to live a good life together is a function of generosity. The spiritual person lives by invitation. The invitation comes from others. Unless others invite us to live, we cannot do so. To be invited is, to a certain degree, to be loved. Unless we are loved, at least to that degree, we cannot live. The spiritual life involves this consciousness of being loved and the corresponding consciousness of being dependent. A great deal of human psychological stress and general misery is attributable to the unwillingness to face such facts.

**Real independence is not to do with circumstance**. The modern effort to ensure that everybody has his or her own refrigerator, washing machine, car, mobile phone and so on is all very well, but it cannot yield the kind of liberation that people are intuitively seeking. This is part of what I mean by saying that faith has become scattered. People may be deceived into believing that material independence will bring freedom of spirit, but it does not do so. Material gain can be a good, but it is not a spiritual liberator, nor can material independence ever be complete. Material things are ultimately outside of our control – they decay in their own good time – and by putting our faith in them we actually multiply rather than diminish our dependency.

My mother knew that she would have more material things and more control over her environment living alone. She gave it up. She did not, thereby, become less independent in spirit. She simply chose a life of productive co-operation rather than one of sterile isolation. She chose love, knowing it to be a risk.

## Faith Rules Lives

**Faith is central to the good life** because the best things in life are intrinsically risks. Love is not under one's own control. Actually hardly anything is entirely under one's control. Circumstantial dependency is a fact of life. It is one of the absolutes. Sometimes people say that a spiritual life is one in which a practitioner attains insight into absolute truth. This is a valid observation, but when we hear such words, the term absolute truth too readily conjures something mysterious and esoteric and people could easily mistake it that this proffered absolute, once attained, will make them immune from the less palatable existential realities of life, like disease, loss, death, and failure. It is not like that. Or, more precisely, it is like that, but not in the manner that the uninitiated imagine.

Absolutes, as anybody who has done a little mathematics knows, are the alternative to variables. The things that are absolute are the things that do not change whereas the variables are the things that do change. For human beings, death is an absolute, whereas the actual time and circumstance of death is a variable. Dependency is similarly absolute. The precise species of dependency within which a person passes their days can be varied. The fact of dependency itself cannot. Those who try to make themselves independent simply choose a different kind of dependency. My mother could see that. She knew that if she stayed in Yorkshire she would have her own space in her own house and consequently would be less dependent upon relatives and more dependent upon impersonal state services as she grew older and more frail. She could vary the type of dependency, but not the fact of it. Similarly, staying in her bungalow she could depend entirely upon her own financial resources, which really meant upon the financial fortunes of the institutions in which her savings were lodged. She understood that. She had seen her income fluctuate massively as government policies and interest rates went through their customary vicissitudes. Living with her family she would give up a portion of this uncertainty and replace it with the uncertainty of her son's equally vulnerable fortunes.

Insight into absolute truth, therefore, means knowing death and dependency. It also includes human fallibility. My love for her could not guarantee that I would always without fail act in her interests or even always know what they were. Such is life. These facts often frighten people into a flight from real life commitments. Then they go seeking spiritual rescue and think that absolute truth will liberate them from all that. In fact, all that is precisely what absolute truth is.

**So it comes back to faith**. The crucial element in the decision became one of trust. How much did she trust me and how much did I trust her? Much of this book is thus about trust, or faith. The basic message is that whether we like it or not faith rules our lives. I could have written a book about faith in the grand sense full of religious theory and high-flown abstractions, but that is not where my focus is most of the time. The faith that matters is the one that shows up in the little details of the passing day, week, and year. Faith is evidenced in our decisions and actions.

To simplify one's faith to the point where it starts to transform one's life into something of lasting value requires a certain wisdom and this wisdom includes an ability to distinguish between the absolutes and the variables. While we keep our eyes closed to this or remain unacceptant of it our faith will continue to be muddled and will not serve us.

Dependency is absolute. Our life hangs upon others just as a coat hanger hangs on the rail. But trusting the other cannot mean trusting them not to die, or not to be dependent themselves, or never to make a mistake, because the absolutes apply to us. In Buddhism, this is called the doctrine of dependent origination and it is to this that Buddhas are enlightened. This is their absolute truth: we are dependent so we must have faith. What we trust in the other is their love.

**Faith is the foundation**. Upon faith grows wisdom. Wisdom is what naturally arises as a person attempts to live a faithful life. One attempts to live in good faith and then things happen and then one gets wise. One also gets compassionate. One finds fellow-feeling as one sees others crash into the absolutes in just the same way as one does oneself. One cannot get wisdom and compassion from books. One can only get them by gathering one's faith in one's embrace and taking the risks of love.

## Shocked, Proud, Sad and Inspired

We arrived early at the hospital on Monday morning. The ward was busy with the customary routines. Mother was, as usual, pleased to see us. I knew that I had to tell her what I now knew and I knew that this was going to change everything for her as it had already been changed for us a few hours earlier when, that previous evening, we sat with the registrar and experienced the shock of hearing the diagnosis.

**The circumstances were not conducive**. A prepared speech was not my style when facing Mother and, in any case, was not possible amidst the bustle and interruptions as the medical staff hurried to get a hundred small tasks completed before the consultant came to do his ward round. The most fundamental things in life are deeply personal and the element of spontaneity cannot and should not be squeezed out of them.

"It's nice of you to come in early."

"It's lovely to see you, Mum. Have you slept alright?"

"As well as you can here. I'm not complaining, though. They are all being very nice to me."

"How are you feeling now?"

"Well, I'm getting frustrated, really. I've been here almost a week and I want to know when I'm going to get better. There doesn't seem to be any real improvement. I would have thought that they could have done something by now."

"Mum, you are probably not going to get better."

There, it was out. My voice was shaking and I was on the edge of tears. She remained composed. There was a slight pause while she took in what I had said.

"Do you mean that I am going to die?"

"Mum, the doctor has told us that there is an awful lot wrong down there," I said, indicating her swollen abdominal area with a gesture.

So now she also knew. I could no longer hold back the tears that whelmed up in sobs as I said, "I love you, Mum."

She was also flushed with emotion, but, in that moment, it was not the dread shadow of death that prevailed, but the intimacy of loving, knowing that one is loved and knowing the mutuality of it.

About then the consultant arrived with his entourage. I sat back as he took the stage on the other side of the bed.

"Good morning, Mrs Brazier." He gave his name, told her he had to examine her and asked if we were her relatives. She consented, explained that we were her son and daughter-in-law and said that she wanted us to remain present. He took her pulse, looked at her charts and examined her abdomen. This was largely theatre, necessary scene setting rather than science. He already knew what he had to tell her.

"Mrs Brazier, this swelling is not getting any better."

"I know"

"Mrs Brazier, is there anything that you are frightened of?"

Momentarily, I was struck by his technique. He must have had to say such things many times. I had myself worked in hospitals. One finds oneself in interactions with people that are massively asymmetrical in that the professional is just doing his or her job, while the patient is hearing something that is a once in a lifetime experience.

My mother replied in the negative and requested further explanation.

"Is there anything that you have thought about your condition that particularly frightens you?"

"No."

"You see, we think that this swelling is a cancer."

"Well, let us hope that it is not, shall we?"

The robustness of Mother's response caught us all slightly off-guard. Chuckles rippled round the assembled group and even the consultant could not help smiling. The spell of gravity had been broken. This was to everybody's relief. This patient was clearly not going to collapse emotionally.

"Yes, yes, we can hope. But I think we will find that it is a cancer."

"How long have I got?"

"At present we cannot tell how fast it is developing. I cannot say." They went on to discuss subsidiary issues.

**I felt proud of my mother's spirit**. I realized that amongst its foundations were her love for me and her realism. One could call it wisdom, and that would not be inappropriate, but one would have to scrub that word clean of the dross of pseudo-mysticism that it too readily acquires. I was shocked, proud, sad and inspired. I felt totally alive, sensing both that a great weight of responsibility was resting upon me and also somehow knowing that whatever I needed in order to carry it would be given. I knew that she also felt corresponding feelings. She was shocked, but not as much. She had been preparing. She was more easily reconciled to dying than I was to her going and, for all her frail vulnerability, she was going to be alive to the very end.

I stayed with her after the doctors had departed. She was gazing out of the window of the ward opposite. Initially I thought she was lost in her thoughts, but then she beckoned me to move closer so that I could look along her line of sight and see what she was looking at. In the courtyard, visible only from the angle of her bed, two doves were perched on one of the roof supports. "They've been there since yesterday," she said. I could see that their presence was somehow deeply comforting to her. She was a lover of peace.

### I Will Not Allow You to Drive Me From My Post

**The appearance of death can bring us to life, or it can be our undoing**. There is a story of one of the Christian Desert Fathers that when asked how he remained so full of spirit he replied, "By keeping death always before me," and similar sayings can be found in many spiritual traditions of the world. It is said that the Buddha always had Mara walking a few steps behind him. Mara is the nearest equivalent to a devil in Buddhist writings, but the word literally means death. The Buddha is depicted as having quite intimate encounters with Mara. Mara rules this world. The Buddha's encounters with him, however, result in Mara vanishing. My mother's encounter with the consultant was like that. Mother is going to die, but Mother is certainly not dead yet. Mara rules, yet Mara is defeated. That is our spiritual task, to live in the world of Death and yet to defeat him. Everything is impermanent – in other words, it is dying – yet, in the midst of impermanence, to find eternal light, life, beauty, truth and goodness and to be exhilarated. Buddha saw the death and the life of things simultaneously. That is the example he gave and that is what he sought to awaken people to. The word Buddha just means awakened.

The form of these encounters in which Mara appeared to the Buddha is that of failed seduction. The appearance of death can seduce or frighten us into being a lesser self or it can stimulate us into filling out a greater spirit. What we call spiritual life is life that attains such spiritedness. The Buddha says, in a passage in the Sutta Nipata, a Buddhist scripture, that the weapons that he has at hand with which to defeat Mara are faith, energy and wisdom. They work in that order. Faith releases unrecognized supplies of energy that was formerly tied up in doubt and self-contradiction. As one lives with that energy from that ground of faith, one learns much and fast. By training disciples far and wide in these three qualities, the Buddha goes about rolling back the frontiers of Mara's kingdom. Although physical death is an absolute for mortals, we do not need to live subject to its dominance – we do not need to take on spiritual death. The spiritedness that a person of faith seeks, therefore, is that which defeats death whenever the latter rises up to frighten or seduce us. Death acts upon us with a force that tempts us to become lesser beings.

**Religion should help us**. The language of religion, any religion, should provide us with vocabulary and a structure of concepts to talk about these issues lucidly so that we can be helped at moments of crisis when the issue could go either way. That is its function. Religion is made by the wise to help those who would be wise. Those who would be wise are foolish beings like myself who need such help. The fact that one religion puts things differently from another does not necessarily mean that they are saying substantially different things. More than one religion can be true because religion is a human artefact, a system that indicates how to live a spirited life, a life that defeats death day by day. There is generally more than one way of saying the same thing and it is important to be able to distinguish what is substantive and what is merely a manner of saying.

**Terrible conflicts have resulted** from the inability to distinguish form from substance in religion. In the south of France, in the country near to the Pyrenees there lived, in the twelfth century, people called Cathars. The Cathar religion was declared a heresy by the Catholics and a terrible crusade was waged in which many gentle people were burnt to death for their divergent faith. I first read about the savage destruction of the Albigensian heresy, as it is also called, when I was a teenager. I remember the acquisition of this knowledge as bringing on a visceral revulsion that played a significant role in my spiritual quest and my original turn away from Christianity.

The Catholics said that man is body and soul and that he has three possible worlds: earth, heaven and hell. The Cathars said that man can be body, soul and spirit and that he only has two possible worlds: this one and heaven. In the twelfth century these differences led to genocide in south west Europe. In fact, however, the language of the Cathars and the language of the Catholics are equally capable of conveying what a truly spirited life is like. That these two communities fell into war and slaughter means that, at that time, they failed to understand what religion is for. It seemed to me that it was like having a war over the difference between six and twice three.

In our contemporary world there are many repeats of this baleful scenario going on. Islam and Christianity are equally capable of describing the good life and assisting people in living it. That they should, in some places and some epochs of history, have been recruited by the forces of greed, aggression and delusion into providing justifications for a bloody clash of cultures is lamentable nonsense. It is worse than nonsense since it also substantially undermines the work of those who actually do want to use those noble spiritual systems for the purpose for which they were really designed, which is the greater good of all.

**Unfortunately there is a considerable confusion**, a Babel, of religious language in the world today and that makes my task of writing a book that might possibly reach across some of these boundaries and speak to people not just of my own faith system difficult. But, then, it also makes it the more necessary and interesting.

The need to defeat death day by day is no greater and no less than it ever was, nor will it ever be. This notion implies, of course, that the gradient of the world is not intrinsically leaning in a spiritually wholesome direction. Good will not prevail simply by our doing nothing. Rather the converse is the case. Therefore the Buddha called endlessly for "striving". In the Buddha's language, a day of striving is the best kind of day one can have. On the other hand, modern people do not want to be told this in this way, so we need to find new languages, new skilful means, that will address the current situation.

Modern people do not want to hear about striving because they feel that they are doing too much of it already and that it is forced upon them. The contemporary manifestation of Mara is called stress. People turn to Buddhism, often enough, because they think that it will relieve them of stress. The last thing they want to hear is that it involves a ceaseless succession of days of striving. The stress inherent in modern life, however, surely has much to do with the modernist project of salvation through rational purity and circumstantial independence, neither of which are viable options. Making more and more effort toward an unrealizable goal is bound to produce stress.

**Buddha meant something different**. What was he pointing out? The Buddha says to Mara, "I will not allow you to drive me from my post." The Buddha has a sense of duty. A spirited person is able to hold firm. A person without such spirit cannot do so. In fact, the person who holds firm does not experience stress. They experience something else. Being told that you are going to die is supposed to be a very stressful experience, but I do not find the word stressful appropriate for what happened in the hospital that morning. Mother's response demonstrated her adeptness at dealing with Mara. She was not going to be vanquished and her demonstration that this was the case gave strength to everybody present.

Such adeptness is not something that one can invent on the spur of the moment. For it to come so spontaneously in such a time, it must be the product of years of cultivation. Cultivation, in turn, rests on the one hand upon insight into the nature of the situation and, on the other, upon faith and persistence. Religions can point us toward the existential realities, but we then have to find out about them for ourselves through experience. It is the weaving together of experience and wisdom in the context of a persistent determination to live and love fully that creates a noble life and nobody persists without faith of some sort.

## Faith is Nourished by Love
**Reason supposedly defeats emotion**, but I cannot believe that a noble life is an emotionless one. In Buddhist iconography there do exist pictures showing the death scene of the Buddha in which the junior disciples are weeping while the accomplished saints, the *arhats*, look on with

almost bored expressions. The arhats, having defeated passion and risen above the vicissitudes of liking and disliking, are immune to grief. This is what the pious artist portrays.

My profession is that of a Buddhist teacher. If you have picked up this book thinking to find here the writings of somebody who remains sublimely unaffected by the ups and downs of life, then I must disappoint you. I would certainly have been among the lesser disciples and I would not want it otherwise. Perhaps that makes me a bad Buddhist, but that is how it is. Pureland is really made for bad Buddhists like me. My emotions flow. I do not know anybody who does not have emotions and I do not think that a state of indifference is really so sublime. Were I to guide you, I would indeed invite you to a place amongst the lesser disciples rather than the great ones, at least in this respect.

Love is not just an emotion, but love appreciates the emotions of the other person. When we feel loved by Nyorai we feel free to feel. A lightness comes into our life because we feel a total assurance. No worry can be of a scale to upset this, but that does not mean that we no longer worry, just that there is something bigger going on as well that puts ordinary worries into a different perspective.

Many Buddhist books begin with a promise of happiness. We are told that everybody seeks happiness and that the Buddhist way provides it. In one sense, this is true. I am a thoroughly happy person and live in a very carefree way much of the time. This does not, however, mean that I never feel sad or worried.

The Dalai Lama often tries to bring out this special sense by drawing a distinction between happiness and pleasure and then by saying that the kind of happiness he is talking about is enduring happiness rather than fleeting euphoria. The pursuit of pleasure, he says, is self-defeating whereas the search for enduring happiness for oneself and others is the proper motive for the spiritual path. Such happiness will be attained when we overcome craving for short-term gains. Such happiness comes from a life devoted to compassion. Buddhists believe that the Dalai Lama is an incarnation of Chenresig, the spirit of enlightened compassion, so the present incarnation is certainly "on message" in this respect.

I substantially agree with the His Holiness, but feel a need to add that happiness is also an ability to enjoy the fleeting things too. The kind of happiness that I have discovered is one in which there is still generally a tinge of sadness in the back of the picture. It is, as the Japanese poets say, the happiness of seeing plum blossom all the while knowing that any moment it will be blown away. Happiness involves awareness of the closeness of death. Paradoxically, happiness involves being able, on appropriate occasion, to experience acute grief.

**The definition of the goal** of the good life has never been easy. Aristotle called it *eudaimonia*, but the translation of this word has been a subject of controversy ever since people started rendering his work into other languages, and even among the Greeks themselves. Often it is rendered as "happiness". A more literal transliteration would give us "well-spiritedness" or life under the influence of a benign angel. Buddhism talks about enlightenment, nirvana and tathata. These terms are makeshifts. They are signposts rather than the thing itself. They have to be. Each points to a particular aspect or facet of the goal, but when one lights up one facet, another is inevitably thrown into shadow.

Enduring happiness is a wonderful thing, but my own Zen teacher, Roshi Jiyu Kennett, said, on many occasions, about the spiritual life, "It does not make you happy." Was she contradicting the Dalai Lama or saying something different? He is emphasising that the advanced spiritual practitioner can take the ups and downs of life in their stride. She was emphasising that when you open your eyes to it you see that there is an awful lot of grief and strife in the world and nobody can rest entirely content while his neighbour suffers. I do not think they are really in disagreement, and both perspectives can be solidly supported by reference to Buddhist canonical teachings.

Aristotle's offering suggests nobility of spirit and I am sure that the Buddha would concur with that, though they might differ on some of the fine detail. Aristotle thought this included treating your slaves decently, whereas the Buddha might have had a few things to say about that whole institution given his known and articulate opposition to the caste system of his own country.

Tathata implies realism: to be what you are and to accept what reality brings. This does not imply complacency, however. Realism is a starting point: let's see what the situation is, then we can decide what to do about it. OK, so I am going to die.... How long have I got? That question is the beginning of a planning process.

Sometimes it is said that the essence of the path is to live entirely in the here and now. I do not think that the Buddha actually says this exactly anywhere in the Buddhist scriptures, but it has somehow become a kind of yardstick for many contemporary Buddhists. What the Buddha actually says is, Do not let yourself become burdened by thoughts of the past or thoughts of the future – or, indeed, by the present for that matter. This is rather similar to the sentiment, "Sufficient unto the day is the evil thereof". We have to deal with the matter in hand.

The Buddha also recommends awareness of what is arising in us at a particular point in time. This is sound advice. The matter in hand and the emotions, thoughts and impulses that arise, however, are only meaningful in a time frame. They gain their identity from their antecedents and their consequences. The fact that we have lived and are going to die are what make each moment of life precious and meaningful.

**Noble spiritedness** does not imply ignorance of the past or lack of concern about the future. A present cut off from the rest of time is meaningless. A person who never plans needs a nursemaid. On the other hand, the fullness of life has to be manifested in each moment. When we experience such a full moment, we know we are alive.

What then of nirvana? The association of Buddhism, in the minds of

Western people, with negativism – nihilism even – is long standing. We are told that nirvana is the condition of a fire after it has been extinguished. If you live in a country as hot as India, having the fire extinguished might seem an attractive prospect. It may also be of some relevance that one of the main rivals to the Buddha's new approach to spirituality was the ancient fire religion of the god Agni. On one occasion, the Buddha is tempted by Mara in the following terms:

> Come, live the Holy Life and pour
> Libations on the holy fires,
> And thus a world of merit gain.
> - *Sutta Nipata 425*

but the Buddha rebukes him and lists the failings of worldly life that he says are Mara's squadrons. The Buddha was not going to stop being awkward and take up a comfortable life since this would mean succumbing to the little hypocrisies, deceits, vanities and malpractice that go with it.

**The Buddha saw himself as putting out a fire** that was raging in the world and what he was saying with the language of fire was no different from what he was saying in the language of life and death. The person who puts out the fire of worldliness is a fully alive one, not a dead one. "Extinguish the fire", means the same as, "defeat Mara".

When Mother was told she was going to die, no doubt some embers of that fire stirred. The "poor me" syndrome lives in us all. Indeed, even the great leaders of the world's spirituality, Buddha, Jesus, Mohammed and so on, each had temptations from time to time. Some of those of the Buddha are recorded in the Marasamyutta, one of the Buddhist canonical books. None of us are perfect, if perfection means that the embers never stir. Their stirring is an absolute element in life. They stir, but the fire need not rage. One feels the embers stir, but then there is the moment when one either feeds the fire or does not do so. To not do so requires faith, and such faith is nourished by love. A person who lives so is by no means emotionless. Rather their emotion is honed to a sharper edge.

## Strong and Vulnerable in the Same Moment

**Now that Mother had been officially declared mortal,** she was moved to a side room. It was a blessing to be removed from the bustle of the main ward. She was pleased to have some peace. It was, nonetheless, an intensely emotional day. For myself, there were times when I was flooded with desolation and other times when appreciation of life welled up. I am sure it was similar for the other players in this drama: Caroline, Heike, and Mother herself, as well as other members of The Buddhist House community who were getting most of their information second hand.

I had several very tender moments with Mother that day. She was sad, yet stoical, dismayed, yet accepting.

"I would have liked to have had longer with you," she said.

I recalled a conversation she had had with me several months before that had begun with her saying, "Now, I want to have a serious word with you, dear. I have a feeling that I may not be going to live that much longer." She had gone on to tell me how she had been putting her affairs in order so that "When I do go, you won't have anything to worry about. I've put all the documents in my box in the wardrobe – the will, the bank books and so on."

I had said, "Well, I hope you're not planning to go just yet. We were counting on having you for another twenty years or so."

She had smiled. "Well, you know, you just get a feeling sometimes."

At moments like that she could seem both strong and vulnerable in the same moment. I had always been aware of her great love and, of course, I admired her spirit, but she could also seem very frail.

"We all have to go sometime," she said.

**Meeting is such a poignant mystery**. "I would have liked to have had longer." Somehow I sensed in that phrase her appreciation of existence. There was nothing negative in it. It was not protest against having to die. It was not really about length of time. It was an acknowledgement that the times we had had were of such a quality that they were precisely what one would want to have more of. One would want to have more of that quality, whether within the world of life or the world of death, whether now or in the future or in whatever time or dimension one might conceive one's sentient existence to take place. What one hungers for is a quality of meeting, an understanding, a mutual sympathy and trust. Here or hereafter – that is heaven.

I have a good friend who is also a Pureland priest. Taira is Japanese, but he has lived in London for several years. We also have enjoyed some very good moments. In his work of conveying the Pureland message to Westerners he has had to struggle with the task of rendering key Japanese concepts into English. He has sometimes discussed at length with me the way to render a particular idea or phrase and these discussions have often been rich times for me. They are rich because the interaction goes beyond the superficial level. It is not just that he is trying to find a technically correct equivalence of terms between the two tongues; it is that he is struggling to express something that is in his heart in a way that will touch the hearts of others who were brought up in a different culture. Not only that, but he is trying to convey to me the difficulty this presents for him. It is when we are invited into another person's difficulties that we start to know them in a much deeper way. In human life, process is more potent than outcome. To know only what a person concludes or professes does not admit you to their sanctum. Only knowledge of what troubles them and of what they are struggling over does that, and it is then, when you do already have some intimate acquaintance with their struggles and vulnerability that the conclusions that they do profess take on radiance.

Caroline, my wife, is also a Buddhist priest. Ordinations involve the taking on of new identity and in Buddhism this is generally acknowledged by the giving of a new name. Thus my personal birth name is David and my Buddhist name is Dharmavidya – "Seer of the Truth". Caroline's Buddhist name is Prasada. These names are in the Sanskrit language, which is the classical language of Buddhism. The word prasada is a very important term in Buddhism and especially in Amidism. The equivalent term in Japanese is *shinjin*. The problem of how to explain shinjin to English-speaking people is more or less equivalent to the problem of how to bring Buddhism to the West. It is the key to the whole business. Understand shinjin and you understand everything.

The common transliteration of shinjin into English is by means of the word "faith". The word faith, however, has a long history in the West and it is closely associated with some of the most fundamental conflicts in our culture. The past two centuries have been occupied by a pointless rift that somehow occurred between religion and science and in the working out of that rift the word faith has, for many people, come to be associated with mental blindness. Yet this is almost precisely the opposite of what it indicates in Buddhism where prasada indicates awareness and clarity.

One day, Taira and I were engrossed in a lengthy conversation on this issue and so I said,

"Well, what is shinjin for you?"

"Shinjin is encounter."

This was a very clarifying moment.

**Faith is situated in encounter**. It is at the point where self meets other, the point where other touches self, that faith occurs. Faith, in the sense of shinjin, is not belief. That is something else. Belief may be an adjunct to faith, but it does not define it. Faith is a quality that inheres in relationship with what is not self. Belief covers what we take to be the attributes of the other and the beliefs that we hold – that the other is friendly or benign, say, may aid us in entrusting ourselves to the encounter. The idea that "God is good" is surely a way of encouraging us to trust Him, but it is the trust itself rather than the belief that matters.

Shinjin is not blind. Shinjin clearly sees the reality of not knowing, which is something quite different. To encounter something that is other is to encounter something that we do not know, and that unknown being touches and changes us. To allow this to happen is faith and without faith we can never enter into a true encounter.

**Belief can indeed be blind** because people can and sometimes do hold onto beliefs in defiance of strong contrary evidence. Faith, however, at least in the sense of prasada or shinjin, is a quality of entrustment that is the essential key to intimacy. The ideal spiritual life is one in which one would have such intimacy with the whole of existence, which is to say that one would have it within every specific encounter that arose in the flow of one's experience. That is the enlightenment that defeats death. Shinjin, therefore, is open-heartedness, not just to other people, but to every experience, and that is what constitutes faith in the Buddhist sense. It is very closely related to tenderness and love.

Death is such an unknowable other. It is an ultimate other. There are those who think that after death lies nothingness – a dreamless sleep. There are others who equally strongly adhere to the idea that after death one is reborn in this or another realm. These are both beliefs. Faith is something else. In fact, death is a mystery. Even if or when we are to be born in another realm, what do we know of it? And what makes us think that our present mode of existence is the only one there is? Must heaven be something like this place, only better? We are bound to think so and to use this convention in order to communicate about it, but it is only a convention. The Pureland scriptures describe heaven in detail. They enable us to face death. But it is the encounter that matters, not the accuracy of this or that postmortem topographic survey. Death is the great moment of life. It is the time when we encounter the ultimate other for real. No belief will protect us from this, but faith will enable us to enter it willingly, open-heartedly, and lovingly.

**Faith is everyday** as well as grand. It bears on relationships with other humans as much as with spiritual beings. Over the years, Mother and I had developed a great mutual confidence. I do not mean by this that she was always right about everything, nor that I was. But we were willing to confide in each other appropriately in a way that gave each of us the knowledge that we trusted and were trusted by the other. The achievement of such confidence requires a degree of modesty. In trusting another, one is not only taking the reckless step of relying upon an other who can never be fully known and who is subject to the absolute existential parameters of life and change, but one is also admitting one's own frailty, lack of omniscience, uncertainty and possible culpability in the twists and turns of life's uncertain drama.

In practice, this had often meant, in our case, an exchange beginning, "I wonder if we could have a little chat." English is a language and culture in which understatement plays a formidable role. A little chat might easily mean that something quite dire and potentially hurtful had got to be confronted. Or it might mean that one of us felt that it was time to review a situation "that has been going on long enough".

I had learnt to enter these encounters disarmed and I consider this to be one of the best things I have learnt. Although, in many of my roles I now carry considerable responsibility and, sometimes, the authority to go with it, I am far from always knowing the best course. Often, too, it can quite quickly come to light that something I have already done has contributed to the problem, or, at least, not made it any easier to solve. I tend to be somewhat impetuous and this sometimes yields big dividends, but it also carries risks. Mother tended to err on the side of caution – "Least said, soonest mended" – but not always – "Something will have to be done about it, dear." Well, such are the fumbling attempts that we humans make to solve what seem like the major dilemmas of life, the indolence of one member of the community, the over-zealousness of another, the confusions of roles and duties, the ricochets of hurt feelings that can bounce around any group.

There is a practical side to human life, and Mother was nothing if not practical. At the same time, that is not the only or even the most important side. The other side is love. Both sides need tender care and they work together. Love that does not manifest in practical consequences means little and practical solutions that do not really express love are not really solutions. There is, therefore, much craft in the art of life, the art of loving.

**Love always has an object** and that object is never the self. Even when people talk about loving oneself, what is indicated can only be achieved by objectifying the self. Of course, the word love is used in all sorts of ways, some of them not really legitimate. Love, however, is embedded in this matter of encountering an other in a trusting way. The other is something that is unknown yet is in a process of revealing itself, of becoming known in increasing degree. The unknownness is never completely eliminated, however, which is why love has potentially infinite depth. We can never fathom another completely. It is only in the ambience of trust, of shinjin, that this process of love ever deepening can proceed.

## THREE

# IRON DETERMINATION NOT TO FAIL

**People Are Changed by Spiritual Experience**
**When you are old, frail and dying, you have to trust other people**.
When they move you to a side room, you have to go. When they come
to take blood from your arm, you have to submit. It may be painful, it
may be against your desire, but you have to trust those who would help
you to some degree. There may also come a point where you withdraw
that consent. Each little step, therefore, involves a choice. It is a choice
whether to trust or not. In very few of these choices does the patient
have enough information to know the situation as well as the people that
are advising her, yet, ultimately it is she that makes the choice. Trust
enters in at every stage.

As it was, Mother was pleased to have been moved to a side ward.

"It is more peaceful. Mind you, they come in every few minutes to
do something or other." Hospitals are busy places.

At this point we were not sure how long Mother would stay in hospital or exactly what would happen while she was there nor if or when
she would come home. I was experiencing a growing awareness that it
was going to be me that would have to make the decisions. Although I
could consult others, it would be me that Mother would trust above all
and were I to make mistakes in this process they would not be easy to
live with afterwards. The scale of the responsibility and the resulting
need for me to take it on squarely were only just dawning upon my consciousness. As they did so I began to feel very calm and quiet inside.
Within this quietness arose an iron determination not to fail in what lay
ahead.

**That afternoon Mother talked to me about the afterlife**. She wanted me to say what I believed or knew about it. She did not really seek information, rather an affirmation that we were on the same wavelength as we set out together on this adventure that was going to be her transition from what we call life to what we call death. We did not speak long, but we knew, beyond the words exchanged, that we shared an understanding.

The lesser problem in talking about life after death resides in the difficulty of finding a vocabulary that does justice to our feelings and intuition. The greater difficulty lies in the fact that we do not know and cannot know what we are talking about. Facing death is the encounter with an unknown other in its most quintessential form. It is the scenario for shinjin *par excellence*. It is also the prototype of all others, so that it is possible to say that all encounters are encounters with death. Day after day we encounter death in the unknownness of the other and the unknownness of what will become of us when we enter into encounter with them.

In the course of serious Buddhist training one experiences some very intense states and in these states there come remarkable and unforgettable experiences. The world is transfigured into a realm of radiance, and one can understand why some mystics speak of lifting the veil that hides the other world from this one. The Buddhist scriptures record many instances of the Buddha bringing his disciples to the point where they had such sightings of the other world. Among these experiences are memories of previous lives and appearances of, on the one hand, the radiant realm that Buddhists call the Pure Land and, on the other, the inferno that is known the world over as hell. In the Larger Pure Land Sutra, the Buddha enables Ananda to see such a vision. Ananda was the most loving of the Buddha's disciples.

As a person educated in the modern manner who has also experienced the Buddhist training, I find myself on the cusp of two contrasting domains of meaning. It is as though a dialogue takes place within me between the representatives of these two domains.

Modernity says, "You should not accept anything without evidence of your senses."

Buddhism says, "Quite so, and you have had a wealth of experience. You have seen the radiant realm for yourself."

Modernity replies, "But can you trust what you have experienced? Is what you have experienced not just projection of your own mind?"

Buddhism says, "You cannot have it both ways. On the one hand you say do not trust without experience and then when there is experience you say do not trust it. If you cannot trust your own experience, what can you trust?"

Modernity says, "Observations must be measurable."

Buddhism says, "I allow you to experience the immeasurable."

At this point it becomes apparent that Modernity wants to believe one thing and Buddhism wants to believe the other and there actually is no evidence that could decide the matter, as it were objectively. This is inevitably so because one cannot go outside life to have a look, collect a sample of the other world, and bring it back for others to see.

On the other hand, there is a sense in which one does do exactly that. Whatever the merits of the modernist paradigm, it is a fact that people who have had what we may call spiritual experiences are changed by them. They themselves are not the same as they were and this change in them can be evidence for others who have not had the experience in question directly.

## The Other World is Close At Hand
**Siddhartha Gotama, the Buddha**, lived in India 25 centuries ago, sought answers to troubling existential questions, embarked upon a spiritual quest, became spiritually awakened, attracted a following, established an order of disciples, and died in a state of fulfilment. Undoubtedly he was an accomplished thinker and speaker, but what

really attracted people to him was a personal magnetism that came from the fact that he lived in frequent contact with the other world and that he was able to bring others to the point where they also saw that world for themselves. He knew Nyorai.

Modern, especially Western, Buddhism tends to down play this mystical side of the Dharma. The widespread secularism that one encounters saddens and inhibits me. I often feel that I cannot fully say what I feel and believe because there is a pervasive taboo upon saying outrightly religious things these days. However, when one stands in the face of death, either one's own or that of somebody close, social convention is not a strong enough reason to do anything if it conflicts with the needs of the moment. Experiencing my mothers death, therefore, has helped to prise me free from the shackles of conventional skepticism.

The popularity of Buddhism in the modern world has come, in large measure, as a result of the fact that Buddhism is a spirituality that seems to be in less conflict with science than any of the other major religions. Buddhism and science share a deep respect for the value of experience. As soon as one presses the matter a little further, however, one is aware that nobody trusts experience completely because we know that it can be deceptive. How, therefore, does one select which experiences to consider valid? Here, the modernist and the Buddhist paradigms sometimes do part company. Religion deals with experiences that certainly happen, but for which science has no real concern and the converse is also true. Religion and science are not in conflict, they are simply different domains. Modernism, however, tends to take the scientific domain as the only one worthy of consideration and in doing so eliminates the most important elements in human experience from consideration. This leads to an impoverished culture, the banality of which is everywhere evident in our times.

**Modernism offers no satisfactory way of coping** with the emotions and experiences that accompany death. Its preference is to try to explain them away through reductionist arguments. These make moderately satisfactory logical games, but they do not satisfy the human spirit and do not ennoble our lives or help the dying person. Buddhism became acceptable in the West in part because of its compatibility with science. This is fair enough as far as it goes, but the projection of Buddhism principally in this frame may lead its contemporary advocates to overlook the fact that what Buddhism has been known for throughout history is its expertise on the matter of death, a subject that has science stumped.

"Buddha" is the best known epithet of Siddhartha Gotama. Another epithet that is less well understood these days is "Lokavid". Loka means world. Vid means seer. Gotama was a seer of the other world – the world of Nyorai. If, like me, you are a mediocre practitioner of the Buddha's path, you may still be blessed from time to time with experiences that only religion has a vocabulary for. The most important among these then become the major landmarks of your life. They inform you. They set the form and direction for what one does. Even though one remains a foolish being full of the normal wayward passions, life is quite different when one has experiences of this kind. They act as lighthouses as one crosses the stormy sea of life. It is not, however, something that is easy to talk about in contemporary polite society, ruled as that often is by a ruthlessly a-spiritual dogmatism.

The modernist paradigm is correct in saying that the experiences that one has of the other world are, as experiences, something that take place inside this world. They are, however, something that transforms one's perception of this world and of one's departure from it and this fact, whatever formulae are used to point it out or account for it, is something that has been known to humankind since time immemorial. Such experience resides in the borderland between the two worlds and there is no time when that border becomes more real than when one sits beside a dying person or when one is dying oneself.

**Closeness to death changes us**. When I was in my twenties I myself had an experience of very nearly dying. After a day's walking I was hot and tired. We went for a swim and when far from land I became exhausted and began to drown. The experiences that I had at that time concur very well with the scientific literature on near-death experiences. One does indeed see the being of light. One does indeed experience a great peace and acceptance. Perhaps it is not so for everybody, but it was so for me and, by all accounts, it has been so for many other people. Now it is possible to give physiological rationalisations for some of these phenomena, but they feel extremely personal. It is probably possible to provide similar physiological accounts of what it means to fall in love, but such accounts do not really add any meaning to the experience any more than an analysis of the properties of paper and ink would add to the experience of reading Keats' poetry. The fact that things happen in a certain medium does not explain away the fact that they happen. In Pureland Buddhism, the being of light is called Amida and in this identity it, or he, is linked with a wide range of other phenomena in which one feels touched by a power that is beneficent and exterior to oneself. The Buddha, however, did not really mind what we call these things. His task, as Lokavid, was to point them out. Call it what you will, our existence becomes most alive when it opens to the other world, to the light in our midst, which is also the death all around us. We live within certain absolute parameters of birth and death. Our life becomes meaningful when it is touched by a radiance that has every appearance of having its roots somewhere beyond or outside of those parameters. The parameters are not just in time. Certainly there is a time before birth and a time after death, but death is also present all the time. The other world is always close at hand.

Each religious system then clothes such experience in its own systematisation and such systems then fall into the hands of many who have never had the requisite directness of experience. Thus opens a

Pandora's box. On the one hand, the most fantastical structures can be erected on the most flimsy foundation. Or, tragically, people can come to fighting over they know not what. Or again, people can refuse to admit any such possibilities into their scheme of things and so close the door to the most precious experiences known to woman and man.

## Entrusting to Death As to Unconditional Love

**The Buddhist account** goes something like this. It conceives of two realms that are not ultimately to be thought of as different or separate, but they serve well as a heuristic device. They enable us to navigate through the vicissitudes of the borderland. One realm is the realm of our ordinary existence, encompassed within birth and death. This is called the realm of the Born. Whatever is born will sooner or later die. Whatever begins will come to an end. Within the Born Realm everything is dependently originated. It comes into being in dependence upon other things that also reside within the Born Realm. This, then, is a realm of flux. Everything that Buddhism says about the Born Realm accords very well with the paradigm of modern science and this is one of the reasons why Buddhism has become an acceptable religion to many modern people.

According to Buddhism, however, the Born Realm is not itself born. It goes through endless reformulation, but time is eternal. Cosmic systems are born and die. Cosmic ages come and go, but the whole process is cyclical without any exact repetition. As in the microcosm of seasons on earth, so in the macrocosm of eternal time. Big bangs there may have been, but there was something before that too.

So much for the physical world. Where this becomes important is that the same is considered to be true in respect to the seasons of our life, from the seasons of a single thought that is born, ripens and fades, through the seasons of a lifetime that is born, matures, weakens and dies, up to the scale of an endless procession of lifetimes stretching long beyond this one existence. Buddhism does not see the drama of a life being extinguished simply because the body dies. The karma of that life goes on. Far from being only concerned about the here and now, Buddhism is also concerned about the fact that our lives have very long-term consequence. There are two distinct matters to describe here. One relates to the fact that Buddhism teaches rebirth; the other to the fact that rebirth is still part of the Born Realm and the ultimate understanding is to establish one's relation to the Unborn.

**Let us deal with rebirth** first. Buddhism teaches rebirth. It does not teach that there is an eternal soul that finds new bodies. It teaches that a new life derives its momentum and character from a former life that has ended. This is rather in the manner that momentum is transmitted from one billiard ball to another. We might ask what it is that passes from one ball to another and, in tangible terms, the answer is nothing at all, and yet the second ball moves and its movement is exactly a function of the momentum of the previous one and the circumstances of the moment of impact. To explain this phenomena scientists and mathematicians employ the metaphysical concept of momentum. Rebirth is rather like that. You may accept this account or not, but whether you agree or not is not really the point, any more than whether you believe in something called momentum is the point of what it means to be a good billiards player. It is a way of describing a phenomenon and, most importantly, it provides a way of orienting oneself to that phenomenon, just as some understanding of momentum enables the player to shape up to the ball. Whatever we believe, we have to face the task of shaping up to the ball of life and death and many of us unfortunately do so seriously ill-equipped.

So I invite you to agree, or at least suspend disbelief for a moment, while I take you a little further into the Buddhist conception of the facts of life and death. Within Buddhism, there are two different accounts of precisely what happens at the time of death. According to the

Theravada, or southern, School of Buddhism, rebirth happens immediately. When a person dies – a process that only takes a few thought moments – the karma of that person immediately transmits to the life of a new, not necessarily human, being. According to the other schools of Buddhism, however, whether of Indian, Tibetan or Chinese origin, the transmission is not immediate, but is characterised by a between-lives interlude of up to 49 days. This interlude is called the *bardo*.

Actually these two accounts can be more or less reconciled if one considers the bardo itself to be a rebirth. If we consider our billiard ball analogy, if there are two balls on the table that are touching each other and a third ball then hits one of them, it may be that it is the other of them that moves while the ball that was hit remains stationery. Momentum can pass through an intermediate medium. The bardo is an intermediate medium, but it could be thought of as a kind of temporary intervening rebirth.

Traditional accounts based upon reports of near death experience and the experiences of those whose intense meditation has taken them into states analogous to death, describe the bardo as a series of stages. The first stage is the well attested appearance of the great white light that Buddhists associate with the figure of Amida. The appearance of this light is considered to be the most potent spiritual opportunity that a person ever experiences and the majority of people only experience it at the point of death. Consequently most people are unprepared for this moment and, unless they have particularly steady faith, the opportunity that it presents is lost.

**At death**, the energies of the person gather and, as the body fails, they separate from it, some say, passing out through the point at the crown of the head. This leads to the experience of the great light, bright as lightning, toward which the person is initially drawn, but which, on closer approach, is too intense for the uninitiated to cope with. The ordinary person, at this point, feels terror. Turning away, they encounter a series of lesser lights and dream-like apparitions, each extremely vivid and compelling, some soothing, some alarming, some seductive. Death, therefore, is rather like vivid dreaming. The forms that appear during this phase have a benign and a wrathful aspect and, depending upon what propensities the person established in their previous life, one or other of these aspects will predominate. These appearances offer a kind of second chance to avoid rebirth within the Born Realm. Generally, however, this chance is not seized and the wrathful manifestations more and more predominate. This is understood as a natural consequence of the operation of the will of the being in the bardo state, constrained by the attachments developed in previous existence and by judgements formed about past acts. In Buddhism, there is no divine judgement – we condemn ourselves. As the bardo state becomes more and more uncom-fortable, the being begins to long to have a material body once again. Inexorably it is then drawn back into a carnal existence of one kind or another. The energy that has thus been transmitted through the bardo medium enters a newly conceived being in the physical world and a new lifespan commences. Such, in very brief outline, is the traditional account.

In this schema, the new birth is a function of the state of mind – or, better, the state of heart – of the person who died. The bright light is equated with unconditional love. It is such love that the ordinary person cannot cope with. They are unable to surrender to it. The inability is a failure of faith or trust. The succeeding apparitions are, like dreams, self-generated. They reflect the life that was lived, just as our dreams reflect, in a rather scrambled way, the anxieties, desires and achieve-ments of our days. When we have dreamt enough, we wake to repeat the cycle, but never in exactly the same way.

The above describes the common case. There is, however, also an uncommon case. This is the case of the person who has shinjin. We have already said a bit about what shinjin implies in the encounters within life. Death is the paradigmatic encounter. The person of shinjin entrusts him or herself to death as to unconditional love that is completely trusted. This, in Buddhism, is what is meant by a good death.

Such a one does not flee the light. Their karmic momentum consequently does not transmit itself through the bardo medium. They enter the Light. This is described as being met by Amida and the heavenly host and carried away to the Pure Land. The Pure Land is not subject to the same laws as the Born Realm. In the Pure Land one experiences only up-lifting occurrences. Everything instructs. Everything is helpful and compassionate. One receives everything one needs. One's activity is that of gathering blessings that naturally fall and offering them in gratitude to one's myriad benefactors – the "Buddhas of other worlds".

Buddhism is not the sort of system in which membership is restricted to those who believe and profess authorised doctrine. Rather it is a system in which a variety of practices are offered to assist us in our passage. The above account is offered to help the dying – and we are all dying. My mother had confidence that she was going somewhere and that it was going to be alright. She hoped that she would be able to look back and see how those she loved were faring, but she also accepted that "What will be will be."

To live one's life in relation to Nyorai is the best possible preparations for the transition that occurs at the death time. If one is accustomed to listening to the call of Amida then one will be ready to go toward the light at the moment when bodily life fails. Nothing is more important than this.

## The Unborn
### The Buddha famously said:
"There is, monks, a basis wherein there is neither earth, water, fire, wind or space; that is not the infinity of consciousness, nor nothingness, nor is it that basis that is called neither entrancement nor non-entrancement;

that is not this world nor the next world; that is not the sun or the moon.

"Monks, I am not talking about coming or going or staying or falling or rising up. I am talking about what is completely without other support, without itinerary, without aim; about that which is the end of dukkha.

"The absolute upright is hard to see

Hard is it to see the truth

Cut through is craving for one who knows

Unheld is he who truly beholds.

"There is, monks, an unborn, a not-become, a not-made, a not-conditioned. If, monks, there were not this unborn, not-become, not-made, not-conditioned, there would be no liberation to declare here from the born, the become, the made, the conditioned. Yet there is an unborn, a not-become, a not-made, a not-conditioned, and therefore there is a liberation from the born, the become, the made, the conditioned to be declared.

"For the one who is dependent, there is quavering. No quavering for the independent. Without quavering there is serenity. With serenity there is no inclination. With such absolute up-rightness there is no coming or going or staying or falling or rising up. When there is no falling or rising up there is no here and there. Such is, as it is, the end of dukkha."

This is how the Buddha talked about nirvana. The context of this teaching, which is given in a Buddhist text called the Udana, says that the Buddha had been talking to the bhikshus with "Dharma talk about nirvana, pointing it out, making them take it up, making them keen, making them bristle with excitement" so that the bhikshus "listened with attentive ears, made it their aim and set their hearts upon it."

**Nirvana is** the "end of dukkha". Dukkha literally means "bad space". Bad spaces are the times when we fall into spiritual danger. The approach of death is such a time. Dukkha times are times when the issue might go either way. One might be ennobled or might be debased. One might, at such a time, fall into bad habitual responses, be overwhelmed with panic or become embittered. On the other hand, one might rise to the occasion, learn profound spiritual lessons, act in a noble way, and provide an inspirational example that lifts the spirits of everybody. The aim of the spiritual life is to cultivate that latter possibility. That is what is meant by the absolute up-right or true independence. That is the possibility that should make us bristle with excitement and it is what we should set our hearts upon. This is surely true for followers of most creeds.

The phrase "end of dukkha" can be taken in two ways. It can be taken to mean that dukkha is ended so that it will not recur. On the other hand, it can also be taken to indicate the end for which dukkha exists. Although it is not the common reading, there are many good reasons for believing that the Buddha used it in the second sense or was deliberately ambiguous. One of these good reasons is that the things that the Buddha himself defined as constituting dukkha do not cease in this lifetime, however spiritually enlightened a person may be. They include sickness, ageing and death, for instance. All three of these are dukkha times. Another good reason is that it fits with the general tenor of the whole of the Buddha's teaching, which is far from escapist. I do not think that the Buddha was advocating that his disciples reached a condition in which nothing ever troubled them again. Spiritual systems of that kind existed in his day, but he saw them as, at most, preliminary exercises not to be taken too far. The Buddha was not telling us about a state in which there is no quavering simply because nothing disturbs. He was telling us about not quavering because one is resolute and unwilling to be driven from one's post.

Life is full of challenges and testing times. The sages do not tell us to avoid them, but to live through them with such authenticity that we truly live. Many people never rise to this. They pass their existence tossed about by circumstance. They never manage to really distinguish between the absolutes and the variables sufficiently to live wisely. The independence that they seek is merely circumstantial and so illusory. The serious trouble in our life arises from that illusion, says the Buddha. On the other hand, there is a different kind of independence that is true liberation. That liberation is not the monopoly of the members of one particular faith community. It is the birthright of all people. A Buddha is simply a person who wakes up to it and points it out to others.

Why is life full of challenges? From the subjective side, which is the side that matters as far as spiritual practice is concerned, the answer is, in order to make us into noble beings. As my mother lay fatally diseased before me, I could feel that ennobling influence palpably calling. I could also sense the other option of panic. Only I could choose. Nobody could do so for me.

## In Poignancy Comes the Sense of Meaning

**All things change**. All things pass. Everything depends. We exist, yet nothing about our existence is certain, except that it will end. In the gap that opens between existence and elusive certainty we may blessedly find faith and so live full and vibrant lives. On the other hand, this same gap may become filled with worry, dread, anguish and so on, in which case we may become paralysed or go round and round in small circles. A great sage, Nagarjuna, who lived in India about 1800 years ago, likened the spiritual teachings to a great ship sailing across the ocean of changeableness. We must entrust ourselves to such a ship.

Here is a story. Once upon a time, long ago, in the age of exploration, there was a great ship with fine sails sailing across a mighty ocean. It was a magnificent craft with a large crew of fine sailors and a skilful captain. One day, land is sighted. The ship approaches a small island in the midst of the ocean and anchors in the lee of the land. A small boat is put down and a party of sailors goes ashore to reconnoitre.

After a time they return to the ship with reports of fresh water and provisions that can be brought on board. They also report that they have found one solitary person on the island.

The captain asks, "Did you invite the castaway to join us? We could rescue him from his solitude." The sailors say that they did indeed invite the islander, but that he is reluctant to leave the island. The captain is interested by this and gets his men to row him ashore so that he can meet the recluse.

The captain and the islander talk. They converse for some time. Eventually the captain works around to asking the islander if he will not consider joining the ship. The islander says, "I cannot leave my companions."

"But my men tell me you are the only person on the island," says the captain.

"Come with me," says the man.

They walk up onto the hillside above the beach, into a wide meadow. In the meadow are a score of stone cairns. Suddenly the outlines of what has happened become apparent to the captain. Once there was a small community on this island. Gradually they have each died and now there is only this one man left. The captain is deeply touched. It seems to him that the spirits of the islanders are still present in this field, as if hovering above their cairns of stone. They seem to speak to him directly.

After they have stood in silence for a time, the captain says, "I understand that you feel you must stay here for them, but my sense is that they are staying here for you. Perhaps you have detained them long enough."

The islander is startled by this comment.

The captain continues, "My ship needs reprovisioning. It will take a few days to take water and supplies on board. We will talk again." The captain then returns to the ship and gets on with his duty.

The islander spent the remainder of the week between the meadow and the beach. He went to each cairn in turn and spent time there remembering the person buried in that place. When he felt ready, he said goodbye. Then he took the stones from the cairn and returned them to the beach. As he took the last stone, he would say, "You are free. You may go now."

Finally there was only one cairn left. This was the site of burial of the person the islander had loved most deeply. He spent a long time sitting before this cairn and shed many tears. However, at length, he was able to say goodbye in this case also. He carried the stones back to the beach one by one. Finally, one small stone he put in his pocket.

By this time, several days had passed and the ship was reprovisioned. The captain came ashore again and met the islander who took him to see the now empty meadow. The meadow was not really empty, however. The grass swayed in the wind. The birds were singing. Insects and small animals were going about their complicated lives. No longer dominated by memorial cairns, the meadow actually seemed full of life. "I am ready to leave now," said the islander.

The captain himself rowed the islander out to the ship.

On board, the man who had been an islander began a new life. He was learning to be a sailor. There were many new people to meet and much work to do. The ship's sails unfurled and caught the wind and the little seaborne community set off for further travels.

Over the weeks and months that followed the new sailor was kept busy much of the time. In the lulls, however, he might sometimes be seen to take a stone out of his pocket and to look at it or to turn it in his hand. A glazed expression would come over his features at such times and an air of sadness hung around him. Sometimes he wept. The other sailors respected his privacy at such times. Then he would return to the task in hand. There was always much to do and many new friends to talk with. As time passed, the times when he took out the stone became less frequent and when he did the sadness was not the only emotion to be seen on his face. Sometimes, indeed, there was a smile, such as one smiles when he thinks of a work completed or a deed well done.

Well, of course, this story should end with the words, 'To be continued' for life goes on. We have all been castaways. We have had losses. We have built cairns and some of us have taken them down again. We may have a number of stones in our pocket. Life is bitter sweet and it is in the poignancy of that bitter sweetness that we find a sense of meaning. This is not something that is wholly 'inner'. The poignancy is amplified for the islander by the fact that he realizes that the captain understands. The whole drama of our life is a series of encounters. Something from oneself reaches out in longing and something from the measureless universe responds.

## Simply Out of Gratitude

**Poignancy is the flavour of a fully lived life**. There is bliss and there is sorrow. Most lives are only intermittently or even rarely like this. The ordinary person develops a range of strategies for keeping the facts of life at a distance in spiritual anaesthesia. This distance neutralises the sting of our frailty, but it also neutralises the love and exuberance we would otherwise feel in life. Our modern rituals that clinicise death categorizing it as a medical failure rather than the consummation of life only add to this problem. Sitting with my mother, knowing that she was dying, took away that distance. This made it a spiritual practice.

Buddhism is practice. Buddhists, like everybody else, have beliefs, but Buddhism is not a belief system primarily. Metaphysical and philosophical propositions have been offered as a way of supporting practice, not *vice versa*. So although Buddhism offers ways of conceptualising the after death state, individual Buddhists may take these ideas more or less literally, and nobody is going to get terribly concerned about it. What matters is the quality of a person's practice, much more than the orthodoxy of their belief. Buddhists, therefore, can recognize that a person from a different belief system may, in fact, be advanced in practice, even though that person's conception of the world and its working, of the meaning of birth and death and so on, may not be Buddhist at all. This is not to say that all religions are the same; they are not. It is to say that particular practitioners may be well established in love, compassion, altruism and inner peace without necessarily sharing the same idea of what will happen to them after death, say, or the same conception of the divine.

Sound spiritual practice does, however, enable us to approach the existential reality of life in an undiminished way. Here we can follow the basic existential dictum stated by Sartre that "Existence is prior to essence". Essence, here, means meaning. Humans create meaning, but they have to exist first; not only exist, but reflect upon that existence. The meanings they create will be a function, *inter alia*, of their ability to not run away from reality. The most potent reality is the ever presence of Death.

**How we love our bodies.** We are infatuated with them. Yet, how frail they are. I sit beside my mother in the quiet side ward. She is old. Soon she is going to die. But I am not that much younger, and several friends of my own age have died already. When Mother has gone, I will be the oldest in the family. In the normal order of things, that means the next to go, and even the normal order cannot be relied upon. Death can be sudden, as it had been for my father a year before. One afternoon he had a pain in the back. He went to the hospital, was examined and was told that there was nothing apparently wrong, but they would keep him in over night for observation. At 8am the following morning he died.

Just before writing this book I attended the Buddhist Teachers in Europe Conference in Germany in September 2004. Some expected delegates could not come because they had had to go suddenly to India to conduct the funeral of a great Buddhist teacher called Bokar Rimpoche.

Several of those who did attend the BTE Conference were shocked by the news. I listened to the story. It was not an unusual one. After some discomfort with chest pain, a decision had been made to send Rimpoche to a hospital for diagnosis and treatment. From the monastery to the hospital was two hours by car. Rimpoche, received some treatment, but died on the way home. He was 64 years old, seven years older than myself. I reflect upon how this great teacher was also a modest man, aware of his own failings and the frailty of life. I also reflect on how many people were helped by his guidance and how many would have wished to be so. When we reflect in this way, the gifts that we have become very precious. Impermanence intensifies value. Perhaps there was somebody who had thought, I would love to study Buddhism with Bokar Rimpoche, but first I must put my affairs in order. This person might feel constrained by worldly commitments, by the sense of not wanting to let others down, by having a mortgage to pay or a cat to feed. And now Rimpoche has gone and the chance has passed. How poignant. Often we intuitively know what we have to do in life, but we do not do it. We prevaricate. Is this not because we do not see Mara deploying his cohorts across the world?

Here is a passage by Bokar Rimpoche:

My previous acts and merit have not been weak: my life is full and free, my spiritual guide is qualified, and I received Lord Shakyamuni's essential doctrine. In this present moment, the best of all worlds, I don't cultivate the experience of genuine Teachings but throw this human life away in fleeting distractions. The deeds I've done form a wide canopy of unvirtuous acts. When I die, I'll be wracked with regrets. Thinking of this, I'm utterly discouraged with myself.

People of this degenerate time are busy and preoccupied; they are unreliable and very unstable. Ignorant of the consequences of their acts, they live unaware of vows, tantric commitments, modesty or shame – they lead themselves and others to eternal calamity. The Buddha, Dharma and Sangha are an unfailing refuge; apart from them, I've not found a reliable companion – I've lost hope in everyone.

We pride ourselves on shouldering the burden of the doctrines of scripture, realization, teaching and meditation practice – excellent education, spiritual activity, monastic lifestyle, and flourishing projects for others' good – yet the impurities of our wish for fame and fortune, and the eight worldly concerns, taint it all. How could this be correct Buddhist practice?

To our conceit toward what we've requested and received of the Teachings We add complaints when putting them in to practice. I wonder if our good-looking guise of spiritual acts will ever result in what we wish to attain for eternity?

Even this saintly man saw himself falling far short of the ideal. What of us ordinary folk? We may want to think we are wonderful, but we are, in fact, rather weak creatures. We know broadly what is virtuous and what is not. If it were simply a matter of learning that it is good to abstain from killing, from stealing, from sexual misconduct, from lies, from malicious speech, from intoxication and so on, and then putting it into practice, spiritual progress would be a great deal easier than it turns out to be. These kinds of behaviours are recommended in all schools of Buddhism, and, indeed, in most religions.

In the moralistic approach, we have to make a lot of effort in order to change ourselves. We try to create a new self, a better grade of self than the one we had before. But then it's about self-improvement rather than real self-subduing. The emphasis is upon looking at oneself and improving that self. When our attention is upon the grace we have received, however, we feel quite differently about the whole matter. We do try to do the things that improve us, but simply out of gratitude.

## Time Running Out

**Mother's body looks very thin** and vulnerable. The hospital staff "monitor her blood". This means coming in at least once a day and inserting a needle into her arm to extract a little blood that they can then test in various ways. Some days they take blood several times.

"They must have an awful lot of my blood in that laboratory by now", she remarks, half humorously.

I feel anguish looking at her arm, lying limp at her side. Against the sheer whiteness of the hospital sheets the areas of blue bruising caused by the repeated puncturing of her flesh stand out. At least half the area of her otherwise pale forearm is disfigured by these painful patches. I feel an inner revulsion at the pain she must suffer.

Across from her bed, we have placed a Buddha image where she can see it. As I am sitting beside Mother, a junior auxiliary comes in to attend to some matter. She is Asian. She sees the Buddha figure and says, "I worship that god, too."

This is interesting as Buddhists never refer to the Buddha as a god. It transpires that she is a member of the Jain community. Jainism is a religion that started in India about the same time as Buddhism. Here in Leicester there is one of the most prominent Jain temples in Britain and there is a substantial community of devotees in the city. The young woman then catches sight of my mother's arm.

"It is terrible what they do in these places," she says, "I'm sure it is not all necessary."

**I am touched by her compassion**. Again, I feel the mixed emotions of appreciating the efforts that different groups of staff are making, each trying to do their best in their own way, yet unable to do good without doing some harm at the same time. The nurses cannot help my mother without puncturing her arm. The auxiliary cannot express her sympathy without, as it were, puncturing the nurses. I feel for them all and, at the same time, I know that the tenderness of my feelings is itself conditioned by my proximity to Mother in her present condition and my sense of the pervading love.

Poignancy again. I love her so much, and she is in pain, yet the pain is inflicted by those who are trying to help her. Such is this life. It is seldom simple. The monitoring of the blood is essentially an act of compassion, and yet it inflicts pain and causes damage. When is enough enough? Our world is put together in such a way that it is often extremely difficult to disentangle what is kind from what is cruel. Sometimes what is kind to one party is cruel to another, as when an animal hunts in order to feed its young. Sometimes even acts that are designed to assist also harm the person who is assisted. Medical ethics are extremely difficult for this reason. Every medicine is also a poison, as one of the doctors remarked to me. "We should not use anything unless we are sure the benefit will out-weigh the damage." A good rational principle, but how is one to be so rational when the future effect can never be precisely known in a given case. One is reduced to statistics and professional judgement.

As a person of religion, this all interests me deeply, because it is the problem of the nature of good and evil and the uncertainty that is an inherent part of our existence. We are cast into a world in which certainty eludes us; yet still we have to act. And, as a son, it is I who would indeed have to act, amidst the uncertainty of conflicting advice, my own ignorance, and my profound feelings of affinity for my hapless mother now caught in the dilemmas of sickness, ageing and death, as we will be in due course. Even the words "due course" belie the reality, since it comes we know not when.

A resolve to get her discharged from hospital was beginning to form in me. The registrar had said, when he gave us the fateful news, that there was no strong reason for my mother to remain in hospital. When it came to actually taking her home, however, there were always going to be more things that the hospital staff would like to do, each of which involved more time. Time, however, was running out. It would be so easy to prevaricate, to let days and weeks go by thinking that one was erring on the safe side. In reality, however, there isn't really a safe side. One has to commit to something and later one will look back and judge. Non-action is just as much commitment as action is. There will always be another medical procedure that could possibly be of some use. Where is one to draw the line? I knew that Mother would like to be home. She would rather die there. I knew also that, when it comes to it, the medical staff may well advise keeping her in hospital. I ponder on what I should do.

## To Act in Wholesome Ways Even When the Times are Against Us

**Everything we do is spiritual practice** if we live our lives in relation to the sacred – in the Buddhist case, in relation to Nyorai. I have begun to talk a little about spiritual practice. Of course, I have to express this in my own way, in terms of my own faith, but the issues are probably much the same in most spiritual communities. The general model common to many schools of Buddhism is one in which a certain method is prescribed for attaining a specified goal. We might be told, for instance, that everybody desires happiness and that there are means to attain it. If we adopt practices that calm the mind, others that bring insight, and others again that cultivate wholesome qualities, our life will become richer and more satisfying.

Or we might be told that enlightenment is the ultimate goal of life and that there is a path that finally leads to it. It may be said that there is a way to perfect our virtues and refine our state of mind through the practices that are recommended. Each school offers its preferred methods and if we can put great effort into those practices then this will generate much merit. And through the accumulation of such merit we will be brought to a point of entering into something called Buddhahood or nirvana. Enlightenment and nirvana thus become rewards. They are the end point. If you ask a question like "What is enlightenment for?" you might get a blank look, because in this means and ends approach, enlightenment is the end point.

We might ask ourselves whether this is not at least a little strange. Was enlightenment attained only to be taught to others? Was it something essentially selfish, an achievement that brought bliss to the one person who understood? Surely enlightenment is a spirit in which a person might act, not a goal in and of itself. Nonetheless, religion needs to depict a goal by some terminology.

**There are other approaches**. Alongside the idea of Buddhism as a path to enlightenment, there also exists a second interpretation that advocates what is called the bodhisattva ideal. A bodhisattva is somebody not yet enlightened, who nonetheless dedicates him or herself to helping others. This altruistic ideal provides an important foundation for the thought and practice of what is called Mahayana Buddhism. You do not have to be enlightened to be a bodhisattva. Indeed, the original implication of the term bodhisattva was "one who is on the way to enlightenment". Thus, the Buddha himself is referred to as the Bodhisattva when one is referring to him prior to his enlightenment.

In general, however, the first model has, to a large extent subsumed the second so that the common idea in the Mahayana is that one attains enlightenment in order to help all sentient beings and, by implication, at least, one's efforts to be of help are not likely to be of much use until enlightenment is attained. Given that very few are thought to attain complete enlightenment, this remains a problematic doctrine. There is no doubt that the impulse to be of service to others is a strong theme running through Buddhist teaching and practice. The idea that one cannot really help until one's own personal spiritual development is complete, however, can sometimes dampen the potential of such altruistic impulses. Buddhism has been criticised for an over-emphasis upon navel gazing.

Another relevant factor is the natural modesty amongst Buddhists that makes people very reluctant to say that they themselves are enlightened or are going to achieve enlightenment in the near future. This has led to Buddhism being structured as a quest for enlightenment rather than as what you do when you are enlightened. Interestingly, this is not what one finds depicted in the canonical texts. In the texts, people get enlightened frequently and go on to do great things. At a very early stage in the Buddha's ministry he attracts the support of a young man called Yasa who soon became enlightened. Soon many of Yasa's friends also become enlightened and when the Buddha has got sixty enlightened followers he sends them forth into the world saying: "Go forth into all the world, for the good of the many, for the welfare of the many, in compassion for the world. Preach the Dharma, lovely in its beginning, lovely in its development, lovely in its consummation. Teach a life of holiness, perfect and pure."

Perhaps we latter day people have become too modest, or, perhaps, as one interpretation would have it, we are a poorer lot who do not have the potential of the spiritual heroes of old. Nonetheless, modesty is no bad thing and it may be that the doctrine has been restructured to accommodate this sentiment.

Be that as it may, the teachings that the Buddha gave tend to be interpreted by contemporary Buddhist schools as depicting, first and foremost, the means to enlightenment. In other words, a method and a goal. This approach is very suitable for people who are new to the faith or are suspicious of religion in general. They can accept a technical approach. In ordinary life people are very used to following instructions in order to attain a given result or objective. This approach is called the self-power approach. By doing something oneself one gets a result.

The eight-fold path of right view, right thought, right speech, right action, right livelihood, right effort, right mindfulness and right concentration, for instance, taught by the Buddha, can be seen as the means to eliminate craving from our lives, and if we can eliminate craving and desire then we will arrive at enlightenment. The problem with this kind of approach is that there are many people who clearly have the qualities that go with enlightenment who have not followed such a procedure in order to become like that. Most notable of these is the Buddha himself. He did not become enlightened in that way. He discovered the Eightfold path as a fruit of his enlightenment not as a means to achieve it. The prescribing of procedures is useful up to a point, but there are many who advocate or even practice procedures who do not have the right spirit. Religion is a matter of spirit. It is something beyond mere morality or technique. A religion that has become technicalised has lost some of its true spirit. It is more difficult to define that spirit than to outline a method, but that does not make it less important to try.

**Faith, in Buddhism**, or, I suspect, in any other religion, is not a procedure. It is a matter of the heart. Not only is it not a procedure, it does not really even mean belief. Belief is a matter of adhering to particular formulations or metaphysical ideas that may or may not be true. Faith is not that, particularly. Some beliefs may be simply a way of avoiding having to confront the uncertainty in life. Faith, on the other hand, is what enables us to do just that. Faith is a quality akin to courage. It is the willingness to trust the instinct that tells us to act in wholesome ways even when the times are against us or the going is difficult. In order to protect my mother in the way that she needed me to protect her, I would need such faith.

## Whatever I Need Will Somehow Be Given
**When we are enlightened** we will have the "divine eye" that enables

us to transcend our ordinary limitations of knowledge. Perhaps if I had had the divine eye then I would have been in no doubt what was best for Mother. I would have been able to see quite clearly what would happen were she to remain in hospital or were she to be discharged and there would consequently have been no difficulty in finding the wisdom to do the right thing. I would have had direct and precise insight into the motivations of all the different people involved and been a master of my moral universe. I would never find myself in bad spaces where moral judgements are hard to call and right actions hard to discern.

Alas, I am not enlightened, not, at least, in that magical sense, but, sitting by her side, I realize that there is a kind of enlightenment that I do have. It involves an awareness of the impossibility of having such magical clarity, and it offers a different kind of lucidity. I am capable of sympathy for the different players in this great drama: a drama in which the conditions in which a person will die hang in the balance. I see clearly that, even though I can consult most of the other players and listen to their opinions, it will be I who will have to make the decision in the end and I know that this is what Mother wants. She wants to be able to put her trust in me as far as the remaining things of this world are concerned because she must now turn all her attention to dying. I feel the responsibility as her charge upon me and I experience it as a substantive manifestation of her love and her faith. She has decided to put her trust in me. Now I have to find the resolve to fulfil that trust.

This realization is a more human form of enlightenment. It means trusting that as each stage of this drama unfolds whatever I need will somehow be given to me. The universe will provide so long as I remain steadfast.

## Supported by Grace
**Is spiritual awakening an achievement or a gift?** In developing the means and ends model of the spiritual life, Indian religions rely upon

the concept of merit. In Western understandings of Buddhism the term merit is not very much used, but the idea of personal accumulation or accomplishment remains strong. The notion that you make a great effort at being virtuous or training your mind and then there is a kind of reward in the form of enlightenment is clearly understandable to most Western people. It fits with the Western way of thinking. You put effort in and you get something out. You invest and you get a return. In the East, merit forms a kind of intervening currency in this process. Accumulating merit can come to be equated with spiritual security.

Merit became a highly developed concept in India. Thinking about merit, however, brings us face to face with the logical difficulty of the reward model. If Buddhism is essentially about overcoming desire, if it is essentially about self-subduing, then why is it, apparently, according to the model, about accumulating something for oneself or getting a reward for oneself? There is something about this structure of ideas that doesn't quite add up. There is a readily apparent contradiction in saying that Buddhism is about giving up desire in order to gain enlightenment, since it implies that if you have a desire for enlightenment then you won't get there, yet if you do not have that desire then you will not make the effort to do so, and then you won't get there either.

**There is, therefore, a third model** to consider. We have already considered the "Path to Nirvana Model" and the "Bodhisattva Ideal Model". The third model involves transfer of merit. There grew up within Buddhism, or perhaps there derived from the Buddha himself, the notion of what is called transfer of merit. Now simplistically speaking transfer of merit means "I can give some of my merit to you", or "you can give some of your merit to me". To some Buddhists this kind of idea is a heresy because karma has inevitable and inexorable results. The person who does good reaps good as a reward and the person who does bad reaps bad as a result, and this, being a fixed law of the universe, cannot be tampered with. That was the classic idea of karma in which the universe is seen as being absolutely fair in the long run. Everybody gets what they deserve. However the real meaning of transfer of merit has to do with what we wish. If we do a genuinely good act our wish is really that others reap the reward, whether they deserve it or not. This is part of the definition of a genuinely good act.

A good act is not really an act in which I'm trying to get something for me; a good act is one in which I am trying to do something for at least one other and ideally for all others. So what lies behind the idea of transference of merit is simply a principle of altruism – to do an act with no thought of self. This is what the Buddhist concept of "non-self", or unselfishness, logically carried through, requires: that what we do is done with no thought of self, and, therefore, is, in the more technical Buddhist language, an act of transference of merit.

Now, why do people do things for others? Why do they do anything at all? Or perhaps a more useful question would be: How do they? In what state can one do things for others or do things for oneself? What is required? Really what is required in order to do something for others – to give something away, you might say – is faith. Faith is the opposite of needing to be in control. When people lack faith they try to build up an independent position for themselves that is defended and secure. They try to ensure that whatever they do brings a profit to themselves. This outlook is associated with anxiety. When times get difficult and there is a problem for or a threat to one's family, one's group, or one's nation, people try to protect themselves. In troubled times, they may run out to the shops and stock up their larder so that they have got plenty in store, just in case. And then they create defences against the enemy, real or imagined. Greed and defensiveness are a function of insecurity. People grab a lot for themselves to guard against difficult times. When they feel secure then they let those stocks run down and the defensive walls fall into disrepair. If we have faith in the universe around us and are at ease in our life, naturally we are less grasping. There is then less self, less accumulation, less of what Buddha called *alaya*.

So one model is that we perfect our virtue and perfect our meditation and from this comes merit and through that we arrive at enlightenment whereas the alternative model begins with the need to establish the kind of faith that takes away the insecurity in our heart so that there is no need to grasp after enlightenment. And, of course, the paradox is that such faith is itself already a kind of enlightenment. With the awakening of faith we enter into a way of living in which the major feature is transfer of merit. The giving away of merit is like the giving away of our spiritual security.

We can give it away when we have more than enough and we cannot have more than enough by relying solely upon our own little stock. We can only give it away if we are receiving it. To have the sense that one is a recipient of merit is another near synonym for faith. We can call the receiving of merit, grace. Real religion is something beyond the means and ends model. It is the faith that comes from feeling perennially supported by grace. Even though my own merit may be meagre, still I am supported by grace. That is the spirit of religion and it is something that goes a long way beyond the spiritual materialism of means and ends. Grace is not something that can be measured. It is unquantifiable and unconditional.

From faith of that kind, virtues naturally arise. Naturalness becomes their foundation. Morality is not then a bridle or a whip. It is simply a description of what comes naturally to one who lives in real faith. Faith, then, is equivalent to enlightenment, and it is not the end product of a path or procedure. It is the source from which the path unfolds.

**Why Not?**

**I live a very full life.** During the last eight years of Mother's life my activities had been focussed into the development of an organisation called Amida Trust. This began in 1996 when a group of people got together to create an organisational structure around Buddhist and psychotherapeutic work that my wife and I and some of our associates had been doing.

It is amazing the effect that creating a name can have. As soon as the work we had been doing became something called "Amida Trust," people started appearing out of nowhere asking to join. We had not really thought about the Trust as a membership organisation, but, why not? People joined. Soon there was quite a collection of members and there was little or nothing that they had in common. While the organisation was embryonic, it was open season for each person who came to project his or her own hopes and ideals onto it. Initially we naively assumed that we would be able to be all things to all people and all would go without a hitch. How wrong one can be.

The initial sudden growth led to new initiatives. At a very early date we sent a team to Bosnia, a country that was then just emerging from a terrible civil war. This was the beginning of a series of initiatives in the field of overseas work. We were amateurs, starting from scratch. Everything we did involved reinventing the wheel. There was an excitement about working with such a clean slate. Everything seemed possible. We continued to offer psychotherapy and to teach it. We organized and sponsored work overseas. We ran classes in Buddhism and gradually evolved a distinctive style of doing so. And the organisation itself required a lot of maintenance. Administration is one of the unavoidable elements of modern life. We were very busy.

Not that that was a novelty to us. Ever since Caroline and I got together and my mother joined us, we had worked hard together. Mother was part of the team. In the early days she did a good deal of the administration and often it was her voice that people heard first when they contacted us. Some criticised us for that, saying that it did not create the right image. Mother could be quite brusque sometimes, but then, so could we. By far the more important element was that many people came to love her and she loved them. Her rooms became "the refuge within the refuge" as one person later described it.

**When our work crystallised into the formation of Amida Trust,** Mother continued to be an essential member of the crew. The number of people coming through the house, however, increased markedly and the range of activities snowballed. This was the situation that she had taken in exchange for a quiet retirement in her own bungalow in Yorkshire: two rooms in what was rapidly becoming the HQ of a bubbling, idealistic, international initiative.

Nor was it conflict-free. Ideals tend to breed conflict. The attempt to be all things to all people was perhaps necessary in the early days, but it was insupportable in the medium or long term. Sometimes it seemed as though every new person who came through the door brought his or her own scheme for reshaping the whole organisation in the image of his or her own project. Yet, in order to make any of these wonderful ideas bear fruit there would have to be discipline, perseverance and co-operation, and, even more daunting, selection. Yet one had hardly started on one project before another was germinating. Even worse, the person who started something off more often than not was unwilling to invest the energy necessary to see it through. It was their idea about what others should do rather than something that they really had the courage for themselves.

In consequence, there were a number of points of serious crisis in the early development of the Trust. At these times, I found Mother's prudence and ability to judge characters to be one of my most valuable resources. Although Mother was invariably kind and polite to visitors, she formed her own judgements and, for the most part, only confided them to me. She noticed little things. Were people kind, gentle and considerate, or did they only think of themselves? Were they the kind who persist and get something done or did they talk big and act small? Mother knew. In my conversations with her, I realized how much better she was than I at making such judgements. Sometimes I took notice of her, sometimes I did not. In the latter cases, it usually turned out that she had been right.

**It became apparent that we could not do everything**. We had to choose between projects. We had to choose between styles of work. We had to choose a single approach to Buddhism so that we could all practise together. We had to choose between people. Choice involves acceptance and rejection and some of the rejections proved painful. Some people were angry that we did not go their direction. It became obvious, however, that if we did not choose, then it would not be possible for anybody to choose us completely either because they would not know who or what we were. To carry through the projects that we had in mind we had to have people who were more committed, people who chose the Amida sangha because it was uniquely what they could identify with. We could not afford to remain amorphous, however politically correct it sometimes seemed to be to try to do so.

Such are the vicissitudes of a small new organisation. It was compellingly exciting. There was a wealth of things to do and some people marvelled at our productivity while others, of course, accused us of being workaholics. We learnt the benefits of persisting. All of this required a vast amount of energy. Such was our life. It was a work of love.

## The Sun Shining Upon us

**Now Mother lay sick**, almost certainly dying. I sat beside her in the little side ward. There was nothing to do. Heike sat in the opposite corner reading her book. From time to time a nurse looked in for one procedure or another, but mostly nothing happened. Mother slept. My mind roamed back over the fourteen years she had lived with us, so packed with events. As she slept I pondered further on the human condition, on our frailty and the grace that supports us through it all.

At the death time, a life can be weighed. What has it been worth? How can one measure a life? Earlier I spoke of merit. To some, merit is a way of measuring a life. Just as we may assess achievements in terms of tangible results, so one might try to assess the moral worth of a person's existence. I am sure we all do this to some extent, but a life cannot really be measured. Rather, a sense of something more profound intervenes. There is the sense of being helped and supported come what may and that, I suggest, is the heart of what we mean by religion. Some people say that Buddhism is not a religion. By this they mean perhaps that Buddhism is an exact translation of inputs into outcomes, something measurable and mechanical. To me, however, it is a religion, not a calculation.

A person who has not discovered the power of faith will prefer the means and ends approach. Later they may discover that there is a much more direct route. Each person, however, must start from where they are. A person mature in their spiritual practice can describe what is going on from any of these perspectives. They are not mutually irreconcilable or contradictory, but they do have a different tone.

Caroline, Mother and I had worked hard together to create something and many other good hearted people had got drawn in. The purpose of the whole endeavour was to make our best effort at service to others. Many people had come to our aid. I could look at the immediate situation in terms of my effort to get the right result, in terms of my concern for Mother, or in terms of my overwhelming sense of how much she and others had done for me.

When looking from the third perspective, I do not feel that any virtues that I have are really a personal achievement. The effort made seems only a slight contribution to redressing the balance. So, although all three perspectives illuminate real aspects of the situation, it is the third that grounds our efforts in the most wholesome foundation. My mother had cared for me unremittingly throughout my life. What did I do to deserve that? She fed me, clothed me, supported me, encouraged me and protected me. Now I had an opportunity to protect her a little. I felt grateful for the opportunity to such a profound degree that I could not fully express how I felt, even to Caroline.

**The most important things in life** come to us as a grace. We might think that we have somehow earned them, perhaps during previous lives, but it is hard to credit that we can ever have done enough to earn the sun rising every morning and shining upon us, which it continues to do no matter how good or evil our actions may have been in the preceding twenty four hours. Mother was such a sun for me.

## Myriad Benefits Have Come Our Way

**The term Pure Land** has gone through a number of phases of development. The original Sanskrit term was *Buddhakshetra,* which literally means a 'Buddha field' and has something to do with the Buddha's ideas about merit: the merit of supporting those who live virtuous lives and the merit that comes to us. If you sow your merit in the Buddha field it will give rise to a great harvest. We can also think of a Buddha-field as being a bit like a magnetic field – the field of influence that a Buddha has. To live in a Buddha field would be to live within the field of influence of an enlightened being, which is to say, within that Buddha's field of merit. Such a situation is the most fortuitous spiritually. It may, however, also be uncomfortable.

When we enter a room that is spotlessly clean we are liable to be suddenly acutely aware of the mud on our shoes. When the land is pure, we quickly see that we are not. When grace is all around, our frailties and failings become glaringly obvious. The person who wants to sustain a high opinion of himself must necessarily live in an environment that is more evil than himself. In order to shine, one must be the brightest light and so one must inhabit a gloomy world. When the sun comes out, the stars disappear. Stars only shine in the dark. Those who want to be stars, therefore, live in the dark. Such a person maintains a sense of his or her own goodness and importance by blaming. All that is bad belongs to others. Only in that way can the self remain holy.

**In the modern world, many people have lost faith** in the existence of divinity anywhere other than within themselves. The problem with such an approach is that the light of self makes the whole world dark. Blame becomes an epidemic as each person tries to avoid responsibility for anything that goes wrong. As blame proliferates, conflicts multiply. A world can be torn apart by such a focus upon self as the measure of things and the source of the only good. In fact, if we look at ourselves soberly, we see that we are far from perfect. We are implicated in many kinds of terrible evil. I sit here typing at my computer in a centrally heated house. I live in the rich world. Although here at The Buddhist House we use North Sea Gas and have energy efficient condensing boilers, we still cannot escape the fact that we are tied into an electricity grid that is still substantially dependent upon oil. Much of that oil comes from lands far away, several of which are currently immersed in war, oppression and tyranny. Much of that evil has been generated in an effort to keep the oil flowing in this direction. I cannot claim to be one of the good and the attempt to become completely pure never succeeds.

Just as this is true in the concrete material circumstances of life, so it is also true in the spirit and the mind. As a practising Buddhist – and as my mother's son – I try to be generous in spirit in all that I do, but I do not succeed. I do not always act in the most generous way and the passions that move my heart are certainly not always sublime.

As we become aware of our own darkness, however, the light around us becomes correspondingly apparent. Buddhism begins with a consideration of what good fortune it is to have been born human. "Precious human rebirth" is said to be as rare as a turtle surfacing in the sea and finding its head in the only floating ring on that ocean. From this we can go on to consider the myriad benefits that have come our way throughout our lives.

So it was for me in the hospital ward. The more acutely aware I was of the grace that had supported my life and the generosity of spirit that my mother exemplified, the more inadequate I felt in the face of the task of making the right decisions for her – the task that was inexorably falling upon me. The spirit of Buddhism, however, is not that of only acting in those areas where we feel ourselves to be master. We act even when we feel our own frailty most acutely. Indeed, getting in touch with our frailty ensures that when we do act we do so in a spirit of service rather than one of self-aggrandisement. We feel, it is not really me that is doing this. This is simply the outcome of the grace that supports me.

## Host to a Multitude of Feelings

**Following the emotional morning** of telling Mother what the diagnosis was, we had to return home for a couple of hours to attend to other things, leaving Heike at the hospital. It was apparent that there would have to be a hiatus in our usual packed schedule of events. We were due to run a nine-day training course imminently. We cancelled it. We were thinking about bringing Mother home. This would involve offering total care. It would be a full time job. At this stage we did not know how long a period would be involved. I was tacitly thinking in terms of three months. It was a big undertaking.

Faith is a matter of not knowing. We did not know how long. We did not know what would be entailed. A week before we had not known that this would happen. We had been thinking that as soon as Mother's medication was sorted out she would get well again. Now, suddenly, priorities had changed completely. Plans we had made were promptly abandoned. A new perspective opened up.

When you live in a world that is made of grace, you assume that all is well. Even though your loved one is dying, all is still well. Death is part of the order of things. This does not mean that it does not hurt. It is devastatingly sad. It provokes the most profound heart searching. Nonetheless, in the fundament, all is well. Death holds us just as life does.

The time when Death reveals his face is a dukkha. It is a time of spiritual challenge, a time when you discover whether faith is really there or not. The mark of its presence is the arising of the words "I am willing". Whatever this is going to take, I am willing. It was going to take quite a few things: willingness to let go of other plans and dedicate attention to Mother's needs; willingness to do a lot of physical nursing work; willingness to act decisively at certain times and to be patient at others; willingness to be host to a multitude of emotions, many of them extremely distressing – willingness to weep; and, above all, willingness to be immersed in love – not just Mother's love, but the love that the members of our community have for one another – love that is not paraded day to day, but which would now come to the fore in many tender ways.

## In Mortal Struggle Against the Fates

**Truth is universal**. I have a sense that, broadly speaking, the truth that religions try to convey transcends particular religions. I do not mean by this that all religions are the same, but I do have a sense of what might be called true or ultimate religion as something that actual religions are groping toward and which a small number of actual people might come close to embodying. Some, but by no means all of those people could be Buddhist.

Nor is religion something static. It is a Way. It is a spirit of action. It is a confidence – the confidence that one inhabits a world of grace, here and hereafter. That grace is not something that will be denied to anyone, yet most people do not allow themselves to receive it. Although grace is eternally and universally present, people live ignoring it. Ignoring it they construct stories about the world as a dark and dangerous place, become alarmed and cling to whatever seems to offer security. What they cling to, however, generally only offers transient support.

**I did not want my mother to die**. A large part of my being rebelled violently against the idea that she was going from us. At the same time, I knew that we all must go sooner or later and her dying was just as natural as her living. The two incompatible sentiments vied for my attention. At one moment, everything in the world seemed right and perfect and I inhabited a kind of mystical communion with all beings. The next moment I would be convulsed with unpleasant emotions as if some part of me was locked in mortal struggle against the Fates. One part of me knew universal grace. The other part clung to my mother and desperately wanted her not to die.

After a couple of hours at home dealing with the most pressing matters, we headed back round the Leicester ring road to visit Mother again. Caroline drove. I sat in the passenger seat, my heart was full of sadness. I was touched by the way that Caroline had started to take more particular care of me. As I needed to care for Mother, so, she realized, I would also need care. Over the following weeks she did her utmost to relieve me of practical responsibilities.

We talked of practicalities. If we brought Mother home, what equipment would we need? What services could we rely upon? What else did we need to know from the hospital? Behind this lay the question: When? We were reaching agreement on the need to bring her home, but when? We had no idea how slowly or quickly the cancer would devour her. I spoke in favour of bringing her home within a few days, but I was not yet certain that this was the right course. We weighed pros and cons and knew that we did not know. We lapsed into silence.

On the roadside the grass verge was a mass of dandelions. Most of the yellow faces had gone and now there were hundreds of clocks of seed heads waiting to be blown away. The light shone through them so that each had its penumbra.

"I love dandelions," I said.

It was a comment charged with resonance. My mother used to go out collecting dandelions to feed to Dennis our pet rabbit. She had the softest of hearts when it came to animals. In our garden nobody was allowed to pull up dandelions unless it was to give them to Dennis.

"Such a splash of colour and then those miraculous clocks."

I was conscious of the subtle irony. Most people regard dandelions as weeds to be destroyed. They are, however, splendid flowers.

"They look like little saints each with his or her halo, just like in the Pure Land."

Caroline started to cry. I imagined that she was thinking that this was just like me. Who else would wax lyrical about dandelion clocks in this way at such a time? There was a tenderness between us.

## The Most Ordinary Person of All

**I thought about the Buddha** as the car drove on. He lost his mother at the outset of his life. I was, by comparison, extremely fortunate to have had mine for my fifty seven years. Perhaps it was the loss of his mother that made Siddhartha Gotama go out in quest of enlightenment. Perhaps, having lost his own parent, the arrival of his son making him a parent was more than he could cope with. I had the good fortune of having my mother's love all those years. He had the good fortune to have lost his mother and been plunged into a spiritual quest that led in the end to enormous benefit for millions of people.

Shakyamuni Buddha was an ordinary person. In fact he was the most ordinary person there has ever been. He did not start off as an ordinary person. He started off as a prince. He started off as the son of a rich family surrounded by prophesies of future greatness. As an important person he had the things that important people get in this life. He had luxuries and sport and sexual partners in abundance and fine clothes and entertainment and the best food and many servants and so on. He had all of that and it brought a certain kind of happiness. The Buddha never denied that such worldly things have a certain attraction and do bring some pleasure. The pleasure is far from unmixed, however. There was always disquiet. He was always longing for something else that he did not quite understand. It did not matter how many palaces he had, they would never be quite enough.

This irritation stimulated his curiosity and led him into encountering the world around him. What he found gave him a shock. He woke up to the universal presence of disease and death, squalor and poverty, and the many cruelties of the world. We read that he was deeply disturbed by seeing how the very process of growing food involved turning the soil and thus exposing worms and other creatures that were promptly devoured alive by birds. The inevitability of suffering bore in upon him grievously.

So what did he do? Did he immediately turn over a new leaf and start helping people rather than living the life of the idle rich? No, he didn't. Feeling himself disturbed and pained by what he had encountered, he set out to find a way of overcoming his own pain. He went out on a quest for his own inner peace. Whatever you may read in apologist books, the fact is that the Buddha's spiritual quest was initially motivated by selfish consideration. He was primarily concerned to find a way to overcome the pain in himself. He went to many teachers – the therapists of his day – and learnt from them about karma and penance and mind purification and a whole range of methods for self-perfection and the creation of inner peace. These were then, as now, the stock in trade of spiritual practitioners and they were ultimately aimed at making one feel good by the pursuit of some technique or other, even though the methods themselves often involved much pain. The Buddha threw himself into this approach and his very effort ultimately revealed its bankruptcy. He became ever more isolated. His efforts to become free and immune simply finished up as self-torture. He became first conceited and ultimately dejected. Eventually we find him literally in the gutter being picked up by the kindness of a passing young woman on her way to make offerings to the forest gods.

At this point a penny dropped. His enlightenment, which soon followed, was, indeed, a turn around. When we read the description of the night of his enlightenment we do not read of him discovering his glorious perfection, encountering his immortal soul, discovering his Buddha nature, nor anything of the kind. We read of him encountering Mara, the Lord of Death. What he was enlightened to was the fact that he was shot through with Death's agents: greed, hate and delusion. He himself was greedy. He himself was proud. He himself was lustful. He himself was envious. And, above all, he himself was capable of complete blindness to his own state – to the reality. The reality that he had to face was the fact that his very nature was corrupt, or, to put it more poetically, that Mara would always walk a few steps behind him. The most imperative insight was the one that revealed this fact. Mara's constant presence was what Buddha awakened to. Death is not something that strikes once in a while. Death is always with us.

**So Buddha awakened to his own darkness**. That is when he saw the light all around. As he did so, because he was an intelligent person, there also came the insights about dependent origination. Blind passion is fathomless because it arises from conditions that are always present and always reforming. We are dependent and vulnerable. We cannot be independent and we cannot, therefore, be perfect. We will always be ordinary. To be a Buddha is to have completely woken up to just how ordinary one is.

When the morning star rose that morning he saw it with new eyes. Being deeply sobered by his night's contemplation upon the corrupt, lustful nature of being a person, he felt miraculously cooled. There was the star, still there. Even though everything in *his* world had fallen apart, *the* world was still intact, still just as beautiful – more so in fact. This put the final dot in place: the dethronement of his former conceit. We are accepted even though we are what we are. When he realized this he knew that he was on firm ground at last. He reached out and touched the earth, calling it to be his witness. The witness he required – reality, not conceit.

**The unimpeded light, Nyorai's grace**, embraces us, but is only apparent when we realize our own darkness. Through darkness there is light. The light that comes from knowing one's own darkness is the great flaming light that eclipses whatever sun and moon may have previously ruled our heaven. Such is the light of Buddha. He was enlightened in the dark of night. Thereafter he knew how Mara walked at his heel and that knowledge stood him in good stead. He did not slip back into being an extraordinary person. He was and knew himself to be the most ordinary person and that is what was extraordinary about him.

The car pulled into the hospital car park. I was jolted out of my thoughts. The thought that we might take Mother home tomorrow was starting to take shape in my mind.

In the afternoon I spoke with the Macmillan nurse. Macmillan nurses are specialists in cancer care. She was friendly, understanding and extremely helpful in giving me details of the different options that existed for Mother's support and treatment both inside hospital and out. She was also supportive of the idea of our taking Mother home and told me about the kinds of reasons that might be advanced for keeping her in hospital or for allowing her to be discharged. This was a thoroughly satisfying experience in the sense that I felt that I was being given the information that I needed with which to make a properly informed decision.

The day suddenly became purposeful. There were many things to find out and preparations to make. I decided that I had to have a clearer picture of what the medical staff had in mind and got the nurses to make me an appointment with the doctor for the following morning. In the meantime, Caroline and I made a range of enquiries contacting the various domiciliary services that can support a bed-ridden patient in the community and finding out what each had to offer.

## I Shall Do Whatever My Son Decides

**Tuesday morning** I woke up in a spirit of determination. Caroline suggested I rest, but I was impatient to be at the hospital. I was steeling myself for the task of getting Mother discharged, but still uncertain whether it could actually be achieved. When we got to the hospital we found Mother had been moved again. By now she had been on four different wards since she was admitted.

The time came for me to see the doctor.

"I would like to take my mother home from hospital as soon as possible. Can you tell me if there is any medical treatment that she needs that can only be administered in hospital?"

"We would like to do a scan and a biopsy to make quite sure of the diagnosis and we could make other decisions then."

I immediately started to envisage extended periods of time being required. I had already been briefed by the Macmillan nurse what was involved in each of the suggested procedures. A scan involves a head to foot x-ray of the patient's body with a machine whose computer can then produce a three dimensional graphic model of the interior of the body. This would show the distribution of the cancerous growth. A biopsy involved inserting a hollow needle into the patient in order to draw out a sample of the cancerous tissue. This latter is the only totally definitive method of diagnosis because it involves obtaining an actual sample of the cancer. However, it is a painful procedure and I had already seen the damage and pain caused by much smaller needles. I decided that Mother should be spared that if at all possible.

"When would you be planning to do these procedures?"

"She is already in the queue for the radiography department so the scan will probably be early this afternoon."

"I am willing for her to have a scan, but not the biopsy. I would like to take her home today, after she has had the scan."

I was surprised at my own decisiveness. It felt extremely bold.

"I would advise keeping her in hospital where she can have full nursing care. Also the biopsy is important."

"But it will not make any difference to her treatment will it?"

"It will help us to have more information that may be useful if there are complications at a later date."

I processed this very fast. If there are complications later they will do the tests again anyway. They are already sure of their diagnosis. None of this will affect her treatment.

"I think we both know that it will not make any difference to her treatment, will it?"

He repeated his basic points, but did not actually say that it would make any difference.

"Well, thank you for clarifying the situation. I am happy for her to have the scan if it can be arranged promptly. She will not have the biopsy. We will discharge her sometime tomorrow. We can provide nursing care and we are already in touch with the local services."

Although opposing views had been expressed it had been a surprisingly satisfactory encounter. The doctor was doing his job. He would err on the side of keeping the patient in hospital because if he discharged her and something went wrong he would be responsible, whereas if we discharged her then the responsibility would sit with us. He was not ruffled. In fact, I think he was reasonable happy to be dealing with someone who had a clear position.

We proceeded to the bedside.

"Mrs Brazier, your son wants to discharge you from the hospital. I'd like to discuss this with you."

"Well, doctor, I shall do whatever my son decides."

My mother has been deferential to doctors all her life. This remark, therefore, came as a shock. I had been preparing myself for a difficult three-way conversation, but it was not to be. She was completely decisive in passing this decision to me, so that was the end of it.

Suddenly I experienced a huge relief. Mother was coming home. Caroline and I were both delighted, though we also realized that a great deal of work lay ahead. We had, in a way, just signed a blank cheque. Mother could live an indefinite amount of time and throughout that time she was going to need intensive home care.

## Looking at the Flowers
**We spent Tuesday morning at the hospital**. Mother was not allowed to eat and at midday had to drink a large quantity of white liquid in preparation for the scan. She found it very difficult to swallow, but did her best. She managed about two thirds of it. I had to sit behind her on the bed to prop her up into a sufficiently vertical position while Caroline and Heike fed her the liquid dye. We had some laughs.

At 2pm a porter came and Mother was moved into a wheelchair. I accompanied her down to the radiography department where the computerised tomography scan would be done. She vomited some of the dye. I accompanied her into the scan room and helped her to get properly positioned on the bed on which the patient is passed through the machine. Fortunately she still had a drip needle in her arm so they were able to give her a second kind of dye without any further puncturing of her skin. By 2.30 it was complete. There was no porter so I pushed her back up to the ward myself. Along the way we stopped at one of the hospital entrances so that she could spend some time looking at the flowers. Then we had to hurry back because she could not contain the liquid much longer and we needed to get to a toilet.

By 3pm Mother was back in her bed and asleep. The experience had been tiring for her. Another registrar came to discuss post-discharge medication. At 5pm we took her home.

That evening she was in her own bed looking out at the lime tree through her window. It felt like an immense achievement.

## I am Just Like Everybody Else

**The sense of coming home** is amazingly affecting. Something deep in the human psyche must carry an archetype or imprint of some kind that responds to the sense of home. I was born in Northampton, but our family moved away when I was aged three and I never lived there again. When I was a child we visited my grandparents who lived in a small terraced house there and this continued until I was about twelve but it was intermittent as we lived abroad for much of that period. Thereafter I did not go back. So logically the place should have meant very little to me. Yet when I visited again after an interval of more than forty years I was overcome with emotion; this despite the fact that I did not know my way around.

Religions have ways of mobilising this sense of homecoming. The goal is often conceived as being the completion of a circle, arriving back at one's original place. The Pure Land of Buddhism is like that: finding our true home.

All my life I was a wanderer. My parents never settled in one place for long. My father was a civil engineer. He preferred to take relatively short contracts. This usually meant jobs that took a couple of years to complete. Consequently I attended many different schools and got used to moving. My mother too had grown accustomed to repeated homemaking.

In Buddhism, there is not just the sense of finding one's true home, however. Homelessness has also become an ideal. The Buddhist friar lived an itinerant life. In principle this style continues to the present day, but in practice, in the modern world, it is not easy to be completely rootless. Nonetheless, the unattached life continues to be highly regarded.

Here again we need to distinguish between two meanings, parallel to the distinction already made in the case of independence. The Buddha spoke a great deal about the importance of aloneness. He thought that one could learn a great deal from the solitude of the forest. However, once his ministry began, shortly after his enlightenment, he was never alone. When he was asked about this he made it clear that there is a distinction between what might be called inner and outer, or spiritual and literal, aloneness. Spiritual aloneness corresponds to the true independence that we spoke of earlier. It is the state in which one is empowered to make decisions and take responsibility for life without depending upon others. That sort of aloneness goes on functioning whether one is in company or not. Literal aloneness is not necessary for a person who is spiritually self-sufficient. On the other hand, the literal aloneness of solitary retreat can help a person to realize this state since when we are alone the habit of blaming others is exposed and it is much more difficult to hide from the truth about oneself.

**Spiritual self-sufficiency** does not mean arriving at complacency. Rather, it means having objectivity about oneself so that one is no longer such a special case in one's own eyes. This is fostered by awareness of one's short-comings. This awareness constitutes an important element in the horizontalizing effect of the Dharma. When we truly realize that "I am just like everybody else" in having passions and failings then we start to feel at home in the human world. The true nature of religion emerges from this as being concerned with revealing the unpalatable truth about ourselves rather than our ascent to worldly glory, and this then leads to the realization that it is precisely in our ordinariness that our true glory lies.

My mother was now home. She was pleased. It was extremely touching to see. Her body was so small and weak now. For a year her world had been becoming smaller and smaller. Now it was confined to this one room. I realized that she would now probably never leave this room again alive. I prayed with all my heart that she would confound everyone and recover as Aunt Margaret had done, but the rational part of me knew that the odds were high that she would end her days here soon.

We had visited Aunt Margaret in hospital twelve months before and everyone was certain that she was dying. However, just before my mother's illness we were able to visit Margaret again living independently in her own house and take tea with her in her garden. Such things happen. However, in my mother's case, I was contemplating only a few weeks and, as it was to turn out, even this was to prove optimistic.

**Just as religion makes us face the paradox of ordinariness, so does death**. In one sense there is nothing special about it – we all do it – but, by the same token, it is the most special thing we ever do. Birth and death are the great times as well as being the common factor. My mother who had borne me was now less than half my size. The physical shrinking of the body somehow emphasises the manner in which we are totally subject to forces over which we have virtually no control and how we are completely in their power. We can do many things in this life, but they seem very small in comparison with the factors about which we can do nothing. How can one be at home in a universe that treats one so ruthlessly?

Although we may say that religion helps us to find our true spiritual home, it cannot do so until we really discover and face the fact that we are not at home. I was vaguely beginning to realize that the twist in the road of my own spiritual journey that I was now entering upon involved confronting anguish and powerlessness. A voice inside me was saying "I don't want her to die," and the more obvious and inescapable the reality became the more insistent that voice grew. With it came the most terrible anguish.

You can see this anguish in small children. Psychologists talk about omnipotent fantasies. In fact the things a child wants are often small enough, but they are not always forthcoming. We learn early in life to cope with frustration somehow. Many of the ways we do so are rather dysfunctional. Generally what the infant desires can be supplied by mother. She does not always instantly oblige and so the child must suffer the deprivation of not getting what it wants. I felt myself to be like a small child. All I wanted from Mother now was that she live, and from all I knew, she was not going to do so for much longer.

Right alongside this anguish there dwelt two other completely different sets of emotions. The first concerned the pleasure we felt at getting her home. It was so satisfying that she was now here in her own room. It seemed like a triumph. The second related to the intensification of the sense of love that comes with awareness of impending parting and with Mother's now near total dependency upon me.

"Perhaps if she rallies a bit we might get her out in the garden," Caroline suggested. Again I was touched by the thought. It was not impossible. Mother was home.

## To Die in Freedom

**On Tuesday evening** my son Michael visited and spent time with his grandmother. I spent the time phoning as many people as possible to tell them that she was home and to break the news that she was failing. After several attempts I managed to get through to my younger daughter who was in Malaysia. She was very distressed at the news. We had a discussion about the situation. I advised her to come home and see her grandmother and offered to pay the fare, but in the end she decided not to do so. "I want to remember her as she was," she said.

Wednesday morning Heike left as she had matters to attend to at home in Devon. I sit in the quietness of Mother's room. She is not eating and hardly taking any liquid. It is exceedingly difficult to give her medication even, but as she says that she has no pain we have not pressed the point. It is dawning on me that it is not going to be weeks, but days. One can see her decline into weakness. Her voice is a little slurred and I realize that it will not be long before she can no longer communicate. We talk occasionally, but there is a certain satisfaction in knowing that everything that needs to be said has already been said. There is no unfinished business. She is free to go whenever she is sent for.

How many people die in such freedom? Having been a psychotherapist I am aware of what scars deaths can leave. So often people die without loved one's having said what needed saying. Often there is unfinished business that can live on for years or even generations. Humans are involved in such complicated dramas. Families are filled with passions. Resentments are harboured. There is a terrible sharpness in hearing the story of somebody who missed the opportunity to clear up a misunderstanding or right a wrong.

**One of the foundational myths** of Amidism is the story of Queen Vaidehi. The events of this story are told in several Buddhist texts. They take place when the Buddha is quite old. He is by then famous. Many people come to hear his teachings and he receives patronage from some of the leading political figures of his day. Among these is King Bimbisara of Magadha. The Buddha is established at a place called Rajagriha, the Vulture Peak, and is giving teachings there. The sequence of teachings that he gives is later recorded in a work called the Lotus Sutra. During this time, however, important political events unfold. King Bimbisara is over-thrown by his son Ajattashatru. Ajattashatru has been incited to this act by Devadatta, a cousin of the Buddha. The King is imprisoned and left to starve to death. Vaidehi, the Queen, smuggles food in for her husband. Ajattashatru finds out about this and is furious with his mother. He has her cast into prison too. News of this reaches the Buddha and he comes to visit Vaidehi in prison.

There then ensues a touching conversation. Vaidehi reveres the Buddha, but is also able to talk to him on a person to person level. She remarks that she has a son who has done this terrible thing and the Buddha has a cousin who put him up to it. Whatever can they, that is she and the Buddha, have done in previous lives to have the karma to have such dreadful relatives in this one? We could take this remark as sardonic, but, in the context of the beliefs of the time, it is probably not meant so. It is rather more an observation that we are all implicated in the awful things that happen. The wickedness of the world is we ourselves. The Buddha does not get into discussion, but induces a vision of the Pure Land in Vaidehi. In fact she experiences an opening of consciousness to myriads of the Pure Lands of myriads of Buddhas and out of these she selects the Pure Land of Amitabha. We can take this as meaning that she becomes willing to die. We can also take it as an instance of how facing the dark reveals the light. Her vision comes out of a complete acceptance of her lot coupled with reverence for the Enlightened One. It does not come out of her virtue, nor out of any ability in meditation, nor out of her wisdom. She is an ordinary woman who had lived a privileged life, but was now cast down by events. She has not engaged in long religious disciplines. However, she reveres the Buddha and this gives her life a basis of faith. This faith enables her to see what a Buddha Land is like and she chooses the land of Amitabha because it is the one most accessible to ordinary people.

There are further episodes to the story. King Bimbisara dies and Ajattashatru becomes king. According to the story, Ajattashatru is visiting his mother in her cell and he brings his infant son with him. The boy has a boil on his leg. Ajattashatru loves his son and tries to suck the poison out of the boil with his mouth – a rather unpleasant task. Queen Vaidehi comments, "You look just like your father. That is what he would do for you when you were little." At this point Ajattashatru's hatred for his father, which is largely based on stories told to him by Devadatta, evaporates. He sends a guard to bring his father to him. The guard shortly returns to say that the King passed away half an hour before. Ajattashatru is mortified.

Later still Ajattashatru, now King, on the advice of his minister, goes to see the Buddha. They arrive at the grove where the Buddha is staying and dismount from their elephants to continue on foot. It is exceedingly quiet. Too quiet. Suddenly Ajattashatru freezes. He turns to his minister and accuses him of leading him into a trap. The Buddha is supposed to be here with a large assembly of bhikshus – how can it be so quiet. The minister reassures him. They continue into the clearing. There the Buddha sits in meditation in the midst of a large assembly, all perfectly silent. Ajattashatru is impressed and, in a rather un-king-like way, sits down at the back. The meditation period comes to an end and the Buddha looks out across the gathering and addresses Ajattashatru. "Great King, come forward." Ajattashatru is deeply moved by the fact that the Buddha addresses him so respectfully when they both know that he is also a murderer and that Bimbisara was the Buddha's friend. There follows a dialogue between the King and the Buddha after which Ajattashatru returns to his palace much edified.

These stories have the quality of folklore. They may be history. The importance of them, however, lies in the spiritual messages they convey. In particular, although Ajattashatru and Vaidehi are royalty, from a spiritual point of view they are ordinary people. The simplest moral here is in the fact that an ordinary woman can see the Pure Land and a murderous monarch can find acceptance and some peace of heart. The Buddha does not act as an ordinary person might. He does not harbour a grievance. He does not get caught up in discussion about his own merit. He simply does as much as he can for whoever stands before him at the time and he even goes out of his way to visit and assist those who have been cast down. We may say that, in acting so, the Buddha is acting in a better way than an average person would. This is true, but it appears to come out of a willingness to meet the other parties on an even level. Although he may appear spiritually elevated to others, he does not consider himself in that way. He meets each person as a person. They may have done bad things – so have we all. A Buddha lives in the grace that holds us all alike.

## Something Subtle Happens

**Because she is so weak** Mother cannot sit upright in the bed but lies horizontal. By inclining her head she can see the flowers that we have picked from her garden that are in a vase beside the Buddha statue on her chest of drawers. She can no longer see the lime tree. This seems like a very significant further narrowing of her world. I look at it, as if for her. There, on the main bough, sit two doves. It is quite uncanny. I had not seen doves in that tree before. They arrived when she came home from hospital. They stayed throughout the time she was on her death bed. I tell her about the doves. She smiles.

The religious literature of the world is replete with stories of uncanny happenings around the death time of significant people. Science has no explanation for such occurrences so modern people are supposed to ignore them and call them coincidences. That does not, however, constitute explanation. This is one of the problems of modern life – that there are many things for which, not only are there no explanations, but even the attempt at explanation is taboo. While science is a wonderful thing it is strange how it has also been used to exclude or suppress consideration of what, for millennia, have been the important matters of human concern.

I am not here talking about superstition or magic, though some would call it such. Rather I am talking about the subtle communication that goes on in our world that goes far beyond the limits of human words and data. Some aspects are commonplace enough. The cat knows when I am talking about her. Perhaps science will indeed encompass such things one day, like the age old supposed superstition that bees swarm when there is a death that is the background fable behind the popularity of Sue Monk Kidd's feminist story book[4] *The Secret Life of Bees*. Modern people respond to these stories, but, in doing so, they are moving to tunes written deep in their folk memory, stories that they now see as merely fiction.

So-called primitive cultures generally believe that there is communication between what is going on in the human world and the animal and vegetable worlds. Traditional literature everywhere carries innumerable stories of "signs". We do not need to think this is magic, but something subtle happens. Modern people have cut themselves off from it by and large. I have to count myself among them. I cannot claim in the least to be a "sensitive". The appearance of the doves was, therefore, all the more startling. Mother's smile remains imprinted on my mind.

## Without the Prince, Sleeping Beauty does not Wake

**So passed many hours**. I reflected on her life and our time together. Around midday she asked for her feet to be massaged and wanted Caroline to do this. As Caroline worked on her toes, Mother slipped in and out of sleep. The battle going on in her abdomen must be consuming almost all her limited energy.

Then she woke up. She looked at each of us in turn and then said,

"I am sure now."

After a moment she added, as if by way of explanation,

"I was not sure before, but I am sure now."

She meant that she was now sure that she was dying. She smiled that same little girl smile that conveyed tenderness and mutual appreciation. She had accepted it.

**I knew that she was at peace** with the ending of her life. My own sense of the time scale had transformed completely. I was now not sure that she would even be with us more than a day more. I knew that she would now "get on with it." Mother was like that. Once she was clear what was to be done she would get on with it. Dying would be no different. I returned her smile. It was yet another moment of mutual recognition, of which there had been so many in those few days. And with each such moment there was not just the knowledge that we understood each other, there was a deepening self-reflection on my side – perhaps also on hers, who can say? – that was sobering.

**Buddhism is a matter of becoming sober**. The Buddha saw that we are as if drunk. We are drunk on self-conceit. This conceit is, in large part, a psychological defence against knowledge of death and the anguish of alienation. Perhaps this would not matter so much if it were not for the fact that the anaesthetising habits with which we fill our lives are non-discriminating. Just as they dull our awareness of our finitude, so they dull awareness of the infinite glory of our world as well. In smothering our alienation they also smother our love. What does it take to sober us up? Encounter with somebody who is not as intoxicated as ourselves. Who would that be? It would be somebody who is closer to death, in the true spiritual sense of the word close.

Somebody close to death does not necessarily mean somebody who is actually dying, though it might and in this case it did. However, a spiritually advanced person is somebody who is closer to death even in their physical prime. Enlightenment is an encounter with spiritual death. It is not something we achieve, however. It is a gift. It is transmitted to us.

The idea of transmission does not just apply to a mystical validation procedure whereby a Buddhist master passes his authority to an anointed successor. We receive the Dharma by transmission. The knowledge of spiritual death and its consequences is not something that an individual can attain unaided. There has to be contact.

**Throughout life we are learning about death**. Mostly, however, the learning opportunities pass us by. Sometimes I have sat in a group of people talking about death or talking about a person who is dying or has died. By looking around the circle you can easily see that some people are tuned in and others are tuned out. With the ones who are tuned out there is little one can do. They will remain in that mental set until something happens in their life that jolts or seduces them out of it and, generally speaking, such transitions cannot be contrived.

This is one of the difficulties of what is called Buddhist training. On the one hand, it is possible for people to follow a course of education and to participate in ceremonies and a way of life and as this rubs off on them they learn something. They may become more considerate of others, more tender and kind, less compulsive or bad tempered and so on. This is to the good. It inevitably remains fragile, however, until it is grounded in a real awakening experience of some degree. This latter cannot be planned or achieved. It is incidental or even accidental.

The most important spiritual lessons that I have learnt from others have not come so much from what people have taught me, but from how they are. People sometimes say that all true knowledge comes from within ourselves. It is true that when one receives some true transmission it feels as though something inside oneself has been awoken and one might like to say that it was there all along, just waiting, like Sleeping Beauty waiting for the prince. Sleeping Beauty, however, does not wake without the prince.

## No Enlightenment Will Eradicate Our Basic Nature
**Buddhist lore personifies death**. There is the negative spirit of death personified as Mara and there is the positive spirit personified as Amida or Amitabha-Amitayus. Amit means measureless. Abha means light. Ayus means lifespan. Amida is short for Amitabha-Amitayus. It means limitless space, time and life. Death, the great darkness, can also give birth to the great light; the great flaming, incomparable light that is brighter than our sun or moon. Rather than face death, however, we get drunk. We may literally get drunk on alcohol or we may get drunk on anything else that is capable of distracting, defending or destroying us.

As my mother got closer to death and did so without fear, I felt myself in the presence of a kind of force field. As gravity pulls things back down to earth, I repeatedly found myself being pulled down into a more sober state. Looking back over my life from this chastened perspective, I could see such a parade of occasions when I had acted in a shallow or arrogant manner. I could feel myself softening.

Such a time is a dukkha. It is a time when things could go one way or another. It would be easy at such a time to get into self-recrimination. "If only I had been kinder to this person or spent more time with that one or not done such and such". Self-recrimination, however, is a way of avoiding real contrition – real softening of the heart. Self-recrimination means that instead of getting softer toward others we get harder toward ourselves. In the end that just comes out as hardness toward others too.

**We soften**. In Buddhism we say that contrition is the gateway to awakening. Contrition is the softening of the heart that occurs when, without recrimination, one faces the harm one has done and the folly that one has engaged in. Contrition is often misunderstood as some kind of self-chastisement. Whilst it is certainly chastening, this is a mistaken notion. There is no punishment in it. One may well experience a natural dismay when one sees oneself more clearly, but it is worth reflecting that even this probably has its roots in conceit.

How is recrimination to be avoided? By letting go of our facade. Generally, when a person has done something hurtful they try not to think about it. When they cannot avoid thinking about it, they "feel bad". A large part of this feeling bad, however, is not compassion. It is the discomfort of realizing that the facts do not support the facade that one is trying to present to the world. Feeling bad is not a species of concern for others. It is a form of self-defeat. Generally it does not lead to deep insight, merely to a resolve to win next time. Winning means keeping one's facade intact.

Contrition is a matter of sobering up about ourselves. When we look honestly at our behaviour we find that there are many situations in which we contribute to harming others. We recognize that the passions that flow in our heart are often unedifying. We are, as Freud said, polymorphously perverse. It is an extremely common occurrence for those who profess the most outrage at scandalous behaviour to turn out to be guilty of as much or worse themselves. Were it not so, many cheap newspapers would not be able to fill their pages. But this is not remarkable. It is human nature.

Contrition, therefore, has two levels. One level concerns the specific acts that one has done. If one is prone to lose one's temper or if one is eaten up by critical thoughts, then these may be habits that one may wish to put energy into breaking. One may be able to retrain oneself. This comes out of sincerity. This on its own, however, is not the core of what contrition is about. Contrition is about depth. Self-retraining can and often is only motivated by a desire to look better. It can still be superficial. This is an area of human life where hypocrisy abounds. Even this hypocrisy is quite understandable. It is unavoidable unless there is a real change in the way one sees oneself and such change does not come easily.

Doing something about specific harmful behaviours, thought patterns, compulsions and so on is important. Even more important, however, is the possibility of obtaining a global insight into one's nature. While humans are capable of nobility, there is also a dimension to their being that is quite repulsive. We are one of the most thoroughly greedy, destructive and self-conceited beasts to walk the earth and no amount of enlightenment will eradicate our basic nature, even though it may give us the incentive to deploy it more constructively when we can.

When I write about these things I am sure to be misunderstood. Many will think it terribly negative to dwell upon the dark side of human nature. However, seeing it does not make it more and not seeing it does not make it less. Rather the reverse in fact. This is the difficulty of spirituality. It asks us to take our heads out of the sand and who is really willing to do so? Very few. I myself am often very reluctant and I can remember a time when I would have scorned the whole idea.

**I reflect upon my own transition**. For many years I was deeply influenced by the ideas of humanistic psychology. Most humanistic psychologists were secularists. I met Carl Rogers on a couple of occasions and felt closely identified with his ideas. Rogers himself was brought up in a religious family and he took most of the basic values of the religious outlook for granted. Taking them for granted he did not write about them. Since his writings did not contain them, his followers did not adopt them. His work thus came to be associated with a secularist philosophy. It was only in his later years that hint of his religiosity crept into a few of his writings.

I still have great respect for Rogers' work. I am less enthusiastic about some of the things that were done with it after he died. Although I remain enthusiastic, I realize that I have come a distance since the time when I met Rogers. I have abandoned the one-sidedly optimistic view of human nature. Rogers was correct in identifying the enormous human potential for good and the relationship between benign conditions and healthy psychological outcomes. This is fine as far as it goes, but there is also a dark side to human nature that, if not acknowledged, will destroy us soon enough. European psychology has been much more ready to acknowledge this dark side than American psychology has and, although American Buddhists have taken much of their Buddhism from Japan, the central role that contrition plays in Japanese Buddhism has largely been over-looked. Now, interestingly, many Buddhists in Japan are very interested in Rogers' ideas. It is a chemistry with a lot of potential.

I continued to sit with Mother, much of the time keeping my hand on the area where the cancer was centred in her abdomen. There is nothing else I can do, I thought. The shadow of death hung over us both. She had become a little shrivelled skin bag full of cancer. I loved her.

# FOUR

# ABSOLUTE GRACE

## Unconditionally Accepted

**Amidism is faith in absolute grace**. In the idiom of Buddhism, this grace is often called Light. The Light (*abha* in Sanskrit, *ko* in Japanese) of Amida cannot be obstructed. It is *mugeko* – unimpeded light. A person can close his heart and mind to it, or may believe they never have encountered it, but there is nothing that can actually make it non-operative. Amida's door is open to whomsoever want to enter. This is the most striking and radical feature of Amidism. There is no judgment and no membership criterion other than sincere intention.

So we say that there is a measureless light (*amit-abha*) or grace that illumines this and all possible worlds. From this light or grace spring the "Four Immeasurables": loving kindness (*maitri*), compassion (*karuna*), sympathetic joy (*mudita*) and equanimity (*upeksha*) and the ethical and compassionate teachings of Buddhism and other religions. This is not a call for people to work at being or becoming loving and compassionate. It is a recognition that those who open themselves to grace naturally become so. They soften. Life becomes more real and more meaningful. Love is not a skill. Love is a response. Unconditional love is a response to unconditional acceptance.

Amida's grace is called a light because people experience it as light. In the mystical experience in which Amida appears before us, one of the most compelling elements is the light. We really do see the world in a new light and that light really is more radiant than the light of the sun and the moon that we usually experience. Religion is rooted in such experience – experiences that come at the point of death and that come to adepts who open themselves fully to them in the midst of life. In

Pureland, we talk of this experience using the name of Amida. Amida is simply a contraction of Amitabha. It is not a problem to Amidism that mystics of other religions describe this experience using the language of their culture and say that they encountered an angel or a messenger from God; one would expect that they would do that. This is confirmation of the ubiquity of the experience. Amida's grace is not just for Amidists.

**Why do we not see the Buddha light** most of the time? Because we scatter our faith. The possibility of gathering one's faith is always open. To do so is to return to simplicity. In practice, however, people's faith is not awakened by their own decision or effort. Even that is an act of other power. When you ask a person if they have faith in something, they look inside themselves to see if the answer is yes or no, they do not make a voluntary decision. All we can do from our own side is to examine our actual situation, recognize our bombu nature and acknowledge the longing within us that calls out for paradise. The stark contrast between what we find ourselves and our world to be and what we know is the desire of our heart of hearts create the dynamic that drives the spiritual life.

In classical Buddhism, spiritual awakening is called *bodhi,* or *buddh*, hence Buddha. Buddha means awaken. Bodhi has more the sense of awakened vision. These are the times when the dark world and the light come into clear focus and one may speak of mystical experience. In Pureland, a slightly different terminology tends to be used. Here we speak of the experience of *shinjin* (Japanese) or *prasada* (Sanskrit). This indicates the awakening of faith aspect of the experience.

In Amidism, the notion of measureless light rests upon equivalence between

the light of enlightenment and faith
the light experienced at the point of death
the light of love and purity

the light of truth

the grace of Amida Buddha

**Because we are bombu, we never see the absolute** truth directly nor can we consciously be in touch with it permanently. It will always be mediated through form and relativity and so will appear to our mind in a specific way at a specific time. A state of permanent absolute clear seeing is conceivable, but not attainable. What would be perceived were this state to be attained is called *Dharmakaya* (literally, "truth body"), things as they are when undistorted by human perception. Human perception, however, is interpretative, even in the highest states of spiritual attainment. We can know as knowledge or faith, however, that the Dharmakaya is simply things as they are. There is a great deal written about the Dharmakaya in Buddhist literature and it is said to be a non-dual state. Pureland, however, is not focussed upon an exploration of the absolute or of non-duality, but upon the spiritual position of the ordinary being of blind passion existing in dynamic relationship with the unimpeded light of infinite love. Amidism is a spirituality of relationship. Everything about it is oriented toward the encounter with otherness, whether the otherness of Amida in contrast with self or the simple otherness of the world around us. It is a spirituality that is extrovert and receptive.

Although seeing the absolute directly is not available to us, a state of relative clear seeing is attainable, though rare. This is the shinjin experience. This is relative in the sense that it is experienced as an encounter, a form of relating. What is perceived in this state is called *Sambhoga-kaya* ("enjoyment body"). Such experiences are transformative awakenings that give rise to settled faith (*anjin*) or serene confidence that cannot be dislodged and so is called "irreversible". This faith is settled because it is based upon an apodictic experience that can never be undone. Although a person who has experienced shinjin may lapse into forgetfulness from time to time, just as the moon goes through phases, the knowledge of having seen the light can never be erased. Shinjin is, therefore, an awakening of faith. It is arguable that shinjin, under different names, is the source of a great many religions. Equivalent experiences are reported by mystics of most creeds from all over the world. The light is interpreted by different cultures in different ways. Religions are like transformers in an electrical grid, stepping down the current for domestic use.

## I Believe

**Encountering the light** may take a variety of specific forms. Even in the most elevated spiritual state we are still foolish beings of blind passion and we see reality through our own filter. However, we can loosely classify shinjin experiences into two types. In the first type the person experiences the world as complete and perfect just as it is. This corresponds to the mystic "All's well and all shall be well and all manner of things shall be well," of Julian of Norwich. Paradisaical descriptions, such as one finds in scripture, hint at the nature of that experience. This is the awakening that came to Shakyamuni Buddha when he finally despaired of the jiriki practice of asceticism. It can be called enlightened vision (*bo-dhi*). Within the enlightened vision one experiences the world illumined by the universal light. Such a world is called a Pure Land, *Sukhavati* (Sanskrit) or *Jodo* (Japanese). In the second type the person experiences being unconditionally accepted by the universe or by a transcendent being. This is the experience of unconditional love (*maitri*). This second type, therefore, takes the form of an encounter with a being rather than a land. These two types of experience both occur, as do hybrids in which both aspects are experienced. The attainment of this type of experience is not unique to Amidism. Amidism is simply one particular way of pointing it out, talking about it and relating to it. Followers of other religions and other schools will have their own terminology.

The being of unconditional love and measureless light is Amida, this being a contraction of Amitabha. Direct religious experience, therefore, is a more or less clouded glimpse of Amida or Amida's Pure Land. In Mahayana Buddhism there are other Buddhas who have their own Pure Lands, but from a Pureland point of view we may see all these lands as instances of Amida's land. Such glimpses may occur during life. They most commonly occur at the time of death. Pureland teaches that the light experienced at the point of death is the Amida light, the same light as is experienced in all degrees of enlightenment experience.

So Pureland understands spiritual experience in simple religious terms. We encounter a sacred realm. It is different from ourselves. It is outside. It affects us. Its effect upon us is a grace. It is freely given. It is not earned. One might be a sinner or a saint. Buddha cares for you just the same. It is living in conscious relationship to grace that makes a life religious, whether virtuous or not. This does not, however, constitute licence since those who open themselves to grace undergo a natural transformation. The knowledge of being truly acceptable – of being seen as noble in the very midst of one's folly and suffering – is pro-foundly affecting. One knows intuitively that Nyorai wants one to live a life of kindness, love, beauty and goodness. One knows also that, due to karma, one often fails to do so. Sometimes we heed Nyorai, some-times we do not. Shakyamuni Buddha says, in the Dhammapada, "The heedful do not die; the heedless are as if dead already." Sometimes we heed, often we do not. This shows us that our relationship to goodness is indeed like a relationship – it functions just like our relationships with other people. Sometimes we listen, sometimes we do not. If the good were our intrinsic nature we would be constant in it. If it were antithet-ical to our nature we could never embody it. In fact we are neither intrinsically good or bad – we are a bundle of karma – but we can heed sometimes. This is because it is a relationship. It is a relationship to a being and to a domain.

**So an Amidist can say, I believe** in the nirvana pointed out by Buddha; I believe in the domain of perfect peace, love, truth and beauty; I believe that from that realm comes help and inspiration; I believe that that is what animates Buddhas; I believe that what Buddhas are engaged in is glorifying that realm – the unborn, unconditioned, uncontrived; I believe that Buddhas are thus portals between ordinary beings and the Unborn; I believe that Buddhas live ordinary mundane mortal lives and yet the eternal shows in them – their eternal life is their true life yet it is not their own; I believe that the life of devotion – of praising and inviting Nyorai – is the best life; I believe that the faith to live such a life is itself a grace – fortunate are those who receive it; I believe that Nyorai will bestow that grace if He can and that it is easier for him to do so in the case of those who see and sincerely lament their own short-comings; I believe that such grace spreads through spiritual friendship, those who have been graced becoming those who carry grace to others; I believe that grace empowers and guides us; I believe that those touched by grace recognize one another; I believe this is the root of religion in general and is the principle upon which true peace between faiths can emerge; war and strife can cease, for the Buddha has taught that everything that is of the nature to arise also has the nature to cease; I believe that Buddhas are empowered to point out these truths with a myriad skilful means because they are themselves basking in the grace of other Buddhas; I believe that everyone is acceptable to Buddha Nyorai no matter what mistakes they have made or what harm they have caused; I believe in love, truth and beauty; I believe in Amida's light enfolding us in life and meeting us at the time of death; I believe in the Pure Land; I believe that we are here to live as a company of spiritual friends for the benefit of all sentient beings; I believe that there is nowhere in the world where that light of grace does not fall; even those who live irreligious or corrupt lives may still be touched by the

Buddha's grace and may find themselves doing the Buddha's work, wittingly or unwittingly. There is grace at work in our world.

**People may ask** whether Amida or the Buddha or the Pure Land literally exist. All we can say is that they exist in the experience of many people. They are encountered and this encounter changes lives profoundly. Spiritual experiences are a matter of fact and in Pureland these are the categories we use to explain them. For instance, in science, categories like energy and momentum explain the way that physical bodies behave. One cannot demonstrate energy or momentum separately from physical bodies moving, nor can one demonstrate Buddha independently of spiritual experience. However, bodies do move and beings do awaken. If we deprive ourselves of the concepts of science we will be unable to understand the physical world. If we deprive ourselves of the concepts of the spirit we will be equally unable to understand spiritual experience. We might have important things happen and believe we are going mad. That would be a great shame and a loss. Religions offer concepts that enable us to understand spiritual experience. One could call meeting Amida meeting Jesus or Moses if one liked. In Pureland we call it Amida or Nyorai. People do manifestly have good deaths and bad deaths. We call a good death, "entering the Pure Land", and this terminology is very helpful. In this life we can only help a person as far as the door of death. We can equip them as well as we can for the journey. Once they pass through the door they have left us and gone on their way. We hope that our invocations may continue to help them, but we cannot know for certain. We can only do our best. We are foolish beings. Some of us believe that the Pure Land is a concrete place that we may enter after death. Some of us believe that the Pure Land is another dimension of reality that cannot be fully conceptualised by mortals during this life. Some believe that the Pure Land is simply an indicator of the way to die well and has no implication for what happens thereafter. We have these diverse opinions because we are foolish beings and do not know. In real life we have to work with what we have. A simple faith in the reality of the Pure Land awaiting one after death can be an enormous benefit, but it is not given to everyone. Even in this, we are not masters of our own life – we cannot choose to believe. Even the question whether one believes or not is not a matter of will, but an expression of some other power. That in history people have been and even today still are being killed because they do or do not have this or that belief only shows the folly of their persecutors. If such persecutors found true faith they would know that the faith of the other person is a grace not something that they must be held to account for by other humans.

People also ask what is the minimum one has to believe to be an Amidist. Belief has always been a dangerous subject in Western culture ever since people could be thrown to the lions for it and all through the terrible times of the inquisition and the burning of heretics. Buddhism, however, is a different kind of approach. One will not be punished for one's beliefs. In order to be a Pureland Buddhist one does not have to believe any particular thing, one just has to do the practice. Of course, in order to do the practice there is a kind of implication that one must believe that saying nembutsu does some good, but one does not need to have a worked out theory about what or how. We say the nembutsu and thereby express gratitude for whatever grace falls into our life and openness to what providence may bring.

**There is no method** by which a bombu can make awakening occur. In principle, a life of non-attachment should make the access of the light more likely, but, human nature being what it is, even those who live such a life outwardly do not necessarily acquire the real spirit of it and those who live in the world do not necessarily lack that spirit. Jiriki very easily subverts even the most sublime spiritual practice into spiritual materialism. We could say, in generic Buddhist terms, that if a practice is not an act of seeking refuge in Buddha then it is an act of feeding one neurosis or another. It does not matter, I think, if you substitute the word Christ or Allah for Buddha in this assertion. The point is that seeking refuge in Spirit is what religion is about. However, though one may seek, this does not in itself ensure that one will find and even those who never consciously seek do sometimes stumble upon it.

Pureland is, therefore, a life for those who have been found by Nyorai. It is equally appropriate for lay and renunciant practitioners. Through nembutsu they express gratitude and all the other feelings that one experiences in a life lived in faith in relation to the light. Sometimes faith comes, as it were, second hand.

In the Buddhist scriptures there are plenty of examples of people who had seen the light themselves and thus become faith leaders and also of those whose faith came at a remove and so were faith followers. A few weeks after his own awakening, Shakyamuni, the founding Buddha, travelled to where his former companions were staying. These five ascetics became his first disciples. One of them, Kondinnya, saw the light immediately. The others could see that something momentous had happened for Kondinnya and were so impressed that they became faith followers. Later they each had their own awakening experiences. Although we might long to have wonderful experiences, even that longing is still only the activity of our greedy bombu heart. The merit of being a faith follower is no less than that of being an awakened being. Both types of faith come through encounter. Faith leaders are themselves followers because they encounter Amida or a glimpse of the Pure Land. Faith followers have encountered somebody else who has faith. Faith, therefore, is something that is transmitted. It is a grace flowing into our lives from Nyorai. Nobody makes up authentic faith by their own effort or contrivance. Faith is given not accomplished.

**Faith has various forms**. In the form called *shraddha*, faith is centred on belief and confidence whereas in the form called *prasada* it appears as clarity and authenticity. Prasada and shraddha are not really different things, however. They are the same thing viewed from different angles. In Buddhism, faith does not stand in opposition to experience. Faith is triggered, affirmed, channelled and directed by experience. The clarification of faith is what makes life authentic. Some people think that they have no faith, but this is not the case. All people have faith as part of what it is to be a human being, but generally a person's quota of faith is squandered upon all manner of trivialities rather than being gathered into a single current aligned to the universal light. When a person's life is aligned, everybody senses that "there is something about that person". Even an aligned person, however, may not be aligned to the greatest good. Some of the villains of history were aligned, but they were aligned to false views. A false faith might, for instance, be expressed in nationalism and the conviction that all will be well when all the enemies of one's own people are dead. Such a belief could be a strongly held faith, but it would be a destructive one. On the tracks of Buddha the first imprint is right view.

Faith also is cyclical. One way in which it is cyclical is that we waver in and out of it. There are times when the spiritual life is extremely alive and compelling. There are other times when it seems to have disappeared for us and we fall into accidie. Although settled faith may go through such barren periods, it never expires. Faith, therefore, is more than a sentiment. Anjin continues even through periods of accidie. This is like knowing that the sun is still there even though the sky may be completely overcast.

We can also describe faith as cyclical in a more systematic way using four Japanese terms *shimmitsu*, *shinjin*, *anjin* and *bodaishin*. Shimmitsu literally means intimacy. It is about the secret in one's heart. This indicates a sense of tenderness toward Nyorai or awareness of Nyorai's tenderness toward one. Shinjin, here used in a narrow sense, refers to the ecstasy of spiritual breakthrough when the light reaches us and we feel up-lifted. Anjin refers to settled faith, which is not spectacular, but persists through thick and thin. Bodaishin refers to faith that reaches out to others. Bodaishin literally means "great, enlightened heart" or "mind of enlightened vision", and it corresponds to the term *bodhichitta* in other schools of Buddhism. For shimmitsu, shinjin, anjin and bodaishin, therefore, we could say intimacy, ecstasy, fidelity and commitment. In this respect, we can think of the spiritual life as like a marriage – the true spiritual practitioner is married to the Light. These four are manifestations of shinjin when the term is used in the broad sense to cover all forms of nembutsu faith.

## FIVE

# DANCING TO TUNES WE DO NOT CONTROL

### Not by Self Will

**Death was coming nearer**. That Wednesday evening a slight rattle started to sound in Mother's breathing. This seemed like the first clear messenger telling us that death was coming. When death comes, one submits. My mother had now got clarity that she would die. Her attention was therefore on dying. Although she would surface in this world from time to time and briefly turn her attention toward us, for the most part, from now on, she would be preoccupied with a more important task. Our role now was to support and not hinder her departure. Nonetheless, there was still a longing in me that against all odds a miraculous change might still happen. Isn't it interesting how we can know and act upon what is right yet still be longing for something else to happen?

The spirit of Buddhism is to turn one's heart and mind toward reality. There are, of course, people enough who think that reality simply means what we experience as living beings during this lifetime. In that case, death would not constitute doing anything. One's attention would remain here until it stopped. As we die, however, something else beckons. When one is dying one does not feel as though it is a non-event. When I myself was near to death it felt compellingly important to do it well, even though I also knew that what "it" was would only be really known as it unfolded of itself.

Death is the great unknown. By the very definition of it, we cannot know its nature even second hand. If a person can still communicate with us, then we do not count them as dead. Of course, there are spiritualists who believe that they do communicate with the dead, but they really think of themselves as communicating with beings who are now alive in a new way. In the Buddhist texts the Buddha and some of his leading disciples, like Maudgalyayana, do seem to have had well developed abilities to communicate with other-worldly beings.

As he lay dying the Buddha is reported to have asked a monk not to stand in front of him saying that the monk was obstructing the view of numerous celestial beings that had gathered in order to be with him in his final hour. These celestials were not visible to the monk or to anybody else present. A materialist will probably conclude that the Buddha was delirious. However, the Buddha spoke to celestials at many times during his life and these conversations were an intrinsic part of the way he lived and the meaningfulness of his life. The Buddha's universe seems to have teemed with life unseen by us and the conversations that he thus had do not seem to have made him crazy, they seem to have made him saner than the average person.

When momentous events were afoot, the Buddha would say, "The devas are gathering." We can see from this that while the Buddha was certainly a great thinker and philosopher, he was also what we now call a shaman. His life was lived on the border between this and another world, or, perhaps, many such worlds.

**The line between imagination and experience** is impossible to draw. Lives are ruled by imagination and the image of a person as a machine is no less potent an act of imagination than the image of a person as a spirit. Many of the most important things in our lives are imputations. People die for their country, for instance, but countries are a purely human construct. They only exist insofar as people agree to imagine them.

People educated in the modern way, like myself, have been taught to be systematically sceptical about anything that is vitalist rather than mechanical, but this is just a training in using the imagination one way rather than another. There is no overwhelming evidence for either way. The mechanical view, for instance, has so far singularly failed in its attempt to explain what life is or how it originated. There is plenty of speculation, of course, but absolutely no demonstration. In order to keep the mechanistic paradigm in business and the vitalist one at bay we are continually being told that science may be just on the point of discovering "the origin of life". Somehow, however, it never actually happens. Life remains a mystery to science. Life reproduces, but it cannot be made from non-living material alone. Living beings can devour non-living material and, as it were, make it live, but non-living material cannot be made to do so on its own. This is a fundamental defeat for materialism, but the consequences of it philosophically have never been fully taken on. Instead, the gap is papered over with the assumption that science will triumph in the end. In fact, this assumption is really nothing more nor less than a dogmatic assertion of belief. Who knows? Sitting beside a dying person, one ponders on such things.

We modern humans have taught ourselves to internalise a great deal. If the Buddha saw celestials, then we will say it must have been a projection of his mind. It must have come from inside him. Actually we have just as little idea of what a mind really is as we have of what a celestial might be, and as for "inside" and "outside", these are very slippery concepts indeed. A human being is not isolated. Waves of communication are constantly flowing through us from many sources. We are much less masters of our own state than we like to think. There is so much subtle communication from those who live around us, from the physical environment and from we know not where that it is exceedingly difficult to know where one's boundary lies. We can talk about atmosphere or about resonance. We are directly affected by the moods of others. A human being is a kind of receptor, like a blade of grass trembling in the wind, responding to every slight change in the surrounding air. When the Buddha was enlightened, what was he enlightened to? What was it that he understood so clearly and consequentially? The content of his enlightenment is recorded in rather formal terms. It is called Dependent Origination. What does it mean? It means that every flicker of feeling, mood, or impulse in us is a response. It also means, however, that these responses are not clean, fresh and new. They are rather stale responses that go round and round in old habitual patterns so that we are blind even to our own blindness.

Everybody, therefore, lives within his or her own paradigm or frame of reference, thinking that thereby they have something that makes life coherent and meaningful, and not realizing the extent to which they are dancing to tunes over which they have not the least control. "Like a flame in the wind – how long can it last" as the sage Shan Tao commented.

**There is a legend** that the Buddha, when nearing death, told his disciple Ananda that if he chose he could use his will to extend his life. Ananda did not ask him to do so. Later other disciples held this against Ananda. However, what was the Buddha teaching by this? There are things we can do by will. Some of them go against the tide of reality. Sometimes there is good reason to do such a thing. No such exertion of will, however, can be a permanent thing or a total solution. Things made by our will are a bit like stretching elastic. It will spring back in the end. Religion teaches us to use our personal will, but, much more importantly, it teaches us how to tap into the will of the universe, which is one way of thinking about shinjin. Pure Land Buddhism is for those who do not achieve the highest outcomes from meditation and other self-power practices, but who, nonetheless, have faith and so can be more at home in reality as it is, trembling blades of grass that we are. And there again, sometimes, it is just the trembling blade of grass seeking nothing that tumbles into the most complete samadhi after all.

In the Pali *Majjhima Nikaya* there is a sutra called *Atthakanagara*. It concerns a conversation between Ananda and a layman called Dasama.

Dasama was a businessman. He was in town doing some business, met a Buddhist friar and asked after Ananda whom he had met in the past. Getting instructions about Ananda's whereabouts, after completing his business he travelled to the town where Ananda was staying and went to see him to ask about Dharma. We can see from these preliminary details that this was more than a casual enquiry. Dasama knew who he wanted to see and he was willing to travel to another town in order to see him. He had a question, but he did not put this question to the friar whom he asked for directions.

**The question that Dasama asked** when he finally got to Ananda was "Is there one thing that the Buddha has taught which, if concentrated upon in a diligent, ardent and resolute way, will liberate the mind, destroy the *asavas*, and give security from bondage?" Ananda says that there is such a thing and, at Dasama's request, proceeds to give a discourse.

Let us think a minute about the question and the assumptions it contains. What is Dasama's goal? It is to be liberated and free from bondage. The assumption here is that we are held in bondage, and therefore not liberated, by things that are objects of our attention and that there may therefore be some particular object that will liberate rather than enslave us. Ananda's reply contains several subtle aspects that are worth thinking upon. The word '*asava*', by the way, literally means 'outflows' or 'issues'. Generally the sutras recognize three issues as fundamental to all others: firstly, sensual desire, secondly, desire for existence or particular states of being, and, thirdly, 'avidya'. Avidya means ignorance or delusion or most literally 'not-seeing'. These are the issues that keep one tied to samsara. To destroy the asavas, therefore, would be to overcome the tendencies in oneself that keep one in bondage to other things.

We can also sense that there is in Dasama's question a hope that he can find something that will enable him to keep himself together. He wants to find one thing that he can hold onto that will be reliable through all the ups and downs of life. There is something in us that longs for constancy. When a friend stays loyal to us through thick and thin we feel deeply moved and our life seems to become more meaningful. Loyalty is one of those things that touches the human heart in the most profound way, yet which runs completely against rationalism. It is rational for people to follow their own interests. Following your own interests does not include backing losers. It is rational, therefore, to support people as long as they are winning and to abandon them when they cease to do so. Behaviour of that kind, however, is felt to be shallow, callous and spiritually feeble. We long for something or somebody that will loyally sustain us. Ananda says that there is such a thing, but as it turns out he is going to have to play Dasama along a bit in order to get him to the point of understanding what it really is, because the nature of that reliable something is not of the kind that we initially intuitively look for.

In his reply, Ananda seems to describe not one thing, but eleven. These eleven items are sometimes called seven *dhyanas* and four immeasurables. All eleven are meditative states. Dhyana means meditative absorption or rapture. The first dhyana is the meditation in which a person thinks in a sustained way about a wholesome object. The second is meditation in which a person holds a wholesome object in mind one-pointedly without thinking about it. The third is meditation that is not particularly focussed on an object, but is serene and pleasurable. The fourth is meditation that is neither pleasurable nor unpleasant, but is a state of complete equanimity. The fifth is meditation in which one reflects upon the infinite nature of space. In the sixth one meditates on the infinite nature of consciousness; and in the seventh one meditates on nothingness. The four immeasurables (also called 'divine abidings') are meditations in which one pervades all the directions in the universe with, respectively, loving kindness, compassion, sympathetic joy, and equanimity. These then are eleven meditations by each of which there is a possibility that the practitioner may arrive at the state in which the asavas are destroyed and liberation achieved.

This list of eleven is a catalogue of the kinds of thing that religious practice typically consists of. Thinking in a sustained way about a wholesome object includes most forms of prayer, for instance. In a theistic religion, one would say that keeping God in mind will stand you in good stead. The theistic person keeps him or herself together by reflecting upon the divine presence. Buddhists do not rely upon God in this way, but keeping the Buddha in mind can serve a similar purpose. Buddhists do this and it is an important part of Buddhist practice in many varied schools of the Dharma. Thus Theravadins recite the noble characteristics of the Buddha regularly and are inspired by keeping them in mind. Amidists do likewise.

Such contemplation is valuable and a support. The characteristics of the ideal are in principle eternal so they are something that can support us through the vicissitudes of life. Ananda provisionally affirms this. However, he points out that there are more and more subtle layers to such contemplation. In doing this he is following a standard Buddhist formula. Contemplation without discursive thought is more subtle than with it; and there are higher states still in which the contemplation is not dependent upon an object at all. Thus he moves Dasana through the sequence of eleven meditations, each more profound than the one before but then, after reaching the most subtle of the dhyanas he points out that even higher than the most subtle contemplation is the experience of pervading the world with love, compassion, sympathy and peace. All these wonderful practices will stand one in good stead.

If this were all there was to the sutra it would be interesting and elevating. We would have learnt how to practise in ways that cultivate steadiness of mind and goodness of heart. One of the main purposes of religion would be well accomplished.

**However, there is an extra twist**. After presenting the first dhyana, Ananda says, "Having attained this meditation the practitioner realizes that it is conditioned, produced by his own will, and therefore subject to "cessation." It is this insight that leads him to move on to the next, more profound step. However, even when he reaches the last meditation, the same reflection still applies. At the same time as learning how, by his own will, to generate the most profound and sublime contemplations, the practitioner learns that whatever is produced by his own will "is conditioned and therefore subject to cessation." This applies to all eleven meditations.

Here we have, therefore, at the core of the teachings that are recorded in Pali, which are common to all schools of Buddhism, the clear assertion by Ananda that whatever is the product of one's own will is, for that very reason, not a truly reliable refuge. Ananda says that it is not so much the meditation itself, but this realization that such a meditation based on the meditator's own will is ephemeral, that leads to ultimately good results. In other words, it is the realization that one must go beyond reliance upon self-power that allows one to find a true refuge.

The results of doing so, Ananda says, are of three kinds.

The first of the three good possible outcomes is that the meditator, realizing that the state he has just attained is ephemeral, may go on to enter the next higher state. Initially this seems like a good idea. However, as soon as he has accomplished the higher state, the same reflection will occur, since the higher state is also based on his will and ephemeral.

The second of the good possible outcomes is that the very insight that even these exalted meditative states are ephemeral may of itself be sufficient to undermine the basic issues. This is because the asavas are essentially forms of ambition and the meditative states are the highest things one can aspire to, so the realization that even they are not permanent may be sufficient to dislodge the whole structure of self-power ambition.

Finally, Ananda says, "But if he does not thus attain the destruction of the asavas, then, nonetheless, his desire for the Dharma and delight in Dharma will destroy 'five fetters' and he will appear spontaneously in the Pure Abodes, attaining nirvana there without ever returning from that world." The five fetters are 'personality view', doubt about the Buddhadharma, reliance upon rules and procedures, sensual desire, and ill-will.

All of this is, of course, in the rather formalistic analytical language of the Pali texts. What it boils down to, however, is that a person who enters any of these meditations is able to do so only because they have 'desire for and delight in' the Dharma, or, what we would call faith, shinjin. If they have such faith then this will in itself be sufficient to ensure that the practitioner 'appears in the Pure Abodes' and be past the point of no return, whether he actually enters those meditations or not. The meditations are a product of the personal will. The desire and delight are a product of being inspired. They are given to us rather than generated by us. The reliable refuge is something that we discover rather than something we create.

This Pali Theravadin sutra is thus in no way out of keeping with the Amidist perspective. Pureland does not put stress upon the achievement of higher meditative states, though it has a place for them. They are their own reward. Beyond them, however, lies a penetrating insight into the nature of the human condition that can only be attained when faith supersedes self-will. Those who think that the Theravadin teaching precedes the Amidist one may like to think that here are traces of the origins of Pureland in the supposedly earlier Theravadin teachings. However, once we are alerted to it, we find that the general sentiment of this sutra actually pervades the whole of the Majjhima Nikaya, a large work of which this sutra is but a tiny portion. In sutra after sutra the Buddha tells us about the meditative states and praises their benefits and then goes on to say that, good as they are, they do not yield the true self-effacement or abandonment of self-will that he wishes for us.

**It would be a mistake to think of Amidism as a later development**. Pureland catches the real spirit of the Buddha's original intention and the devotion of his earliest followers. It is for those who do not necessarily achieve the highest outcomes from meditation and the various self-power practices, but who, nonetheless, have faith and authenticity. They desire and delight in the Dharma and, as a result, appear in the Pure Abodes and this itself ensures that they do not fall back into corrupt ways. They do not rely upon their own personality, nor upon rules and procedures, nor do they have doubt about Dharma. They are aware that they have sensual desires and ill-will, but these are softened in their force by the overwhelming importance that the practitioner attaches to entrusting him or herself to the Buddha.

In most books on Amidism, even those written by Pureland Buddhists themselves, the idea is presented that Pureland's other-power doctrine is a later development of Buddhism. When Amidists want to stake their claim they will say that Pureland is the culmination or final development of Buddhism. What I feel, however, is that Amidism is original Buddhism. Not only is it original Buddhism, but it is the original spirit shared by many religions dressed in a particular terminology. Religion aims to help us realize other-power as the profoundest influence in our life and to help us to despair of self-power as a spiritual liberator. Self-power has its place in the activities of everyday life, but it can never be the foundation of our life, any more than a person can lift themselves by pulling on their boot laces.

This then is an interesting sutra for Pureland Buddhists. We do not expect these eleven meditative states to open doors to nirvana for us, we expect them simply to be beneficial in their own right. This helps us to distinguish between two types of practice. There are practices such as these meditations that generate secondary faculties and there is practice that is directly associated with spiritual awakening. The former is what is called self-power. The latter has to do with other-power. The former can be dispensed with.

We do expect that the "desire and delight" that Ananda refers to will stand us in good stead, being manifestations of faith. They create a place in the Pure Abodes, not just for ourselves, but for all those who are touched by the universal light that the Buddha indicates to us. Buddhism is not, therefore, to be identified with meditation. Buddhism teaches meditation and acknowledges its value. This value does not, however, extend to equation with the enlightenment that Buddha brought. This is clear in sutra after sutra.

However, this has to be discovered through experience and the discovery typically comes through the frustration of our spiritual ambitions, just as Ananda points out. This is how it was for me. I studied Meditation Buddhism for many years hoping for great experiences and I had quite a few. I also met some wonderful people. I wanted to have what they had got and so I practised what they taught. I believed that if I made sufficient effort I would get the reward. This belief was half true. The practice of intensive meditation yielded many wonderful things and penetrating experiences. I recommend it for that, but in the end, whatever state of experience I can bring about by my own will can never be completely convincing. One may have experienced visions of other worlds or of past lives, but one can never know that they are not just projections of one's own mind – wish-fulfilment dreams. They may be profoundly meaningful and unforgetable and they may give shape to your life, but something still remains missing, something that comes from the other side.

**There is another step**, but it is not a step further up the ladder. It is a step down – backwards or sideways. Amidism is for those who find the doors of perfection ultimately closed. Faith is a last resort. We do not take to it until we have exhausted everything else. We would much rather be' in control. There are, however, different ways to be freed from bondage and it is not always the direct ascent up the sheer face of the mountain that yields best results. Pureland offers a subtler, sweeter, horizontal approach.

Whatever human will power can achieve, it is temporary. This is not to say that we should not do anything, but we should recognize the limitations – be honest about ourselves. We are all going to die. Everything we create will fade one day. We should not forget that almost every Buddhist epic begins with "He gave up his castle and his kingdom..." It up-ends normal values. Status and achievement are not the goal of religious life. Buddhism is thus a breaker of popular icons. Castles are also prisons. Only by seeing the situation clearly will we walk clear of them and that clear seeing is not something we achieve by will-power. However, through experimentation and the resulting frustration we may chance upon it. One of my mother's favourite poems was Shelley's *Ozymandias*.

## Beautiful, Young, Inexperienced and Happy
**I stayed in Mother's room** through the night. We fixed up a folding bed in the bay window. I sat with her until late and then lay down, sleeping from half an hour after midnight through to just before 4am. In the early hours I sat with her again. She slept. Dawn came. The household began to stir.

Here is an entry from my diary:

"It is 8.30am on Thursday 13th May. Mother is sleeping noisily. Caroline has been reading up green funerals and has passed the job on to Willemien, another member of the community. Caroline and Willemien have decided that it is time for breakfast and have set it up in Mother's sitting room. They have both been wonderfully supportive. Caroline has helped with all the caring tasks including giving Mother bed baths. She was very touched when Mother said to her that she had been an excellent daughter-in-law and that she made a good wife for me. We have got a commode and have to lift Mother on and off her bed, which is rather high, in order to use it. Then we clean her. For the second time in my life I have seen my mother naked. I recall two incidents. The first is recent, when she was in hospital a fortnight ago. We were visiting her and she said that she had had an experience she had never had before in her life. We enquired what it was and she said, "I had a man wipe my bottom." She was highly amused at having received this service from a male nurse. The second is long ago. I remember as a child of eight playing in my room in the afternoon siesta time. We lived in Cyprus. It was hot. After lunch one had a sleep. Mother would put me to bed. When I woke up I would slip out of bed and play with my toys on the floor. As there were few English children, I was quite accustomed to playing on my own. With my toys I could create whole worlds and immerse myself in them for hours. For some reason, however, on this day, I needed something. I cannot remember what. I walked out of my room across the hall, feeling the coolness of the tiles under my feet. I pushed open the door of my parents' bedroom looking for Mother. Both my parents were lying on the bed naked. They were lying side by side. At the time I had only a hazy idea of what I had walked into. My Mother got up, put a dressing gown round herself and ushered me out. I remember the event quite vividly and with the memory comes a collection of feelings. My parents took it in their stride and acted "like modern rational people". They acted as though they thought that a child seeing them naked was perfectly natural, yet somehow I knew that I had crossed a taboo line. Why else do I still remember it? I think that was the day that I began to distrust rationalism."

**Is this not something we most of us feel?** On the one hand, we try to be sensible. When we use words like "the real world" we mean the exigencies of work and money – having a job and a house to live in. We think that these are the real things. When people come to our Buddhist community and spend a period there and the time comes to leave, they may say that they are now going back to the real world. That real world is the place where people are sensible. It is supposedly an unsentimental place where people are responsible. In that world there is no life after death and minds are just epiphenomena of brains. Everything is done for sensible reasons. However, when one tries to find out what this rationality is founded upon, one searches in vain. Rationality is to life rather like nuts and bolts are to a steel bridge. They hold the bits together, but no amount of understanding nuts and bolts will help you to know what a bridge is or what it is for. When a person has decided what they want to do, rationality will help them work out how to do it. It will hold the different bits of the exercise in place. However, rationality will not tell us what we want to do in the first place. It will not tell us what life is about. We have to find that some other way.

Bodies are just bodies and one can attempt to be sensible about them. They need washing periodically and sometimes medical attention is in order, but what are bodies for? One thing they are for is making love, but making love is an intimate mystery in which rationality plays only a very peripheral part. Bodies are also for giving birth and for dying. When they do so even on-lookers feel caught up in something immensely powerful and bigger than themselves. It is impossible to be completely unsentimental about such things at the time. Watching one's child being born is compelling. By what power is one so compelled? Certainly not the power of reason.

When I was eight years old and I saw Mother's body, it was the body of a young woman in love with her husband. It was a smooth healthy body full of vitality and charm. Now, I was seeing it again, wrinkled, sagging, shrivelled, with skin thinner than paper, knotted like a plum tree, with bones showing through. Looking at it then I felt things that only poetry can express. Can this just be dismissed as hormones or synapses? Life has meaning and although meaning may be played out in the medium of space, matter, energy and time, knowing about that medium does not explain the meaning.

Rationality can help us to do what we want to do, but much of what happens in life is not what we want. What happens in life is that we age. Decay accompanies us along our pilgrimage toward death. We do not choose it. We do not want it. Life is more pathos than reason.

On the far side of Mother's bed I could see a picture of her as a young woman. She had always had that picture on view. She did not like people to take pictures of her, but she kept that picture out. It shows her aged about twenty. There is still a touch of the child about her face, which has not entirely lost the adolescent fat from the cheeks. She looks beautiful, young, inexperienced and happy. I know that that is how she experienced herself. She occupied the body of an old woman, but that picture was a picture of how she felt inside. It is the picture of the woman she was when her husband first loved her, when her life lay ahead of her, when her own parents were alive, and when she had wings on her heels. I prefer pictures of her old and full of the experience of life, but I still melt thinking about how she experienced herself.

## Be Fully Alive

**One of the most famous poets in Japanese history** was the Pureland monk Saigyo (1118-1190). The name Saigyo means "Westward journey". The Pure Land of Amida – Nyorai's paradise – is said to be far away in the west, so the name Saigyo indicates travelling toward Amida's land. This in turn implies both travelling toward death and toward spiritual emancipation.

Here is one of Saigyo's poems.

| | |
|---|---|
| *Ogurayama* | In the village |
| *fumoto no sato ni* | At Mount Ogura's foot |
| *ko no ha chireba* | In the tree tops, |
| *kozue ni haruru* | The leaves having fallen; |
| *tsuki o miru kana* | I now can see the moon. |

The poem conjures up the image of a little village nestling at the foot of a great mountain as autumn comes. The little village and the great mountain suggest the smallness of humanity and the vastness of nature which, to the Japanese, symbolises, or is virtually synonymous with, the spiritual power. Amida Nyorai is associated with the autumn, as with the sunset in the west. The year coming to an end, melancholic feelings rise. Yet, the falling of the leaves makes room for the moon to be seen. The moon symbolises Quan Shi Yin, the bodhisattva of compassion, who is Amida's assistant. Just as the moon reflects the light of the sun, so Quan Shi Yin brings us Nyorai's reflected light. Quan Shi Yin is associated with the principle of active compassion.

**This poem has many levels**. Superficially, it reports what Saigyo noticed while he was establishing himself in a village in preparation for his winter hermitage. More profoundly it draws out the contrasts between life and death, dark and light, spiritual abasement and elevation. It does so without establishing any particular primacy of light over dark or life over death. There is no vertical ascent in Amidism. There is no invitation in the poem to climb the mountain. Rather we get the sense of the mountain sheltering the village. Meanings, superficial or profound, are part of the turning wheel of reality. The texture of the poem, and of many of Saigyo's works, is such that one cannot even really say that the trees, moon, mountain, seasons and so on are symbols. It is not so much that they point to spiritual realities beyond themselves as that they become inseparable from those realities. Spiritual reality actually is the rocks and plants, the little village and the trembling hearts of its denizens preparing for winter. The falling leaves reveal the moon just as the ageing of the body reveals the presence of Death, not as a concept, but as a tangibly experienced presence. The identity of the concrete and the metaphysical, typical of the spirit of Pureland, here finds its expression in the sensitivity and beauty of Saigyo's art.

The quality of bitter-sweetness found in Saigyo's poems is, in Japanese, called *yugen*. Yugen is the flavour of Amidism: to be aware of sweetness, beauty and tragedy, all in a single glimpse. To see the young woman in the old body and the soon to be shrivelled body in the young beauty. The spirit of Pureland is, therefore, not one of surmounting or transcending opposites, but rather of appreciating inseparability and irreconcilability in full intensity and with great vividness. It is to be other-worldly and this-worldly all at once.

Life is not measurable. Only non-life is measurable. In life, opposites enhance one another, they do not cancel out. Life has a different logic from non-life. Life is the logic of the immeasurable. The worldly way attempts to reduce life to non-life. Religion seeks to reverse this.

The Buddha called his Dharma the Middle Way. The Middle Way is not a weak compromise between extremes, but simply a refusal to become one-sidedly attached. It is up-right, not in the sense of ascending, but in the sense of not inclining. It is to have the faith to remain poised. Life is not only wonderful, nor only terrible, it is both at once. We cannot and should not try to cut ourselves off from the mundane world, nor can we extinguish that part of us that responds to the thought of Nyorai's Pure Land and longs for refuge.

**Siddhartha Gotama, the Buddha to be, was born at Lumbini** in the foothills of the Himalayas. His mother Maya was from the Koliyan people and she and her sister, Pajapati, were both wives of Suddhodana Gotama, the leading elder of the Shakyan clan. It was traditional for a woman to go back to her parent's home to give birth but Maya came into labour early and the child was born en route by the roadside, Maya delivering her baby while standing holding the bough of a tree. However, there were complications and seven days after the birth Maya died. The party returned to Kapilavastu, the Shakyan capital, with the new baby and his dead mother's body. You can imagine, therefore, the mix of emotions that surrounded Siddhartha's arrival in this world. His father was all at once overwhelmed with joy to have a son, a first child, and stricken with grief to have lost his wife. Siddhartha would be brought up by Pajapati, his step-mother-aunt, and she would later also play a highly significant role in the establishment of the new Buddhist religion.

Everybody must somehow come to terms with the diversity of life experience they encounter. Suddhodana had to cope with great joy and great grief both at the same time. How can one do so? Only by being fully alive to both. How might one not do so? By suppressing both or by thinking that each neutralises the other. Siddhartha was brought up in a family for which his birth and his mother's death were both powerful formative events outside his control. One did not cancel the other out. Both were stark consequential realities. Life is like that. We can admire the grace of the leopard as it springs and simultaneously grieve for the young buck it slays. To live with an open mind, an open heart, is poignant. It is yugen. It is to be repeatedly torn apart. There is, however, a continual temptation to close down one's sensitivity. We would rather not have to see the terrible aspect of life. We would like to make ourselves comfortable and escape from the sharpness of reality. Our embeddedness in existence is a fact. Our longing for a paradise is also a fact. If we can hold both these seemingly contradictory lights, there will be a great brightness, but if we let them cancel each other out, there will be only gloom. The Buddhist word for that gloom is *avidya*.

Vidya means radiance. It implies seeing things clearly. The word is from the root vid that we see in English words like video and vision. A-vidya means lack of radiance, implying ignorance in the sense of a motivated refusal to see. We can induce avidya in all sorts of ways from over eating, idle chatter or light entertainment, through complex psychological defences, inhibitions and compulsive habits, to, in the extreme, serious addictions, mental illness and suicide. Avidya is endlessly shape shifting. It even invades our religious life. In fact, the progress of the religious life is generally marked by a series of essays in which one unconsciously imports into whatever spiritual practice one has adopted the habitual patterns of attachment upon which one is used to relying in one's non-spiritual life. If one belongs to an effective spiritual community, each of these attempts will fail. Each failure is painful and confusing. Generally, when this happens, the adept picks him or herself up and starts all over again. There is always the possibility, however, that the falling of the leaves may reveal the moon that has always been shining behind them.

There is a haiku poem by the modern Pureland teacher Zuiken Inagaki that captures this possibility:

*Chiru toki ga*              Time to fall
*Ukabu toki nari*          Is time to float
*Hasu no hana*            For a lotus blossom.

Each of us is a lotus. It is when we fall that we get the chance to float. It is only in our downfall, in the leaving of our castle, that a doorway to salvation briefly opens.

**The word Buddha means one who is awake**. In other words, one who has vidya, radiance, and who sees the radiance all around them. The opposite, avidya, implies dullness, escapism, and refusal to engage with the fullness of life, good and bad, beautiful and ugly, inner and outer, light and dark, just as it is. The Buddha's own story exemplifies the dynamic just discussed. He left home and entered upon a spiritual quest. The way he went about it was, however, just as one might expect, contaminated with the same personal dynamic as the life that he thought he was escaping from. He sought perfection. He sought freedom from suffering. He was spiritually ambitious. He was willing to go to any lengths to achieve his goal. When teachers offered him a comfortable position based upon partial achievement he ruthlessly rejected the possibility. He seemed like a spiritual hero. In one sense he was. But, at the same time, he was still just being the same old proud stubborn self he had always been, only in a new arena. Just as he always won the archery contest as a youth, so he now intended to win the spiritual contest as an adult. He was still just striving to get to the top. In place of worldly palaces he now wanted celestial ones. Awakening was not the success of this project, it was the fruit of its failure. What Siddhartha Gotama had to find out was that he was just Sid. He was an ordinary being. The Dharma that he sought on the highest pinnacle turned out to be horizontal.

The world, just as it is, is multi-tone. Our own lives are tossed about upon a sea of circumstance moved by currents outside our control. We never know what will befall. Everything is contingent. Everything can change. It is in this world just as it is that we are invited to be fully alive, to live, love and die.

We too are, in ourselves, like little worlds. Within ourselves, in just the same way, many currents are flowing and we are at the mercy of them. In this circumstance, people seek salvation (refuge) in many ways, both worldly and religious. Religious paths sometimes demand great effort and achievements in terms of moral purity, wisdom or meditative realizations. The Purelander, however, simply entrusts himself to Amida, knowing that Amida already accepts us exactly as we are. We are what we are and we are already children of the universe.

**Empty Handed**
**Thursday morning Mother slept** in until about 10.30. Then she start-

ed to become restless and disturbed. She was distressed but one could not discern what the problem was. We conjectured that this was perhaps the consequence of her morphine wearing off. Caroline phoned for help and the local doctor supplied more morphine in liquid form, which Caroline fetched. However, by the time she returned Mother had settled again. She lies there on her pillows rattling. From time to time she becomes briefly lucid and then glazes over again.

Little by little we are losing her. Her attention is rarely toward us now. It is as if her journey into death is already beginning and she is turned that way not this one. I remember this from my own near death experience when I almost drowned as a young man. Once it is clear to you that you are going to die, you leave the world behind. Attention turns in the new direction.

**Death is the great leveller**. The Dharma is also an equaliser. When I am dying, I do not care about my worldly status or my possessions. When I am dying I am no different from anybody else. It does not matter at that time whether I have been a good man or an evil one. We should not judge the dying. A death is a death.

When people encounter the non-judgmental attitude of Amidism they sometimes find it alarming. Does it really not matter whether one has been good or bad? Are we not destined to be reborn according to our karma? Or are we not going to the judgement seat of God? And, interestingly, I find it is often the people who profess not to believe in God or in rebirth, who are the most alarmed of all and the most concerned to assert that it should matter.

But let us ask soberly, why should one do good? One does good so as not to cause harm. One does not do good for the sake of a reward or status. If it is not a good unto itself it is not a good at all. Good acts are complete in and of themselves. They have no carry over. That is the nature of a good act. The good person carries nothing over. They die empty handed.

What of the bad person? From the Buddhist perspective the bad person is no different from the good person, save that he or she is misguided. The bad person is trying to do good, trying to establish a certain kind of order in their world, but doing so in a way that happens to be destructive – sometimes terribly destructive. But whether you are Genghis Khan or Mother Theresa, when you are dying, you are just a bag of skin and bone, essentially no different from my mother lying here. Genghis Khan and Mother Theresa would probably recognize that, whereas most ordinary people would not. Temujin and Theresa both lived fully. We judge them differently, but they both took risks with their lives that most people shrink from and that made their existence meaningful. I have long had a deep respect for really bad people as well as for really good ones. They each teach us something very important about life and about ourselves.

My Zen teacher used to say, "If you are going to sin, sin vigorously." That way, you learn fast. Religion has more to do with living to the full than necessarily always living virtuously. Virtue is what you learn by doing so. Virtue is then grounded in experience and the virtue that is grounded in experience is alive and robust, whereas virtue that comes only from a conceptual knowledge of how life should be – a set of mere ideals – tends to be fragile, brittle and judgmental.

In any case, on a strict basis of measurement, we are doomed. If karma is a calculus, then we are all in serious debt. The benefits that we receive, day in and day out, are immense. The sun shines upon us. Food arrives. We are sheltered from the elements. There is ground to walk upon and air to breathe. We did not make any of this and we certainly did not earn it. It is the fruit of billions of years and the work of innumerable beings. The virtues that we practice are not usually that great and in no way do they come anywhere near matching the benefits we receive. All of us have done harmful things. I remember that as a child I became rather skilled at killing flies. If karma prescribes that I must be splattered to death an equal number of times to that which I inflicted on those creatures, then the outlook is rather grim. We are all implicated in immense cruelties. If you drink milk you are implicated in supporting an industry that kills calves. You might become vegan, but your bread is from wheat and in the harvest a huge number of tiny creatures are crushed or cut down. Even by the most ruthless purification regime you will not put yourself in karmic credit.

My mother did not live a life that was conventionally religious. Nonetheless, she was consistently kind and humane. She could make people feel welcome. One could say that she had many virtues, but it would be truer to say that she had a broad mind and a wealth of experience, coupled with an amalgam of practicality and kindness. In her ordinariness she embodied many special virtues. However, during the Second World War she had been a radar operator. Radar was state of the art science. It was, in effect, the most lethal weapon that the allies possessed. It provided the guidance that enabled the Battle of Britain to be won. It was the key component in an effective killing machine. How many German pilots were burned to death as a result of my mother's skill?

### What do you want, Mum?

**Many people loved Mother**. Her room was gradually filling up with cards and flowers. Every half hour or so, the doorbell would go with a new contribution. Word had got around.

Mother is restless today. She keeps trying to move but does not have the strength. I try to help her but am really at a loss to know what to do for the best.

Then, in a semi-lucid moment she says, "Don't take me anywhere. Let me do it myself." She is now trying to sit up, but she makes only a small movement and then falls back.

Another lucid moment:

"You don't know what I want, do you?"

"What do you want Mum?"

"I don't know... Hold me."

She reaches out her hands. I take them and she pulls against them manoeuvring herself onto her side. She settles for a time.

Caroline and Willemien are in the other room discussing burial arrangements. Mother has asked for a green burial and some research was needed to discover how to arrange it. Mother is busy dying. It looks like hard work for her at this stage, but also quite joyful at times. I sit and watch over her.

## The Importance of Ritual

**Each person has a part to play**. At ten to one the undertaker calls by and leaves his information. He is exactly what you expect an undertaker to be.

"We can do whatever you want, whenever you want it," he says in a softly melodious voice, "The answer is always 'yes'. 'No' is such an unnecessary and unpleasant word, I always think, don't you?"

As a priest, I find myself operating again on two levels just as when I watched the consultant tell Mother that she was dying. I have a professional interest as well as a human one. It suddenly becomes real to me that soon I will be conducting Mother's funeral. As yet I have no thoughts what it will be like.

Priests and undertakers must work together when somebody dies. They have to agree who will do what. When, as now, it is the priest's own relative who is dying, the rational world and the emotional one intersect.

**This point of intersection** suddenly seems very significant. Much of Buddhism is concerned with such intersections. Spiritual literature abounds with references to Oneness. However, there are two different kinds of oneness. There is encompassing oneness and there is centring oneness. Encompassing oneness refers to the unity of all. Centring oneness refers to the point of intersection of what appear to be opposite or contrasting dimensions of life, existence and time. Thus, in Mahayana Buddhist mythology the ultimate oneness is personified as Vairochana Buddha. In Japanese, Vairochana is called Dainichi. Dainichi means great twofold wisdom, *ni* being the Japanese word for two. Dainichi exists at the intersection of the two wisdoms, or, we could say, the two dimensions of human nature.

There is much concern in contemporary Buddhist philosophy with something called non-dualism. Philosophically, this is through and through a paradoxical matter. To say non-dualism immediately implies that there is something called dualism. In other words non-dualism is set off against what it is not. This something and something else thus constitute a dualism, so non-dualism implies dualism. Although at first this seems absurd, it points to something more practical. We can conceive of non-duality, but in practice we live in duality. We can conceive of Oneness that is all embracing, but in fact we live in one specific place or another. We can conceive of the point of intersection between the different sides of our nature, but we rarely and only fleetingly arrive at it.

Although Amidism is a form of Buddhism and so acknowledges the importance of these ideals, it is a characteristic of Pureland that it does not expect people to occupy them very much. Where most forms of Buddhism involve intense effort to understand the nature of and attain the enlightened state, Amidism is, more typically, an enquiry into the dark side. Where most Buddhism presents as an upward ascending ladder, Amidism takes us into the basement of human nature.

In this particular moment I am divided between my emotional dimension, enmeshed in the process of being with Mother, and my professional dimension, listening to the undertaker. I rather like the way that he over-plays his part. It reminds me of a salesman who once sold me a computer system:

"Mr Brazier, this system has everything,"
then, turning to the next one...

"and this one has even more."

At one level it is absurd, but what do you want from a salesman? He clearly enjoyed his work and the enthusiasm was infectious. He not only sold you things, you enjoyed buying them from him. What we want from people really is not that they perform like rational robots. We want spirit. We want what Bergson called *elan vital*.

**All of life is ritual**, in a sense. Being an undertaker is certainly ritual, but so is being a salesperson. Ritual is behaviour that has meaning consciously added. At a purely rational level all that is required of an undertaker is that he dispose of bodies. At the rational level it is no different from being a refuse collector. We all know, however, that such an approach would never work. Death is important in terms of what it means, not in terms of what it is. In philosophy these dimensions are called epistemic and ontic. Humans operate epistemically. Their lives are shaped by meaning, not merely by facts.

When Mother was younger she would say,

"I don't care what you do with me after I'm dead."

But as the time of death approached, she thought more carefully. Sitting beside her now I knew that she wanted to be buried, not cremated, and she wanted the burial to take place at a natural burial ground. She had researched the matter. There were two natural burial grounds close to Leicester. In a natural burial ground, the grave is in a plot in an area of unconsecrated ground that is intended eventually to become woodland. In many cases, a tree is planted on the grave.

The undertaker was quite familiar with this system. He could also offer a range of bamboo completely bio-degradable coffins. Being from Leicester, one of the most multi-cultural cities in the UK, he was also used to doing funerals accompanied by non-Christian ceremonial. Clearly it was all going to work. More importantly, it was going to be what Mother would want and it would express well to those who attended some of the important things about what made Mother's life meaningful: her love of nature and natural things, her sense of the poetry and of the process of life and death, growth and decay, and her basic modesty about the human condition. All these things are to do with meaning. Life becomes satisfying when the factual ontic side of existence is expressive of such meaning. Ritual is important.

**Yet death is also a practical matter**. Caroline had spoken to the doctor and he had told her about the signs of impending death. She passed this information on to me. It was clear that we were not there yet. Mother might well live a couple more days.

My elder daughter, Emma, phoned. She and her husband Dave, and my son Michael would visit that evening.

Throughout the day the phone went repeatedly both with people who knew nothing of what was happening and people who were phoning because of it. Friends also called in for brief visits.

From my journal: "I seem to have stopped being emotional. All the activity seems to flow over me. I seem to be in a kind of mindless state, just doing whatever needs doing."

In the afternoon Mother had diarrhoea. We tried to cope with it without getting her out of bed but there was too much. I, therefore, lifted her onto the commode. When she seemed to have finished, I lifted her into a semi-standing position. However, it then all restarted so I sat her down again. Although she is small, it was not easy to lift her. We went through this several times. Each time I lifted her it seems to reactivate her bowel. Not all of it went into the commode. There were liquid faeces everywhere. Mother was exhausted and so was I. Caroline commented that when it comes to my turn to die nobody will be big enough to pick me up the way I pick up Mother.

Eventually Mother is back in a newly made bed, soiled sheets are in the wash, the commode has been cleaned up, Mother sleeps and I also doze. What a messy business bodies are.

At 2pm, Caroline came in and said that Jenny was coming. Jenny is Caroline's younger daughter, my step-daughter. Caroline had delayed telling her what was happening until now as Jenny had been in the midst of her final exams at university. As soon as she heard she said, "I'll catch the next train." Jenny has always been quite devoted to my mother. She had known of Mother's hospitalisations and visited her, but it would have been deeply painful for her to hear that Mother was dying.

**When the Buddha was dying**, his disciples gathered. Even though he died at an out of the way spot, they congregated around him. When a death is anticipated people gather. It is the same the world over. Members of our community have worked in Zambia in Africa on the other side of the world, but there it is just the same. The tribe gathers.

The scriptural account of the Buddha's death makes it clear that he was anticipating his death for about three months. This gave plenty of time for people to gather, even when this meant walking considerable distances. The Buddha was travelling with his cousin and close companion Ananda. He decided that the place to stop was a grove of sal trees near Kusinagara. There he lay down facing west, on his right side, with his head in the north. Petals fell upon his body.

He told Ananda that he could see many celestial beings that had also gathered, but they were invisible to the assembled humans. Because people were distressed that they would be unable to visit and greet the Buddha in the future after his death, he told them that they could do so by honouring the four places associated with his life: the place of his birth, the place of his enlightenment, the place of his first teaching and the place of his final passing. He gave instructions upon what should be done with his remains and talked about the merit and importance of a *stupa*.

A stupa is a reliquary, often in the form of a burial mound erected to enshrine the remains of a saint, a disciple, or a world-benefactor. The importance of such monuments is that people can come to them and think upon the person who lies there. It is important that people attempt to practice the Dharma that the Buddha has taught – that is the rational aspect of the spiritual path – but it is just as important that they have a relationship with the person who is the source and conveyor of that Dharma. These are the two dimensions of our nature that we seek to unify. Consequently the earliest Buddhist sites display by their architecture that they were designed for memorial. There is generally a central reliquary and a circular walkway around it. It is fairly obvious what the general form of early Buddhist devotion must have looked like. People would circumambulate the relics, either silently or intoning the Buddha's name, the name that inevitably became holy to Buddhists.

**When we think about ourselves biologically**, humans have layers to their brain. The surface layer or cortex has evolved most recently. It is the cortex that processes information and can operate rationally. Beneath the cortex, however, there are older layers that reflect our evolution out of mammalian and even reptilian ancestors. An enlightenment that operated only in the brain cortex would not function more than intermittently. It would not mobilise the powerful emotions that make life feel real and significant. It would have nothing to do with the meaning of life. We should not, therefore, view the enlightenment that Buddha taught as an elevation of rational principles to a supreme and exclusive status. It is certainly true that the Buddha was a clear thinker who knew how to marshal an argument, but he was also a wise teacher who understood that relationships are at the heart of what it is to be human. For this reason he provided for memorials by saying,

"Ananda, there are these four places the sight of which should arouse emotion in the faithful."

Ananda is extremely distressed that the Buddha is dying. The Buddha, however, calls him and comforts him and before the assembly praises him for his unstinting service both to the Buddha himself and to the whole Buddhist community.

Then the Buddha was visited by an enquirer called Subhadda. At first Ananda is reluctant to let him trouble the Buddha at such a time, but the Buddha allows him to come and teaches him Dharma. The Buddha has a rule that postulants must wait four months before being ordained, but he is struck by the sincerity of Subhadda and ordains him there and then. Subhadda was thus the last disciple of the Buddha.

The Buddha says that after he is gone, they should not think that they are without a teacher since the Dharma that he has taught will continue to be their teacher. Then he gives instructions on a variety of matters, tidying up unfinished business and loose ends. Finally he asks the disciples if there is anything they still wish to clarify or about which they have doubts. He speaks his final words to them, enters meditation and then passes away.

## Blessings are Not Just for the Good

**Buddha comes and Buddha goes.** When the Buddha died different disciples reacted differently. Broadly we can distinguish two patterns, which correspond to the two meanings of the word *Tathagata*. The Buddha is commonly referred to as the Tathagata. Tatha means "thus" and can also be taken as short for tathata or "thus-ness", which we discussed earlier. Gata means "gone". Agata means "come". Tathagata can be construed as tatha-gata or as tatha-agata. Behind this difference of terminology lies a basic choice about the way we view the significance of the spiritual life. These two basic options correspond to the different dimensions of human nature that we have referred to recurrently and that the Buddha catered for in the instructions that he gave on his deathbed.

If we take the perspective of tatha-gata, meaning "thus gone" or "gone to thusness", we are dealing with an interpretation in which the

Buddha is seen as a spiritual pioneer or trail-finder. The Buddha has gone ahead. He has found a path and showed the way. Now he has gone and it is our duty to follow. In this model, the spiritual practice involves carrying out the Buddha's instructions, accomplishing the things that he accomplished and, ultimately, becoming a Buddha oneself. This is one of the basic paradigms of spiritual life whether it is the imitation of Buddha or the imitation of Christ or whoever the paradigmatic figure may be. This path involves great effort and striving at perfection in ethics, meditation and wisdom and the mastery of the many stages of spiritual development. This is the ascetic or "training" side of spirituality. Finally one will arrive at thusness, which is ultimate reality or nirvana. One's life purpose will then be fulfilled and there will be nothing further to be done. One will never again need to be reborn into this world. This is one approach to Buddhism.

On the other hand, if we take the perspective of tatha-agata, meaning "thus come", or "come from thusness", we are invited to see the Buddha as a saviour. He has come to us. He has brought something wonderful into our lives. He is like an emissary from the other world. We are not so much invited to emulate as to celebrate him. It is the relationship that is important. The person who approaches Buddhism in this way is likely to be filled with gratitude rather than with striving. It has to be said that the great majority of the Buddha's disciples, especially his lay disciples, saw him this way and this is the way that the vast majority of his followers in Asia approach Buddhism to this day. What had been most important for them was meeting him. That had been far more impressive than what they had achieved by their own efforts and meeting him did not seem like something that they had worked for or achieved. He was the Thus Come One and as such he was the greatest gift that had ever fallen into their lives. The Japanese word Nyorai means tatha-agata.

Amidism clearly derives from the second mentality. Thusness

corresponds to the Pure Land. To be with the Buddha is to be in the Pure Land, whether you are a top grade saint or a bottom grade sinner. Pureland thus envisages universal salvation, not merely the salvation of an elite few who attain particularly elevated levels of practice.

**The great Pureland sage Honen** who lived in Japan eight hundred years ago pointed out that if salvation in Buddhism depended upon study, then only the intelligent and educated could be saved, yet the intelligent and educated are few while the unintelligent and uneducated are many. If salvation depends upon lengthy meditational practices and attainments, then only those with the leisure for them can be saved, but the leisured are few and those who cannot do such practices are many. If salvation depends upon generosity and good works, then only those who are rich enough to afford them can be saved, but the rich are few and the poor many. If salvation depends upon goodness, then only those who have lived virtuous lives can be saved, yet the virtuous are few and the unvirtuous are many. If there is a form of universal salvation in Buddhism it must be something that is available to all, not just to the good, the rich, the leisured or the intelligent. The world already rewards the good, the rich, the leisured and the intelligent. Religion is not primarily made for them, though they are not to be excluded either. Religion is primarily made for those who are not necessarily privileged or talented in these ways. It is for ordinary people who may have been trodden down by life, who may not have been endowed with great cleverness, whose life circumstances may have been such that they have not always acted in highly ethical ways. They might be beggars or fishermen or prostitutes. They might have had to fight and kill. They might have lived in destitution. What does religion offer to them?

In the approach that sees Buddha as Tatha-gata, there is a scale of achievement. Some do better than others. The ladder is very long. At the very top there is Buddhahood. On the way there are the stages of bodhisattvahood. Traditionally there are ten of these. Even the bottom rungs, however, seem well out of reach to most ordinary people. In fact, one would have to have a pretty high opinion of oneself to think that one was going to climb to such heights of perfection. This reflection nearly caused Honen to despair.

He wrote:

"The Buddha Dharma has many aspects, but its fundamental basis lies in *sila* (ethical precepts), *samadhi* (meditational absorption) and *prajna* (transcendent wisdom). These three trainings are established in Theravada and Mahayana Buddhism in both esoteric and exoteric schools. On close inspection of my own case, however, I see that I have not succeeded in keeping any of the precepts nor reached any of the meditational attainments. A master has said that one will never enter samadhi without first purifying body and mind through the precepts. Furthermore, ordinary people's minds are easily distracted. Their minds are like monkeys that swing from branch to branch, confused, wavering and unable to concentrate. How can wisdom emerge? And without it, how can we extricate ourselves from the chains of unwholesome karma and evil passion? How can we avoid just going round and round through birth and death in the delusive world? How can we be released? All this is very disheartening and sad."

Now please do not think from this that Honen was a lazy man. He was extremely diligent. He was ordained as a boy and noted as a hard work-ing scholarly and virtuous practitioner – a saint, in fact, famous in his own lifetime for his virtue and piety. He was dispassionate enough about himself to be able to reason that if even he who had the leisure, the facilities, the intelligence and the motivation could not reach the exacting standards required by the sutras, then probably there would be few indeed who could do so, since the great majority of people lacked these qualifications.

Honen eventually experienced a profound awakening upon reading the work of Shan Tao. Shan Tao was a Chinese Pureland sage who lived six hundred years before Honen. Shan Tao taught that the essence of Buddhism was devotion to Nyorai Amida. It was by reading Shan Tao that Honen learnt how to stop trying to follow the Tatha-gata and learn to celebrate the Tatha-agata. This insight revolutionised Honen's life. He left his monastery on Mount Hiei and began a career of preaching to the masses. His fame spread throughout the country and the schools of Buddhism that descend from him are still the largest in Japan.

**My experience** of introducing Amidism in Western countries is mixed. Typically people react in one of two ways. Either they express great relief or they express confusion and hostility. I am sure that some of the latter response is attributable to my own inept methods of communication. Nonetheless, to some extent it must also reflect the two different types of personality – those that respond to the Tatha-gata and Tatha-agata respectively. Those who respond with relief say such things as, "Then I don't have to be perfect." This causes them to relax and become more at ease. Others find them easier to live with. They are no longer caught in the grip of puritanical moral injunctions. On the other hand, those who are confused or hostile fear that such a teaching will lead to licence and a slackening of effort or feel at sea wondering what then should one do.

Honen encountered a similarly mixed reception in Kamakura Japan. He was extremely popular, but he was also persecuted. He was especially popular with ordinary working people, but he also found friends at court and enjoyed imperial patronage. On the other hand, the established schools of Buddhism saw him as a threat and near the end of his life he was actually exiled for several years and at least four of his disciples were executed.

We are, therefore, here talking about extremely powerful forces that move people to great passion for good or ill. Honen opened up a new way. Shakyamuni Buddha appeared in our world. He was a human, not a god. Although he was a human, there was something remarkable about him. How are we to conceptualise his special gift?

Shakyamuni pointed something out to people. We could call that something by a number of rather grand names like the Ultimate Truth or the Absolute Reality, but I am rather inclined to believe that setting up big headline words like that confuses people more than it enlightens them. Nobody knows what they mean.

Although we may say that Buddha gave a teaching, it is probably more important that he gave an example. Buddhism flows more from the Buddha's example even than from his teachings. A teaching needs to be embodied in order to be real. We may say, therefore, that, even at the abstract level, the Buddha Dharma is a certain sort of person.

The sort of person that we are talking about is a universal person. A Buddha is a person who really is endowed with a sense of universal equality. He or she also lives in service of others. We saw above how Buddha was still ministering to people and thinking of their needs even on his deathbed. Now we can try to emulate that person. We can try to convince ourselves of that principle and put it into practice. We might succeed, but it is more likely that we will simply suppress whatever aspects of ourselves do not fit the image of what we want to adopt. We are much more likely to become an imitation Buddha than a real one and behind the facade all kinds of trouble may still loom.

Buddhism coming to the West has suffered from this phenomenon. There have been guru figures who have gone off the rails and some writers have observed that people seem to be able to be enlightened yet still neurotic, successful meditators who are yet still liable to get their lives and inter-personal relationships into a mess. Several leading writers have concluded that perhaps Buddhist training needs in many cases to be supplemented with psychotherapy.

On the other hand, if we encounter Nyorai, not as a model but rather as a source of blessing, we will naturally be influenced in a positive way. We might be more ripe for this experience or less so and so the progress may be faster or slower, but unless we cut ourselves off completely, we are bound to be influenced. This is because it is extremely difficult to keep up a script of superiority or inferiority in communication with somebody who naturally and authentically does not play that game. As we become intimate with Nyorai what needs to happen will happen naturally. A relationship influences us, but we do not enter a relationship as a strategy to get influenced. One does not get married thinking, "I will associate with this person and thereby learn his/her talents." Indeed, the best relationships are often complementary ones where the partners are not necessarily alike, yet each is matured and completed through association with the other without trying.

If there is a relationship that is central to our life then many of the things that we encounter along the way remind us of it. Sometimes we commune directly with the beloved, but even when we do not we find reflections everywhere. As a Pureland Buddhist one sees tokens of Nyorai in the setting sun, in natural beauty, in little acts of kindness done by others, in the myriad benefits we receive. Two of the most powerful tokens, however, lie in the experience of being born and dying or of being intimately close to somebody who is doing so.

Once one has accepted that it is the time of birth or the time of death there is no strong investment in being anything other than a human being doing what human beings do. The problem for most of us is that we have great investment in being all sorts of things. We try to set ourselves up by our own will. Relying upon such self-power, we can never realize our ordinariness fully. The person who is dying, however, may have dropped those worldly pretensions, for the simple reason that they are no use to you when you are dying. Being with my mother as she lay dying, I experienced being with an instance of Amida. I am sure many other people do so in parallel circumstances.

## There is No Efficient Technique That Will Ensure Salvation

**Buddhism is a soteriological religion**. It is about salvation or liberation. The Buddha achieved such liberation and offers it to others. Each
school of Buddhism conceptualises that liberation in its own way and
offers related practices that dramatise that conceptualisation. Some then
present these dramatisations as methods or techniques. From an Amidist
perspective, however, one is inclined to doubt whether that is what they
really are.

As the Buddha's message is understood from the Amidist point of
view, there is and can be no efficient technique that will ensure the
achievement of the liberation or salvation that Nyorai bestows. The fact
that we find many methods that look like techniques in the sutras does
not change this fact. The Buddha in the sutras does not say that any of
the methods produce enlightenment. Rather they constitute things of
intrinsic worth that religious people may want to do.

Buddhism offers the possibility of enlightenment or awakening
through refuge. The awakening involves seeing into one's true nature.
We could say that it is a fruit of self-reflection, but the crucial reflection
does not really come about as a consciously undertaken method. It
comes about as a result of the kind of encounter that cuts the ground
away from under our previously tenaciously held assumptions about
ourselves, many of which we were probably not even conscious of.
Self-reflection that is undertaken as a deliberate policy can certainly
yield improvements as can all the methods presented in the Buddhist
texts. None of them, however, yields full awakening. Awakening is in
its very nature a negation of the will by which any specific practice
could be deliberately undertaken.

For this reason, religious practice is better regarded as a dramatisation or ritualisation of the conceptual framework within which the par-

ticular religious school has couched the soteriological discourse. In the Zen School, for instance, people sit in meditation for long periods of time. There is great emphasis upon correct posture. Adepts sit facing a wall. One might think that this is a method for attaining enlightenment. However, really it is a dramatisation of what Zen Buddhism thinks that enlightenment is. Enlightenment in Zen is the perfect poise of the meditator facing his own impenetrable barrier.

**The enlightenment of Zen is no different from the awakening of faith** in Amidism, though, in a sense, it is its mirror image. In Pureland, the ritual is to recite the nembutsu, "Namo Amida Bu" or "Namo Amitabhaya". Namo refers to the ordinary foolish being that calls out. Amida refers to the unattainable Buddha ideal. The Amidist calling out across the unbridgeable spiritual abyss is essentially the same drama as the Zen adept trying to penetrate the iron wall. He may call out in longing or in gratitude, in hope or in despair, in faith or in doubt. The nembutsu encompasses all the dimensions of what it is to be human. There is no right way to call the nembutsu. The nembutsu is always right just as it is and we are always foolish beings. The wise one is the one who knows it.

The ritual of the traditional Buddhist friar was to go on alms round. Here we see dramatised the liberation of acting in a way that is completely dependent. The alms round dramatises the fact that each of us depends upon others for our life. It is up to others whether they put food into the bowl or not. This is not a means to enlightenment so much as a dramatisation of the human situation. Wisdom is to know your foolishness, weakness and dependency. In Tibetan Vajrayana they practice tantric sadhanas. Here the practitioner visualises a deity, becomes one with it and then dissolves it into empty space. Any of these practices may be presented as if they are means of achieving something, but in fact that is not their real nature. Rather they re-enact the central myth of the school. The same is true in other religions.

There is nothing wrong with this. What happens is that a person enters such a school, learns its mysteries, practices them and, sometime along the way, may stumble upon awakening. The thing that they stumble over is the person or circumstance that proves to be the source of transmission for them. What the transmission does, however, is quite different from what was expected. Instead of demonstrating the success of the practice, it demonstrates something else altogether. After awakening the adept may well continue to practise, but now does so in a quite different spirit from before.

# SIX

# PRACTICE

## Bombu Shin Gyo

**Gyo means practice**. At the beginning of this book I called Pureland "Bombu shin gyo" – faith and practice for foolish beings. Now it is time to take a closer look at the practice aspect. Buddhist schools are sometimes classified as practice schools and philosophical schools. Philosophical schools include some practice and practice schools include some philosophy, but there is a difference of emphasis. Pureland is a practice school. Among practice schools, as we have just discussed, some present their methods as a way of reaching awakening. Amidism, however, asserts that there is no method by which a foolish being of blind passion can make awakening occur. Awakening is a grace. It is not something that can be achieved by jiriki. The occurrence of awakening is therefore said to be an instance of other power (tariki). Just as when the sun rises in the morning, it is the light that awakens us, not we who awaken the light, and it will do so in its own good time. Whether we have had shinjin experience or not, however, we can still have faith in the dawn.

Amidism's fundamental practice is keeping Buddha in mind and this is specifically enacted by saying the nembutsu, which is the practice of calling the Buddha by name out loud, thus entrusting oneself to the light. Throughout the vicissitudes of life, we have the nembutsu. Nembutsu is the prayer by which the light is invoked and celebrated. Nembutsu takes slightly different forms according to language and custom. In Japan they say "Namu Amida Butsu" or "Namandabu", in China, "Namo Omito Fo" and in Vietnam, "Namo Adida Phat." The common Anglicised form is "Namo Amida Bu", Bu being a contraction of Buddha, to retain the six syllable form of ancient tradition. There are other alternatives. One can say "Namo Amitabhaya", which is Sanskrit. In Theravada Buddhist countries they say, "Buddho, Buddho" or "Namo tassa, bhagavato arahato samma sambuddhassa". There are also longer Sanskrit and Japanese forms. In our Amidist community in England we use many forms, but the basic one is "Namo Amida Bu".

**This practice is exceedingly easy**. One does not have to learn complicated doctrines to do the practice, nor does one have to have the leisure to sit in meditation for many hours. One just has to say the nembutsu with a mind of simple faith. Even the framework of doctrine set out in this book is not actually necessary. Although it may be elaborated into any number of forms, the saying of nembutsu is essentially so easy that anybody can do it no matter what demands their lifestyle puts upon them. Buddhism prescribes that we should choose a moral and honourable lifestyle if we can, but we are constricted by worldly circumstances in varying degrees and the awakening of faith is not limited to people in one category of occupation. People may choose to be monks and nuns in order to free themselves of other ties so that they can dedicate their life to going forth for the good of all beings, but they do not need to do so to be saved by the unimpeded light. Even if they have been conscripted into the army or forced by economic or coercive power to work in some immoral trade, if they have a simple faith and say the nembutsu they will arrive at spiritual emancipation quite naturally.

Namo Amida Bu. Namo Amida Bu. Getting up in the morning, Namo Amida Bu. Greeting a friend, Namo Amida Bu. Before eating, Namo Amida Bu. After eating, Namo Amida Bu. Namo Amida Bu. As a way of saying please, Namo Amida Bu. As thank you, Namo Amida Bu. When bad things happen, Namo Amida Bu. When good things happen, Namo Amida Bu. When one feels an influx of spiritual love, Namo Amida Bu. When one is lost in depression or despair, Namo Amida Bu.

While standing, Namo Amida Bu. While walking, Namo Amida Bu. While sitting, Namo Amida Bu. While lying down, Namo Amida Bu. Amidist practice is Namo Amida Bu.

In Amidism many of the things that in other schools of spirituality may be conceived to be means toward the achievement of enlightenment are, here, regarded as outcomes of the awakening of faith. We should reflect that in stories contained in the Buddhist scriptures, people did not spend many years becoming awakened. After meeting the Buddha they pretty soon either awakened or they did not. Once they were awakened the Buddha sent them forth to do some good in the world. Nembutsu faith is a basis for an active life of service. It is sustaining, portable, direct, and sufficiently irrational to bypass the ego.

Nembutsu has a wonderful ability to transform people. Saying, "Namo Amida Bu" we are invoking the influx of Nyorai's love. Actual human Buddhas, such as Shakyamuni Buddha who lived and died in India 25 centuries ago, are conceived to be instances of this love-light. When we take refuge in Buddha we are not taking refuge in a corpse, we are taking refuge in the light that that man's life corresponded to: the light that awoke him and animated his ministry. That is Nyorai.

**Buddhists talk about faith as refuge** (*sarana*). We take refuge in *Buddha*, *Dharma* and *Sangha*. Complete Buddhas are those who have awakened to Amida's Light, live in reliance upon it uncompromisingly, and point it out to others. The Dharma is what Buddhas point out. The essence of Dharma is Nyorai Amida and the Pure Land. Dharma is all the teachings that are given by which Buddhas seek to make Nyorai apparent. The Sangha is the community that lives by the light, comprising both the awakened and the faithful, whether monks, nuns, laywomen or laymen. The life of the Sangha is inspired by the Pure Land and it takes form in the creation of communities that aim to be models of harmony, like reflections of the eternal ideal to which we aspire but which lies beyond our grasp. In Amidist spirituality there is a principle of complete equality between men and women, rich and poor, and even between good and bad. The Buddha's love encompasses all in exactly the same unconditional way. It is deplorable that religions, including some branches of Buddhism, sometimes condone or even encourage sexism, nationalism, or racism. The purpose of spirituality is to enable people to be lifted above such things; however, we are bombu. However much we criticise others we fall into similar faults ourselves.

Since there is a correspondence between the Pure Land and the material realm, we can encounter Nyorai reflected in the multifarious circumstances of life as they present themselves. This does not mean that all is well with this world in the ordinary sense. It means that there is scope for love and wisdom in all situations and that, if we are aware of the correspondence, we will be learning about love through everything that happens around us. Working with others in a spirit of friendship, we will sometimes find ourselves resisting oppression, sometimes assisting the afflicted, sometimes creating communities that correspond more closely with the Pure Land vision, and sometimes simply learning patience. In every instance, when we call Nyorai's name, his love comes to our aid, and without conscious effort we naturally harmonise with or are used by his compassionate will. Even as foolish beings we can still fumblingly play our part, trusting in the larger scheme of things

The different modes of religious life help the Dharma community to function and help individuals to express and deepen their faith. There is no fundamental inequality, however, between lay and ordained. In regard to faith in the measureless light, all are on the same footing. All are bombu. However many times a person may have had a shinjin experience, on a given day they may still be overwhelmed by old habit energies and lost in darkness, and even though a person may never have had such an experience, on a particular day that person may be full of faith and joy and an example to the whole community.

Literally, Namo means "call upon" or "take refuge in", so Namo

Amida Bu is the Amidist way of expressing taking refuge. Taking refuge is the act common to all schools by which one formally becomes a Buddhist. A person who recites the nembutsu, therefore, is becoming a Buddhist over and over again, implicitly recognising that one falls away equally often. The nembutsu, therefore, is a way of expressing the situation in which a bombu relates to Amida. The human situation is, on the one hand, that of unassuageable longing, and, on the other hand, of inexpressible gratitude. Pureland practice has nothing to do with achievement and everything to do with expressing this bitter-sweet sentiment that is the feeling accompaniment to the spiritual life.

**Nembutsu may be practised in any circumstance**. Where conditions allow, it can be said out loud. Where they do not, it can be said silently. The practitioner becomes saturated with nembutsu, besotted with Nyorai. From the Pureland perspective, all other Buddhist practices are auxiliary to nembutsu. Thus, such practices as bowing or making offerings can become forms of nembutsu with the body in contrast to nembutsu with the voice. A full range of Buddhist practice may be followed, therefore, including recitation of sutras, other ceremonial, meditation and so forth, but in Amidism these are not means to attain anything, they are ancillary forms of nembutsu. This way of regarding things is not meant to be offensive to other schools, it is simply the way that Pureland conceptualises the spiritual path.

The Chinese Pureland sage Shan Tao (613-681) divided practice into "concentrated" and "widespread". Concentrated practice occurs when practitioners gather to practise formally together. It usually takes place in a dedicated place, such as a ceremony hall. Concentrated practice generally includes such elements as invoking Nyorai, chanting nembutsu, walking and sitting contemplation, making prostrations, and sutra recitation. There may also be singing of hymns, making offerings, and Dharma talks. There may be a prescribed etiquette. Our most fundamental practice is walking nembutsu. In this practice we walk slowly while chanting the nembutsu, usually circumambulating the Buddha statue. Walking nembutsu can also be done outside and does not have to be slow. There are also forms of *odori* (dancing) nembutsu that derive from the practice of itinerant Pureland teachers from the Japanese middle ages who were called *hijiri*. Walking nembutsu is a very ancient practice, circumambulation and chanting having been done by the earliest Buddhists. If one visits the Ajanta caves in India, one sees that the earliest shrines were designed to facilitate the practice of circumambulation. The practice symbolises that Amidism is an "on your feet" spirituality, not just a contemplative one, and that our faith revolves around the Buddha and from that source goes out into the world.

Widespread practice refers to practice outside the ceremony hall in the midst of daily life. Here again, nembutsu recitation provides the foundation. Widespread practice also includes works of service to the community and gatherings in which practitioners share their experiences and explore their religious feeling together in a natural or spontaneous way. These meetings for mutual support and testimony have a democratic character, deriving from the sense that all practitioners are on a similar footing vis-a-vis Amida and are bombu. We have things to learn from one another and sharing from the heart in a group can be a wonderful support to faith and love. None of us is particularly wise alone. By listening to one another we come to a much deeper appreciation of what faith means. We find that people that we initially could not understand have secret treasures of kindness and understanding. One learns to respect what is different from oneself and this helps to make us modest, taking away the sting of judgement that can poison relationships so easily. Relating to one another in tenderness is also a way of appreciating the light, each other person becoming a reflection of Nyorai.

**The Pure Land is made of unconditional love**. We are incapable of such love, but we have faith in it. We remember that the Buddha preached against animal sacrifice, opposed the caste system, raised up the oppressed, tended the sick, and advocated the relief of poverty by granting people the means to establish an occupation that contributes to the good of society. Even Buddha could not eliminate these evils from the world of his time, but he carried on in faith acting in correspondence with the light to the best of his ability. Shakyamuni Buddha put forward his teaching on ethics in great detail. These teachings are summarised in ethical precepts. The precepts summarise what the life of an enlightened person is like. The transmission of the precepts is, therefore, the transmission of the life of the Buddhas. To receive the precepts is to have a dynamic force implanted within one. We cannot keep the precepts by our own power, but this dynamic force works within us simplifying our life and opening it up to the influence of unconditional love in a much more powerful way. Amida Buddhists do not keep precepts in order to accumulate merit. They receive all the merit they need freely direct from Nyorai. Rather the precepts are tokens from Amida's world of love, making life beautiful.

Shan Tao also taught shinjin in terms of *chih*, *quan* and *nien*.

*Chih* means stopping. This is the mode of shinjin that stops the constant onward flow of self-preoccupied thought, imagery and feeling. One suddenly becomes aware of Nyorai in one's life. This is like falling in love. Again, chih is a dropping away of preoccupation with one's body, speech and mind. In ordinary life we easily become pre-occupied with our bodies or with justifying our speech and ideas or with protecting our mind and feelings. These preoccupations tend away from faith. They are aspects of seeking refuge in self rather than in what is greater than self. The Sanskrit word for chih is *shamatha*.

*Quan* means seeing, sometimes called insight. This is the mode of shinjin that investigates. One investigates one's own darkness. This is also the dawning of contrition. Through empathy and fellow-feeling one also comes to deeply understand others. One feels the tenderness of being in the same boat together. Quan enables us to see how conditions operate in our life – how much we have received, how much or little we have given back. One also investigates the Pure Land. When we turn our mind to the features of the Pure Land described in the sutras or given to us in our own experience, the light sometimes spontaneously enters our life and we feel greatly uplifted. The Sanskrit word for Quan is *vipashyana*.

To some extent, chih corresponds to the "Amida Bu" of the nembutsu and "quan" corresponds to the "Namo". Chih is the sense of awe that stops us in our tracks. Quan is the investigation that we make into our own blind nature. Chih and quan thus form a kind of cycle. Each supports and informs the other. As one becomes more aware of one's own darkness, one is more ready to open up to a greater light and as one feels embraced by Nyorai "never to be forsaken", so it becomes much easier to look at the state one is in.

*Nien* means mindfulness. It means having shinjin in one's heart right now, moment by moment – having a sense of Nyorai close at hand, or a sense that one is only separated from the Pure Land by the thinnest of screens. It begins with saying nembutsu. In due course, we realize that this is not really something that one is doing so much as something that is happening. Nyorai starts to be with us more and more of the time. Our life relates more and more strongly to the Pure Land and the Buddha's influence on our life grows. Moments of great joy then occur spontaneously. The Sanskrit word for nien is *smriti*. A person of shinjin is *smritimant* – magnetised. The "nem-" of nembutsu is the same word as nien. Nien is from Chinese and nen (or nem-) is Japanese.

Chih, quan and nien can lead one into states of rapture (*dhyana*) or visionary awareness (*samadhi*). These are states of bliss that reflect a tiny sample of the Pure Land. They are intrinsically beneficial, like having a healthy diet. Chih, quan and nien are also ways of being with others. Chih then refers to breaking out of our self-preoccupation sufficiently to be with another person. Quan refers to the process that we go through with them, accompanying them on their exploration of their world and discovering its dark side and its radiance. Nien is the place we get to with them, where there is a sense of fellow-feeling for one another within the sense of being held by the greater meaning of life.

These practices have their roots in the meditative and mental cultivation methods common to most schools of Buddhism. They have, however, undergone a special development in the Pureland tradition leading to what is now called nei quan or naikan. This is a practice used in the preparation of Pureland priests and devotees in which a person undertakes a systematic and intensive period of introspection involving a review of their own life, especially their relationships with parents and significant others. This process generally leads to an experience of cathartic contrition and a general emotional softening of heart. The naikan method is sometimes used as a form of psychotherapy.

**The nembutsu-mind** is described in the sutras as having three dimensions, referred to as *sanjin*. These are called sincere mind (*shijoshin*), deep mind (*jinshin*), and unconditional merit-transferring mind (*ekohotsuganshin*).

Sincere mind refers to genuineness and honesty about ourselves. When we are honest with ourselves and with others we are not pretending to be wiser or better than we are. We are willing to be an ordinary being, a bombu. In relations with others, a sincere person is likely to tend toward becoming transparent and modest, full of fellow-feeling, but, in reality, we are afflicted by habits of long standing that too often mar our relations with one another. So sincerity tends to support all virtues as well as revealing all non-virtues. It keeps us humble.

Deep mind means being willing to look at things in more than just a superficial way. Some understand deep mind as referring to penetrating insight. Human beings are complex. We ourselves have many conflict-ing thoughts and feelings. Often there are subtle hidden motives in what we do. The person of deep mind is willing to face and examine these, even when they are not self-flattering. A person who has, through sincerity, realized their own dark world, is able to penetrate the dark world of others without blame or condemnation. The deep mind can also be understood as the mind that appreciates Nyorai's intention. The sense that Amida always intends the best and that this intention is always at work even when we do not understand it imparts a sense of depth to life. When deep mind is understood in this second way, then jinshin corresponds to "Amida Bu" and shijoshin corresponds to "Namo" We can thus see a set of correspondences as follows:

quan
shijoshin
Namo

chih
jinshin
Amida Bu

nien
ekohotsuganshin

Ekohotsuganshin is the unconditional mind, which grows out of the deep mind. As we explore the depths of our own and other hearts, we stop measuring things by scales of good and bad. We appreciate the suffering and pain of all beings, victim and persecutor alike. The unconditional mind has the features of merit transference and aspiration for birth. Merit transference means that we are not seeking to accumulate merit for ourselves. We are happy to find merit in others and to bestow it upon them. Aspiration for birth means that whatever happens, the practitioner's mind is on what is conducive to the birth of a Pure Land.

This is the intention to be of service to sentient beings. For a person of true nembutsu faith, merit transference and aspiration for birth are constant through the ups and downs of life, so they are called unconditional. Unconditional also implies a love for all that is not a function of conditions. The ideal Buddhist loves others, whether they are rich or poor, healthy or sick, sane or mad, Buddhist or non-Buddhist, good or bad. Because we are bombu, none of us fulfils this ideal, but we find that when faith has been awakened, many aspects of it come naturally with ever increasing frequency. Also, of course, the term unconditional is very similar in meaning to the word Amida. It is a matter of not measuring against any scale of judgement. Amida has such an unconditional heart. Thus there is no judgement in Buddhism, other than what we inflict upon ourselves.

Another way to express sanjin is in terms of the relationship between faith and doubt. In common speech we tend to think of faith and doubt as opposites and mutually exclusive. However, doubt is a very important part of faith in a number of ways. It takes faith to doubt. Faith without an ability to doubt is dogmatic bigotry, which, according to Buddha, is the source of all ill. Doubt is, therefore, an essential element in Buddhist method. Everything that a bombu believes is, by definition, doubtful. At a personal level, it is the sense that one could be wrong that so often opens the door to awakening, and immediately after awakening, the danger of falling into attachment is most particularly intense. The most important element in awakening, therefore, is not the understanding that one may gain about love and wisdom, but the profound insight into oneself as a foolish being of blind passion. To really know that one is a foolish being is to know that everything one believes, even one's precious awakening, is questionable. If one does not think so then one does not really believe that one is a foolish being. Instead of true awakening, one has fallen into the hell of spiritual pride. This is a great pitfall for all religious.

Amida faith, therefore, is not belief. It transcends particular beliefs, including even the ones suggested in this book. Frameworks of belief are artefacts of foolish beings such as you and I. To trust Nyorai is to trust enough to be able to doubt. Even if what I believe turns out to be mistaken, in a deeper sense, all is still as it should be. The truth reveals itself only partially. As we walk the spiritual path we see ever-new vistas and perspectives. Walking in Nyorai's love we can afford to enjoy these views without clinging to any of them. On the spiritual path, you do not need to take your camera.

Real shinjin, therefore, is not a simplistic elimination of doubt about the propositions of this or that sect, but a deep confidence given to us from a realm that, from its own side, is not defined by doctrines. Doctrine, even Buddhist doctrine, is simply skilful means (*upaya*) by which those who have awakened seek to bring aid to those who are lost and confused. One should not, however, mistake the maps they provide for the territory they walk in. Maps are useful, but they are only maps.

One of Honen's greatest disciples, Shinran Shonin, said: "For me, Shinran, there is no reasoning; I believe only what my venerable teacher taught: 'Just call the name and you will be saved by Amida.' The nembutsu may lead me to rebirth in the Pure Land or may lead me to hell; I simply have no assurance. But even if I were deceived by my teacher, the blessed sage Honen, and fall in hell as a result, I would never regret it. The reason is that were I the kind of person who could become a Buddha through other, strenuous religious practices and yet fall in hell through the nembutsu, I might regret having been deceived by my teacher. But because I am absolutely incapable of any other religious practice, hell is definitely my place". [5]

This shows that Shinran's shinjin was not based on a tenacious certainty, but upon insight into his own nature as a foolish being. Making a commitment is not equivalent to having no doubt. It is having doubt and doing it anyway. This is the existential dilemma of the human being. We are here. We have to commit our lives one way or another. There is no such thing as doing nothing. Religion offers a path with instructions and a map, but, as Shinran also says, "You yourself must make the choice."

**Doubt is also closely related to contrition**. The heart of contrition is really another way of expressing the three minds. Contrition (*san-ge*) is the change of heart that comes about through seeing one's own nature, particularly seeing one's own failings, frailty and vulnerability, in a context of confidence that one is loved anyway just as one is, sins and all. Contrition is to be in touch with one's own dark world. Essentially contrition means that something hard in us becomes soft. Contrition is closely related to repentance, but we need to distinguish between a true and a false variety and we need also to see that contrition has two levels.

False contrition is really a form of pride. In false contrition, people feel bad about something they have done because they feel they have let themselves down. The feeling exists against the background of an inflated view of oneself. One believes that one is not the sort of person who does bad things and so palpable evidence to the contrary is uncomfortable and hard to swallow. True contrition is concerned not with self and self-image, even at a subtle level, but with actual harm caused and the painful realization that one does cause such harm.

The two levels of contrition are the specific and the general. At the specific level, one may notice that one has a certain bad habit and resolve to do something about it or one may see that one has committed a harmful or unskilful act and resolve to do better in future. Specific contrition is a valuable thing. It can help a person become a better person in some precise ways. The general level of contrition, however, is really the more important. The general learning that one may gain from noticing a specific failing is that one learns, I am of such a nature as to do such things. Specific contrition may remain attached to a rosy illusion to the effect that really, in one's true nature, one is not like that and the wrong thing that one did is just a passing aberration. In fact, however, we are of the nature to do such things. We are not of different nature from the bad people that we read about in the newspapers. If we have Buddha nature, then we also have Hitler nature, and, indeed, if we rely upon our own merit power alone, most of us will assuredly turn into little Hitlers quite readily when the circumstances are conducive to it. Awareness of the potential of our Hitler nature is a much more useful mindfulness than self-flattering thoughts about our own latent perfection. Contrition, therefore, helps us to gain insight into our bombu nature. The contrite heart is thus no different from the sincere, deep and unconditional mind.

These attitudes of heart and mind, which are the filling out of what faith means in day to day life, are the basis for ethics in Pureland. Buddhism has extensive ethical principles. There are schools such as the Vinaya School in which the starting point and goal is the perfection of ethics, with faith and enlightenment being encountered along the way. In Pureland it is the other way about. Faith and the deep sentiment of tenderness and love associated with it is the alpha and omega and ethics are realized as the fruit thereof. Pureland and Vinaya are, therefore, sometimes seen as complimentary.

## Emptiness

**It is because doubt** plays such a central role in Buddhist faith that Buddhism is commonly seen as being not incompatible with science. Historically, the fullest development of the theory of doubt in Buddhism, aside from the words of Shakyamuni Buddha himself, can be traced to the work of the sage Nagarjuna (c.50-150CE). Nagarjuna is regarded as one of the spiritual ancestors of the Pureland schools. Nagarjuna showed that all beliefs are questionable and all belief systems have inherent contradictions. This points, philosophically to the groundlessness of human life that is our biggest spiritual challenge and opportunity. Nagarjuna calls it emptiness (*shunyata*). This groundlessness does not make beliefs useless, but it does enjoin a particular attitude toward them, one that holds them appreciatively yet lightly. It also shows us that Buddhist faith is not exactly the same thing as belief.

We all have beliefs, of course, as a result of experience, of logic, of conviction, or of having been influenced. We might believe that this person loves us and those people are our enemies, but with every belief of this kind, we may find we are wrong. Those who we thought were our enemies may help us and those we thought were our friends may let us down. We might think that a certain belief system is our friend and another our enemy. We have to make such commitments in order to live at all. We should, however, have the faith to hold such convictions in such a way that we do not become blind to contrary experience nor intolerant of the views of others. This path of openness is a middle way.

Amida-shu, therefore, advocates the faith to go beyond mere belief into an existential commitment to live in correspondence with unconditional love with neither the comfort of certainty nor that of thinking one will be successful. Each person must take stock of what is important and commit his or her life. Leaving behind a life of worldly craving, one may enter a life of faith. Although one does not know what lies ahead, one may proceed in faith. Namo Amida Bu. Discovering one's bombu nature, one may arrive at fellow-feeling with others. One may experience intense gratitude and tenderness, the joys of contemplation and of service, living in dependence upon a love too vast ever to be fully comprehended, that, nonetheless, unfailingly comes to our aid in its own mysterious way.

### In summary
**Amida Buddhism is a religion of light and love**. It is life affirming without being complacent about basic human nature; respectful of uni-

versal spirituality but not dependent upon ideas of divine creation or divine judgement. It honours and appreciates the bitter-sweetness of the spiritual struggles of ordinary folk who are attempting to be truly human. It allows for a life of full time devotion without setting up an over-privileged priestly class. It is an engaged spirituality, centred on the prospect of the Pure Land paradise. It is suitable for all people, having a basic practice that is accessible to anybody. It is a path of sudden awakening centred uncompromisingly upon faith. It derives from the very earliest Buddhism and from a direct encounter with the Buddha of all time. It is grounded in the doctrines common to all Buddhist schools, yet offers a unique perspective upon them, and, furthermore, does not require the mastery of those doctrines as a condition of awakening. It emphatically asserts that the practice that matters is the utterance of nembutsu in simple faith and that alone. Understanding of the doctrinal framework and support may be satisfying, but is ancillary to the main spiritual project, which is eminently simple. It does not stand in opposition to other faiths, but reveals the generic nature of faith itself as the wellspring of eternal life. It holds that no religion can be ultimate since even revelation must pass through the medium of human nature. We are foolish beings of blind passion, living, knowingly or unknowingly, in the presence of infinite light, that reflects in us as faith. That gift of faith we either squander or gather in. We express it through ceaseless nembutsu expressing a contrite heart and a mind that is sincere, deep and unconditional. Such is Pureland.

# SEVEN

# HEADING FOR HEAVEN

## Heaven Hell and Mother's Milk

**We are feeding Mother on milk**. It is the only thing we can get into her. I still want her to take some nourishment. Even now I still want her to recover, even though the rational part of me knows that she will not. A friend goes to the shop to see if she can obtain goats' milk, which she says is more nutritious. In order to get the milk into Mother it has to be siphoned. We were using a pipette for this, but a straw proved more effective. It is like feeding a baby animal.

I reflect on the cycle of life. Mother is now in many ways like an infant again. I remember looking after my own children, feeding and changing nappies. I think of how she must have fed me. I feel very tender toward her. I can remember times when I was off school with some minor ailment or other, how she would look after me. I know that she would make a calculated compromise between looking after me and not making me so comfortable that I would never want to go back to school again. School was a challenging experience. I enjoyed learning, but I found the social dimension extremely difficult. Children could be cruel. A day at home with Mother once in a while was a welcome respite. Now, here she was, in my care.

Just as Mother continued to think of herself as a young woman despite her four score years, I too feel much younger inside than my physical age. I often find myself among people who are in fact younger than myself experiencing the situation as if I were the junior. Is this because part of me is psychologically arrested at a younger stage? Perhaps so. I don't mind if it is. When my mind goes back to those days, something tender stirs in me and I cherish that tenderness.

**The point that I keep coming back to** is that it is the ordinary things that matter. Feeding somebody is a perfect act. Mother was now dependent upon my feeding her just as I had once been on her feeding me. That is love. When we love, that is enough. We may be growing or we may be dying. We need to be fed.

In the text called *Majjhima Nikaya*, to which we have referred before, there is a discourse of the Buddha called the *Alagaddupama*. It is sutra number 22 and it is very famous. It contains two famous similes used by the Buddha, which are the simile of the snake and the simile of the raft. These two similes have each become of enormous importance in the history of Buddhist teaching.

In the simile of the snake the Buddha talks about how a person might go out in search of a snake and try to catch the snake. It is likely that the Buddhist friars used snake venom in the making of medicine. The snake is thus an interesting symbol encompassing both healing and danger. In our own culture the symbol of two serpents is often used as a medical sign. If you catch hold of a snake in the wrong way, however, it is likely to climb back up along its own length and bite you with serious consequences. To catch a snake you have to know the right method. Specifically, you have to grasp it at the right end, which is the head end, generally after immobilizing it with a forked stick. The Buddha uses this simile to point out how the Dharma must also be caught hold of in the right way or it will do more harm than good. The context for this teaching is an encounter the Buddha has had with somebody who purports to be following the Buddha's teaching, but in fact believes that so long as one has the right frame of mind one can do anything one pleases without deleterious effect. The Buddha says that this is a complete travesty of what he has taught.

The second simile is the simile of the raft. In this simile the Buddha says that the Dharma is like a raft in that it is a method to get you to the other shore. We can imagine a river that has to be crossed. A person might make a raft and use it to get across. But having crossed, would that person be wise to now carry the raft on their back? Would that help them now that they are on the other side. Obviously the answer is, 'no'. The raft carried on the back while walking on dry land is a hindrance not a help. In the same way, religious teachings are a means to get one across. For the person who has already crossed, there is no need to go through the whole procedure again or to continue to use the method. What this means is that religion may bring us to life, but if we are already alive we no longer need the specific practices of religion. It may show us what it means to love deeply, but a person who already loves deeply does not need to learn that.

These two similes contain a great deal of wisdom. There are, however, still other treasures to be found in this sutra. Thus, in the very last verse, the Buddha says, "those who simply have faith in me, who simply love me, are all headed for heaven." This is the conclusion of the whole sutra.

**From the very beginning there have been two ways** within the Buddha's religion. There is the wonderful way of the great practitioner who accomplishes the samadhis, perfects the virtues, matures in wisdom and attains nirvana. Then there is the path of those who simply love the Buddha. The former enter nirvana. The latter are headed for heaven. Pureland, of course, springs from this latter way. Throughout most of Buddhist history it has been regarded as the lesser path. It is the way for those who are not up to the discipline and rigors of the holy path of great practitioners. Of course, people who are proud will think that only the great path is for them; no lesser way will do.

In the few verses immediately prior to this wonderful statement, the Buddha has been talking about the prospects for disciples of different levels of attainment. In some of the Buddha's discourses it is difficult to discern sometimes when the Buddha is speaking seriously and when ironically. In any case, he details how those who are superlatively virtuous and full of understanding will get enlightened, no doubt. Finally, however, he makes this lovely remark "those who simply have faith in me, who simply love me, are all headed for heaven" and that is how the sutra ends.

So some may take this statement as referring to a lesser path or a path for lesser beings. This may be so or it may not. In any case, as Amidists we are willing to take the lesser path and to see ourselves as lesser beings. If those who simply have faith and simply love the Buddha are in some way lesser, then I am quite content to be among the lesser. In any case, I know full well that my ability to rise to the level of the superlatively virtuous and wise is rather limited.

Woven into this passage is a distinction between disciples who are characterized by "the power of wisdom" (Pali: *pann-indriya*) on the one hand and on the other hand disciples who are characterised by "the power of faith" (Pali: *saddh-indriya*). In the Theravada and Mahayana commentaries priority tends to be given to those who have the power of wisdom. They are superior. Amidism, however, is directed more humbly to those who have the power of faith.

There are many passages like this that show that the distinction between a path of wisdom and a path of faith goes back to the very beginning of Buddhism. Sometimes we hear that the idea of 'two gates' was introduced by Nagarjuna (c.50-150CE) or by Tao-Cho (562-645), but in the above text we see that it is in the earliest Pali texts too, which certainly pre-date Nagarjuna, and, furthermore, it is linked with being headed for heaven.

I am sure that there has been a faith-based Buddhism from the very beginning and even in the earliest days there was a distinction between the 'path of the sages' and the 'path of faith followers'. The latter was less associated with asceticism and more with Buddhism in the world. The Buddha did not love his lay followers less than his monks.

To be 'headed for heaven' does not only mean that heaven awaits at the end of a long time. It means that we are right now facing toward heaven instead of facing toward hell. As nembutsu practitioners we are not unwilling if the Buddha were to send us to hell. No doubt there is work to do in hell as well as heaven, but even if we must work in hell, we will do so with the heart of one "who simply has faith in me, who simply loves me" and then even in hell we will be headed for heaven.

I am sure that there has been a faith-based Buddhism from the very beginning and even in the earliest days there was a distinction between the 'path of the sages' and the 'path of faith followers'. The latter was less associated with asceticism and more with Buddhism in the world. The Buddha did not love his lay followers less than his monks.

**Mother fed me on her milk, now I am feeding her**. Feeding milk to Mother also put me in mind of the story of the Buddha visiting his own mother in heaven. Queen Maya died seven days after giving birth to the Buddha. It is said that she went to a heaven of radiant light. The Buddha longed to see her. One day Manjushri Bodhisattva went to the heaven on the Buddha's behalf and sang a song to Queen Maya in which he said that the Buddha wished to repay his debt of gratitude to her by teaching her the Dharma. When Queen Maya heard this song, milk began to flow from her breasts. She thought, "If it is really my son that Manjushri sings of then this milk will enter his mouth." The milk flowed from both her breasts and entered the mouth of the Buddha. Queen Maya then left the heaven of radiant light in the company of Manjushri and went to visit her son upon Earth. She declares that she has never felt as joyful as on this occasion. The Buddha sees her approach, welcomes her and exhorts her to practise Dharma. She says to him that if he wishes to repay his debt of gratitude for having received her milk in numberless past lives, he should cut off her roots of evil passion. She declares her total reliance upon him. At once, through the power of the Buddha, Queen Maya enters the state of non-retrogression. She declares her pleasure at this liberation, rebukes her own mind for having kept her in the thrall of greed, hate and delusion for so long and praises her son for his liberating wisdom, urging him to assist all beings in the same way as he has assisted her.

This story is full of fantastical goings on, like a dream, which, perhaps, it was in origin. We can imagine the Buddha having such a dream and we can imagine what a healing effect it would have. In the Buddha's day, people did not think that dreams came out of one's own mind, they thought that the characters that appear in a dream are real visitations. If Maya appeared in the Buddha's dream it would be that Maya had indeed come to visit him from her heavenly dwelling place. The visitors from other worlds often bring us wisdom and healing and the Buddha seems to have been a master of healing of this kind. Why should he not have healed himself, or himself been healed by visitation from the other world? It seems likely that he would be. Nowadays we might use different language and speak of psychology, archetypes, projection, catharsis and so forth, but do we really know any more about the actual healing process than the Buddha and his contemporaries?

I syringe Mother another straw-full of milk and wait as it slides erratically down her throat. It is a slow task, but there is plenty of time.

## That's Better

**That evening we had an emergency**. Some of the milk went down the wrong way and Mother suddenly had great difficulty in breathing. In effect, she was drowning. Having had some experience with children suffering from cystic fibrosis whose lungs frequently become clogged, I decide that the thing to do was to turn Mother up side down over the edge of the bed. This seems like an extreme thing to do to an elderly lady on her deathbed, but I did not want her to die in this distressing way.

I tell Caroline what I intend. Her immediate expression says, "You can't do that". Time is of the essence and I do not want a long discussion so I say, "We have got to do it." I can almost hear Caroline say, "Well, she's your mother." Anyway, we turn Mother over and hang her torso over the edge of the bed, head down toward the floor. I press her back and some liquid comes out of her mouth. I press again and she is breathing. We lift her and put her back on the bed.

"That's better," she says. As it turns out, those were the last coherent words she uttered.

Her breathing was still quite difficult and her face was gradually turning blue. We were now engaged in a life and death struggle. We could lose her in a matter of minutes. The folding bed was still in the room, so we let down the legs at one end so that it sloped and I carried Mother over, lying her on the bed with her head at the lower end. This enabled us to give a measure of artificial respiration by pressing her back. In this way we got some more fluid out. However, she was still going blue.

I was thinking clearly and fast. Although not a medical person, I have some relevant experience from having been a medical social worker in the past. I got Caroline to phone the emergency doctor. I knew it would take a little time for him to arrive, however, and we might not have that much time and, in any case, he might not be able to do what was necessary. What we needed was oxygen. I knew that there was one way to get it and that was by calling the ambulance service who would send a specialist team within minutes. However, they would also want to remove Mother to a hospital, which we definitely did not want to happen. I conveyed all this to Caroline very swiftly.

"You have to decide," she said.

"Get me the ambulance service."

As I had anticipated, the paramedic team arrived in minutes. It was highly dramatic. Four people in what looked like space suits appeared in Mother's bedroom carrying a mass of equipment. Within moments the room was transformed into a temporary intensive care unit. Mother got oxygen and quickly turned pink again. So far so good.

**Now the difficult part began**. The leader of the paramedic team began to assert strongly that they had to take Mother to hospital. I could see this was going to be difficult. I pointed out that it was not helping my mother to have this altercation in front of her and insisted that they go through to the other room. I would speak to them in a minute. Basically I was playing for time. Mother was still receiving oxygen. At this point Caroline had to leave as Jenny was due to arrive and needed to be collected from Birmingham railway station forty minutes drive away.

The paramedics conducted a range of tests on Mother and recorded it on their charts. Mother was breathing fairly normally now, so the oxygen mask was removed. After ten minutes she was still stable. This was a great relief. I was, by now, doubly determined that she was not going to go to hospital. Arriving in a casualty department at this time of night would very likely be fatal and almost as bad a way to go as drowning in milk.

Negotiations resumed between the team leader and myself. They have their operational procedures and these say that they must get the patient to hospital as soon as possible. This, of course, is quite understandable in general and I could see that, from their perspective, they would be leaving themselves open to a range of complaints if they did not end their work by handing the authority for the patient over to a responsible medical officer. At the same time, I knew that it would be a completely unacceptable course for Mother at this juncture. I mustered all the assertiveness skills I could remember, appreciated their difficulty and reasserted that she was not going.

**There was no way out of this impasse**, and the discussion was getting rather tense. Relief was at hand, however. Just as the confrontation was reaching its crescendo, the doorbell sounded. Another member of the community went to the door and after a couple of minutes the stand-by doctor came up the stairs.

It was like the relief of a besieged fort. The paramedic's instructions say that they must take the patient to a hospital because they had to pass their responsibility over to a doctor who could take charge of the patient's care. Now that a doctor had arrived they were relieved of their charge. I thanked them and they departed.

The doctor was completely sympathetic. He talked with me about the dying process and told me what to expect. He gave me a form to give to her general practitioner after she had died. He thought that she might live about another twenty-four hours.

Just as he was leaving my children Emma and Michael and Emma's husband Dave arrived.

It felt very strange welcoming the family at that moment as they had not been part of the drama that had just taken place. Nonetheless, they had a good visit. Each spent some time alone with Mother, though she was past communicating, and we spent some time all together with her. Mother seemed to have moved into a new phase. She would raise her arms and then let them fall again. Emma, half humorously, said, "I think she is practising flying."

They had each had previous opportunities to speak to her in person or on the phone so this was the time to pay last respects. Neither intended to be present at the actual death. About 10.45pm Caroline arrived back with Jenny. Emma and Dave departed about half an hour later and Mike, Willemien and I stayed with Mother into the early hours.

## I Specifically Am Loved
### "Namo Amida Bu. Namo Amida Bu...."
The basic Amidist practice is to say the nembutsu. I imagine that this was originally a Buddhist *crie de coeur*, a way of asserting the universality of the Buddha light and the determination that the Dharma would endure. Amida, the measureless, is a contraction of Amitabha-

Amitayus, measureless light and measureless life span. Light means space. Life span means time. This was, therefore, a way of asserting that Nyorai is everywhere always. This everywhere-always aspect of Buddha is called *Joko*, the ever-present light. Joko stands in contradistinction to *Shinko*, the heart light.

Joko is the light that is always present and that shines on everybody. Even when you have forgotten about Amida, Amida's Joko still shines upon you. It even shines on those who have never heard of Amida or even of any religion. Joko is everywhere. Even if, in the midst of the emergency, I am not thinking about Nyorai consciously, Nyorai is still shining on me. This, of course, is a completely mystical idea. It is not psychology or science. It is a metaphysical assertion. It makes a lot of sense. Somehow we are held, through our tribulations. From time to time we are aware of Joko. We realize that some power has been operating through our life. I am somewhat amazed, looking back, that I was able to think with such clarity and speed and handle the situation. That feels like a blessing – not something that I can really take credit for myself. At such times, it can feel as though a power enters into one. That power is Joko. Joko is like potential love. Just as we know that there is a lot of electricity in the air and many radio waves and that if you have the right receptor you can tune in, so the idea of Joko suggests that there is love energy everywhere just waiting to be tapped. This, of course, is not science, but it is true to life's experience. Awareness of Joko can make our lives happier and more compassionate. It speaks to the meaning of the situation, not the mechanics of it, and that is what we humans are really concerned about.

When we become aware of Joko we may say "Namo Amida Bu." The nembutsu is many things. It is a way of celebrating. It is a way of consoling. It says, "Thank you" and it says, "Please." The nembutsu is a way of having a relationship with Amida. Once one has entered into the nembutsu, however, one may experience Shinko. Shinko is not just universal light, it is a direct beam from heart to heart. It is not just a sense of "I am one of the people and Nyorai loves people, therefore, I too am loved." It is a sense of "Nyorai loves me, no matter what I am, what I have done, I specifically am loved." Joko and Shinko are not really two different things, they are two different ways of experiencing grace.

Joko and Shinko are thoroughly mystical religious ideas. They cannot by any means be reduced to rational or materialist processes. Such processes go on, but Joko and Shinko represent a different way of thinking about what is going on. They are a way of understanding the salvation that comes through Buddhism.

We have already seen that a common way to teach religion is to specify an ideal state and to describe the way to attain it. If the religion is Buddhism, then the ideal state may be called nirvana and the way to get to it may be the practice of ethics (*sila*), meditation (*samadhi*) and wisdom (*prajna*). The religion then becomes the prescription of these methods and of that ideal. That is one way. It appears to be rational and relatively mechanical. However, in practice, the human mind does not proceed in a linear way. It goes round in cycles. We have moments of spiritual elation and also times of depression or even despair. The fact that we have had a great insight or revelation does not necessarily mean that we will remain in that state indefinitely, nor does the knowledge that problems will be solved when we attain the ideal necessarily help us much when we have not attained it or have fallen away from it again.

Authenticity requires recognition of this aspect of human nature. Recognizing that we are foolish beings of blind passion does not mean that we do not attain elevated states. Sometimes we do; but the old darkness of habit creeps back in again. Sometimes this happens very quickly, as when we attain something and then feel superior because we have done so. We need a way of practising that relates realistically to the cyclical nature of human experience.

## Firmly Established in Pureland Practice

**It is 5.45am Friday morning**. Mother is sleeping peacefully and has done so since midnight. Her breath is slightly laboured and she makes a small "Ha" noise every few breaths. The number of breaths varies and I find myself waiting for the next "Ha" wondering how many breaths it will be each time. Over the past three-quarters of an hour it has been getting light. I have opened the curtains in the hope that Mother may be able to glimpse the lime tree when she wakes. Mother is still on the folding bed. We have now folded the bed legs at the foot end so that she is lying on a slope with her head up – the opposite to how we had it when we were clearing her trachea of fluid the previous evening. The room, as she would say, "looks like a bomb hit it", but the disorganization is brightened by the many bouquets of flowers. Outside, the doves coo. Caroline comes in and gives me a hot drink and then departs to attend to the cats and other domestic duties. Willemien has sat with Mother all night. She decided that it was the only way to get me to take some sleep. I am immensely grateful. I probably had four or five hours and it has done me a lot of good. In due course, Caroline drives Michael to Coventry where he is working today.

I feel particularly touched by Willemien's kindness. In the community, Willemien is often teased for her love of sleeping in. Then, on this night, she stayed with Mother, staying awake right through the night, and insisted that I go to bed, at least for a few hours.

"Why did you do that, Willemien?"

"So you would sleep."

In things like this one knows one is loved and one feels the strength of a community.

**When Amida Trust started**, eight years before, there had been no initial intention to form a religious community. At first it was a loose association of people who were either interested in socially engaged Buddhism or in Buddhist psychology or had been involved in other projects that Caroline and I had set up in the past. It was not a homogeneous group. Initially we were over-optimistic about people's ability to get on together across group boundaries. We wanted to encourage the spirit of kindness in a global way. To us, psychology and social action, for instance, were two sides of the same coin. Each was an attempt to put the compassionate principles of the Dharma into effect in a particular arena of activity. However, we soon found that the kind of people who were attracted to one were different from the kind attracted to the other. Implementing a universalist vision was more difficult on the ground than it seemed in principle. In order to work together people had to get on. As time went by we realized more and more the qualities that mattered were commitment, loyalty, kindness, practicality and willingness. An even temper also helped, but few of us were actually capable of it for extended periods. We had a lot to learn.

In 1998, two years after the Trust started, we held an event that proved to be formative. At our retreat centre in France we held what we called an Activist Week. This event grew out of an Activist Weekend that we had held in Birmingham in England the previous November. We were broadly aware that if we were going to be involved in socially engaged activities, we needed training and development. We did not think that there were many experts around in what we were trying to do so it would have to be a home grown affair in which we set up some conditions and worked together to help one another.

The week in France attracted about a dozen people. We structured the week into three types of sessions. Some were practical activities, some were study sessions, and some were groups for mutual sharing and encounter. The practical activities included fieldwork, going out to the local villages and finding out about their social needs, as well as on-site exercises in which sub-groups were given resources and a task that could not be completed without negotiation with other groups that had other tasks. The study sessions focussed on the Buddhist ethical precepts. They were not so much classes as "what does this mean to you?" sessions. Finally the groupwork periods provided a time for people to talk about their life experience and, as the week went on, increasingly, to challenge themselves and one another in various ways. The whole week thus took on the form of a personal introspection and group encounter that became steadily more profound as the group grew in confidence.

Now, it happened that, ten days before this event, an Amida member had drawn my attention to a remarkable woman called Linda Dhammika. Linda came from the city of Manchester, but she had spent much of her life working in Africa. Initially this took the form of doing teaching on Voluntary Service Overseas schemes. Latterly it had involved starting a project from scratch in Zambia. Together with a Zambian friend she had gone to a village in a poor area where there was a half built, but abandoned, clinic and, starting with no resources whatsoever, they resolved to get the clinic finished. They had heard that if a village completed the building of a clinic, the government would supply a nurse. To Linda it seemed like something that needed to be done. The project that they started they called Tithandizane, which, in the local language, means "We help each other".

Now Linda was taking a short respite from her labours and had returned to her home town partly to get a break and partly to gather support. As it happened, I was due to lead a retreat in the Manchester area that weekend, so I also arranged to meet Linda, visiting her house. We conversed, it felt like we were on the same wavelength, and I told her about the Activist Week we were planning. "I'll come," she said.

Also at that same week was a woman from Hawaii who had done a good deal of group work in the US and proved to be a very helpful facilitator at the event and another called Louise Duguid who had recently come to live with us at the Amida house in Newcastle in order to help with the work.

During the week the three women established important connections with one another. By the end of the week, our friend from Hawaii had decided not to use her return ticket, but to go to the Zambia project instead. Louise, who took the Buddhist name Modgala, would also subsequently spend a period working in Zambia. Amida Trust has continued to support the African project ever since.

Even more importantly for the development of our community, however, people attending the week evidenced a growing desire to commit themselves, in varying degrees, to keeping the Buddhist precepts as a basis for their life. Carried by the momentum of this wish, before the end of the week, we held a ceremony in which my wife Caroline, Linda and Louise all took Buddhist vows and received the names Amita Prasada, Amita Amrita, and Amita Modgala respectively. Thus began the Amida Order that was finally ratified by the trustees of Amida Trust in May 2003.

**The next few years** saw many further events and initiatives. By no means all of them prospered, but we were learning. We were also gradually evolving a way of life. A process of definition was inexorably forcing itself upon us. People wanted to know what we were and what they would be committing to if they joined us. Our initial impulse was to keep things as flexible and open as possible. Gradually, however, it became apparent that the advantages of clear definition often outweighed the initial difficulties involved in getting that definition established.

I found this process interesting and challenging. A group comes together and through co-operation has the capacity to accomplish things together. The struggle to agree a course may, however, alienate some members. On the other hand, when something is done, it defines what the group is and that in turn tends to attract new people. Slowly things shape up. In the early years we had some tense situations and by no means all the founders stayed with it. As our direction and way of life have become clearer, however, the community has steadily become more harmonious and more effective.

Not only internally has there been a harmonization process at work, but externally as the Order has become established we have learnt to co-operate with other groups and to act in an ecumenical way both in relation to other Buddhist denominations and other faith communities.

This description does not really, however, do justice to the real process at work. The real development has come in our collective deepening of understanding about what faith means in practice. The changes that have happened that have pulled us together into an effective team could not have been accomplished simply by the application of good management methods.

The Amida Order has evolved steadily over the years that have elapsed since that week in France. When Amida Trust joined the European Buddhist Union in the autumn of 2004, it was as a clearly designated school of Pureland Buddhism, with a reputation for being socially engaged, but with its primary sense of identity firmly established in Amidist practice.

## Why Pureland?

**"Why are you Pureland Buddhists?"** we are sometimes asked. After all, Pureland is not yet that common in Europe.

As I am the teacher of the community, there has to be an answer in terms of my personal history and as we are a community there is also an answer in terms of our evolution and our relations with other groups in the Buddhist world. As Pureland is a specific interpretation of the Buddha Dharma, there is an explanation in terms of the merits of that interpretation. Ultimately, however, I have to say that we have been led to Pureland and it is this sense of being led that makes us Pureland. Nyorai reached out to us.

In terms of my own history, I am Amidist because the Pure Land has appeared to me a number of times during my life and spiritual history. It, therefore, feels natural and apt for me to discuss the spiritual life in terms of my own experience. I am continually made aware of the proximity of that other realm. From an early age I have been a person of faith and although I have been through the same processes that lead so many modern people to lose their faith, I seem to have come through. In terms of our history as a group, we have found the Pureland perspective on faith and on the nature of the person to be most authentic for us. Carrying Buddhism out of the cloister into the world can sometimes be a bit like going to the moon. One needs oxygen cylinders. Our oxygen is faith. Faith is what keeps us authentic when we are in the midst of other influences that would otherwise corrupt or dissipate our energies. Of course, this is true for any Buddhist – if they do not keep faith with the Dharma when interacting with the world then they are not really Buddhists – but for us it is a core truth that we particularly emphasize, perhaps because our engaged activities make us particularly exposed. Also relevant and not inconsiderable in our history, it has been Pureland Buddhists who have been particularly supportive and helpful to us. Their friendship has meant that we have felt welcomed in the wider Pureland community and we feel at home there. We have gradually built up close friendships with communities that follow other denominations, but this has come more slowly. Again, this process of friendship building seems to have become easier as we have presented a clearer image of what we are. Finally, we have become more overtly Amidist because it is an interpretation of the Dharma from the perspective of the ordinary foolish being of blind passion. We feel we can identify with that. It takes away the pressure toward affectation and permits us to be what we are.

The January of the year Mother died Caroline and I had been in Japan. We were hosted there by a variety of different Pureland groups, both Jodo-shu and Jodoshin-shu. In particular, we were hosted by Saiko Sensei, a teacher who had a depth of understanding of both Jodoshin

Buddhism and of psychotherapy. He arranged that we should be entertained most graciously and that we might participate in various public events. Saiko Sensei was 81 years old and he had been telling his disciples that one day a teacher would come from Europe who would later convey the Amidist teachings to the West. Saiko Sensei placed that trust in me. We departed from Japan. Sensei went into hospital happy and died soon after. Some of his Japanese disciples think that he had kept himself alive extending his life until after our visit. This kind of occurrence makes a deep impression upon one. Although I feel completely unworthy of it and wonder what can possibly have made Sensei chose me, still I feel greatly empowered by the fact that this happened. Whether I or our community will be able to fulfil Sensei's dream remains to be seen, but surely these things are simply reflections of the working of Nyorai's love and if that is the case then we will just as surely be guided as necessary.

Most of our Amidist spirituality begins with an attempt to get closer to the raw human condition as we find it. Humans are not perfect. To put it bluntly, we are all sinners. The fact that there has grown up a modern taboo against even using such a word as 'sin' should not blind us to our own capacity for being at fault. The contemporary consensus in Buddhism suggests that we are all perfect in our essential nature. The task of religious practice then becomes the realization of that perfect nature. Well, it might be so, but even if it is then the perfect nature is so well buried in most of us that it is not something we are going to unearth in the near future. Practical spirituality requires a willingness to face the real situation rather than dogmatic adherence to a doctrine of inherent purity widely removed from what we see actually going on in the world and even in our own hearts. We live in a world torn by the most terrible things and it seems a lot saner and earthier to face our own dark side than to comfort ourselves with a myth about its ultimate non-existence. The most dangerous people in the world are those who are unaware of their own darkness. The kindest are generally those who feel themselves to be nothing special.

**We are Pureland because we feel our own frailty**, vulnerability and foolishness and we also feel the grace that supports us and enables us to do Nyorai's work. We do not, therefore, have to wait until we are enlightened before we start trying to be of some service in the world. We know we are far from perfect and always will be, but that does enable us to have fellow feeling for the mass of ordinary humanity. Nyorai's grace is for ordinary people and if we trust he will lead

Furthermore, ordinary people are mortal. As I sat beside mother, I could say that my concern and care sprung out of fellow-feeling for her – from sympathy. However, it seems much truer to say that what held me there was something coming in the other direction. The dying person has cast off the clutter of everyday life. Their existence, lying there on the deathbed, is clean. It is purified of the attachments and schemes that distort our usual relations with one another. This means that from the dying person there emanates a power that penetrates one as few other things do. It is like being in the presence of the Buddha.

### Did Your Life Become Real?

**The emotions came back**. That Friday morning I was several times overcome, crying bitterly. Somehow the kindness of the people around me seemed to act as a trigger. While I was sitting beside Mother some kind of balance would be sustained. As soon as I left the room I would weep.

Mother woke about 9am. She lay with her head slightly inclined. The window, the tree and the doves were in her line of sight, but I could not tell whether she saw them or not.

I feel full of gratitude. Mother has been my best friend. She has been a teacher and a confidant. By all accounts I have been extremely fortunate. I have heard so many accounts of fractured relationships between people and their mothers. I remember her saying to me on one of the days that I visited her in hospital,

"We have never fallen out, have we dear? That is something rather special, isn't it?"

Now, as she approached death, it seemed momentous. Was it really possible that such goodwill could have been sustained for a whole lifetime? Certainly we had had disagreements, and I could remember times when I had been exasperated with her. Generally, however, what caused my exasperation was her unwillingness to be drawn into any kind of serious quarrel. When I was young I disparaged her meekness. Now I appreciated what lay behind it. Sometimes it takes great courage to be meek when all about you are working up a storm. Sometimes the storm-maker had been me.

**That Friday morning I felt more alive than I had ever experienced before**. What was happening was more real than anything I had ever felt. It was real, I knew, in part, because it was wholly against my will. "I don't want her to die," went through my mind again and again, each time triggering off more tears. At the same time, I knew that she was dying. Reality is something we come up against. It is not answerable to us. We are answerable to it. Did your life become real? If there really were a judgement after death, I am sure that would be the question that would be asked, but in Pureland we do not believe in a judgement day in the future. In one sense the judgement is here and now. At that time I felt completely alive and authentic yet there was no sense whatsoever that that was something I had accomplished or brought about. It had been forced upon me. I had been loved and now the person who loved me was being taken away. Dukkha.

Dukkha is the occasion when we might become real. I wrote in my diary, "This time is a watershed in my life." It is a truism that we do not fully appreciate something until it is taken away. A month earlier I had been talking with a group of Buddhist friends and, in the attempt to explain a point about impermanence to them I had pointed to Dennis, our rabbit, nibbling grass on the lawn. I had said, "If you knew that Dennis was suffering from a terminal illness and was going to die very soon, would you not view him there nibbling grass with a more special affection and tenderness? He is just eating grass, but just eating grass would seem a terribly poignant thing if it was going to end very soon, would it not?" The listeners understood this message. As it happened it also proved prophetic. Dennis the rabbit died less than two months after Mother.

The Buddha understood impermanence. I am sure that he did not talk about impermanence so much in order that we become immune to it and learn how to casually say, "Oh well, that was impermanent too." The value of impermanence lies in the fact that we hate it. The cherry blossom hangs on the tree. We would like its beauty to endure forever. The breeze blows and it is gone. But without the breeze, it would never have been so fine. The most real things are those in which we perceive the fragility.

When Buddhism puts an emphasis upon the "here and now", surely it is not in order to shut out the past and future. It is so that one can appreciate the fragility of this moment. The most ordinary things seem precious when they hover on the point of being blown away. So seemed my mother to me that morning. So seem all of us in the eyes of the Buddha.

When I think of Nyorai I am, at least partly, thinking of how he sees me. He sees clearly enough all my failings – sees them more clearly than I do. He sees them, but he does not judge me for them. Rather he sees how I too am a fragile petal, just hanging on. Any moment a chill spring breeze may take me away. In this I am as all the rest and in being so I am exquisite to him. That is how Buddha sees me. That is what Amida means. In the Buddha's eye there is a tear for each of us. He knows the pathos of our lives.

"But is there really a Buddha who sees us like that," you may ask, and I will say, "Oh yes, there are many. And anyone can be an instance of that universal Buddha, now and then, just for a moment, when the true reality of the human situation breaks through upon them." Just for a moment I am in Nyorai's eye. Just for a moment Nyorai's eye may be me.

**Mid-morning the family doctor arrived**. We had just cleaned Mother up again after another bout of diarrhoea. This one had wrecked the foam mattress she had been lying on on the folding bed so we had now got her back into her own bed that is fitted with a waterproof mattress cover. Willemien and I finished cleaning her while Caroline dealt with the incessant phone. Two other distant members of our community have phoned to say they are coming to help out, one travelling from Devon and the other from Newcastle. The doctor came in just as we were finishing. He was ready to roll up his sleeves and help, but we were done.

He examined Mother, discovering nothing unexpected. He then said that he was greatly impressed by how we had handled the situation. There were several members of the community present and I felt very happy for everybody to hear this affirmation. It felt proper that they be acknowledged by somebody who, like the doctor, carried some weight of authority, as I had been constantly aware of how supportive the whole community had been. It was very satisfying to hear them praised in this way.

He then took my hand and said that he could see that I was "a wreck" from lack of sleep and constant care work. Then, turning to the others, he said, "but he hasn't become bad tempered about it in the least." It was a homily and also intended as an accolade for me.

I said, "Mother has always been my best friend," meaning that I could not have acted any other way.

"And she will go on being so in your heart," he replied. This was so touching that we all cried, the doctor included. I think he had been moved by the palpable atmosphere of love in the room and we were certainly deeply affected by his response to it.

This was a tender moment. I knew that it had been important for him as well as for ourselves. We were in real time. This, to me, is what religion is about: being fully alive, whether it is pain or whether it is joy, and in that aliveness, meeting one another. Such moments are just for the moment, but they also have an eternal quality. When it really is real time, just-for-a-moment time, then it is eternal. They impart to us something of the unmeasurable light and life. In the very surge of tears that burn one's eyes there is the meaning of life.

**In a way, what happened there was a ritual**. The doctor played his part. He said his words. There was, however, not a trace of insincerity. He meant every syllable. It is sometimes like that. We cherish those occasions when the words that are meant to be said are genuine and completely appropriate. Also, in such moments, it is acceptable to be spiritually naked, to just be the completely foolish being who weeps to lose his mother and is touched by a kind word, passion flowing like spilt water from an upturned vase. It is not that there is a time when there is a foolish being and another time then there is or might be a Buddha. The Buddha appears only when the foolish being is completely a foolish being. The light can only be seen in the darkness. The equality of all moments can only be experienced in the specialness of this one moment when the heart is so touched that one is turned inside out, emptied with nothing remaining.

## Love and Grief Rescue Us from Ourselves

**Love is the important thing**. There is an approach to Buddhism that says that it is all about non-attachment. If you never attach then you never lose anything. If you never lose anything you never grieve. This, we may be told, is the object of the exercise – to live a life that is immune to grief.

I, however, am immensely grateful for having the opportunity to grieve. If a person never grieves, they have surely left half their life unlived. Grief is the pain of becoming real. The spiritual path is about becoming real rather than ideal, and there is no way to skip the pain.

A person is not inanimate. A person is a subject, not just an object. A person may be an object to another person, but the spiritual life is the life of the subject, and it is in the nature of a subject that it cannot be self-sufficient. A subject is subject to all manner of things. A subject is dependently originated. Our life energy flows out toward the object world, which is to say, toward the other subjects, and so risks acceptance and rejection. The life of the subject is not self-sufficient or self-enclosed. It is open to being affected. The more we live as subjects rather than as objects the more tender our life becomes. The life of a subject is not the life of self-regard, but the life of risky engagement with what is other. We are brought to life by love and love necessarily entails the risk of grief.

Popular psychology is concerned with self-regard. We are told to cultivate self esteem – even to love ourselves. Regard, however, is regard for an object. To have self-esteem one must be an object to oneself. This objectification is not true spirituality. True spirituality is to be a subject and a subject is unselfconscious. A subject risks all on each throw of the dice of life.

**The development of our spirit** is not equivalent to the perfection of the super-ego. Rather they stand in opposition to each other within our nature. The super-ego seeks control and rationality in the conduct of affairs. It makes us an object to ourselves. The spirit seeks gratification in involvements that are fresh and rash. Spirituality grows out of the wild side of our being, the side that risks grief by taking the risk of loving. When this out-flowing spirit is repressed, one succumbs to depression. The super-ego is fundamentally part of the death instinct. The highest development of life can, therefore, never lie in the complete triumph of super-ego demands.

Consider the question of the ethics of killing. If I do not kill because "Thou shalt not kill," then the blood lust in me is not assuaged. It is likely that it will leak out in some other manner. On the other hand, if I do not kill this particular beast because I feel sympathy, compassion or love, then the dynamic of the situation is quite different. The super-ego and the spirit are not the same. Ethical behaviour may flow from either source, but in a quite different way. Both are also capable of producing unethical behaviour. Many of the most terrible things in history have been done in the name of righteousness.

As we mature, there is a dialectic between these two different sides of our nature. Unfortunately many people have come to see religion as a child of the super-ego rather than of the spirit. When the doctor said tender words to me and I wept, he was evoking my grief. Grief like that is direct spirit energy. There is nothing depressive about it. That is why I felt so alive at that time. There is much depression in our society because people have forgotten how to really grieve. Is it not that they did not really take the risk of truly loving in the first place?

**We need love in our lives**, both to be able to give and to receive. This involves us, however, in needing others and so becoming vulnerable. Did Buddha point out dependent origination so that we could avoid it or so that we could recognize it more deeply as the inexorable reality of our life? When one we love goes or dies we must grieve or we will turn in on ourselves. Love rescues us from ourselves. The loved one holds our attention so that it does not fold back upon itself. When the loved one is gone, we may fold back and fall into depression, or we may grieve. In grief the loved other remains in focus, even after they have gone. Buddhism is powered by the grief that Shakyamuni's disciples felt when he went.

The folding of attention back in upon oneself and the construction of an ego seems to be an attempt to achieve security in this uncertain world. Ego is the avoidance of grief by setting up the illusion of self-sufficiency. Buddha's pointing out of dependent origination punctured that illusion. It is painful to keep one's attention on the lost other, but it is also true that the pain keeps us focussed. In Buddhism we recognize something called "great grief". In this world there is not just our personal grief, there is a universal grief. Far from withdrawing attention for the lost other, the Buddha, when confronted by a grieving person, would broaden their perception to encompass all the lost others of the world so that even the very last vestige of turning back upon oneself as object was extinguished. My loss is an instance of the great loss. If a person were to open their heart to the world at large, loss is everywhere. I feel my own personal loss deeply. You feel yours. Everybody has losses. Religion does not help us to flee from this, but to see its universality. Shinko is joko. What is most personal is most universal.

## Things That Hang by a Thread

**Mother had grieved**. She had grieved over her own mother. She never talked about it, though. I remember my grandparents as an elderly couple living in a little red brick terraced house in Northampton in the English Midlands. Northampton is not very far from Leicester where I live now. Grandfather was usually ill. During the First World War he served in an artillery regiment. Proximity to repeated detonations had damaged his ears. Then, one day, his unit was attacked with gas, some of which he inhaled. His lungs were permanently damaged. When I remember him, I remember coughing.

I remember that the house was rather dark. Although it was a small "two up two down" terraced house, the front room was never used. As the first reception room it contained the best furniture and this was kept covered with dust cloths. It was always ready for that special big occasion that never seemed to come. Perhaps it had been used, but I was never present for such an occasion. So when we visited we would pass the time in the back room that connected with the kitchen. There grandfather sat and coughed. As a child, I never appreciated what a struggle his life must have been.

Much more interesting to me as an eight-year-old was the fact that there was a cellar. It was a dark place, half full of coal. Access to it was from the kitchen. In the other direction, beyond the kitchen, there was a garden where they grew vegetables. The garden was a long strip. Standing in it you could look along the row of house backs in either direction, each house having its strip. This was also where the washing line hung and, at the back of the house, outside the back door, was the mangle. This piece of equipment also held a certain fascination. Two wooden rollers could be turned by the metal handle to squeeze the water out of the washing before it was hung on the line. The rollers clearly also had the capacity to flatten little fingers, so my interest in it was a source of anxiety to Mother.

**I did not much like visiting the grandparents**. Grandad was gruff and there was not much to do. We did not go very often. Probably a lot less often than my Mother would have wished. My memories are fragmentary. I liked the corner shop where there were varieties of fizzy drink that were unobtainable where we lived. I remember watching Nanna cutting bread, which she would do by holding the loaf in mid-air with one hand and the knife with the other and cutting a horizontal slice. The knife she used had been sharpened many times and the edge was correspondingly wavy. The slices of bread that she cut were extremely thin. The sight of the sharp knife brought the same kind of *frisson* of excitement as contemplation of the mysterious powers of the mangle.

I was too young to fathom the dynamics of the various relationships. I did not know what my grandparents thought of their son-in-law, nor even what bond there was between them and their daughter. My perception of the situation was completely self-centred.

During my childhood we lived some of the time in England and some of the time abroad. I do know that my mother had mixed feelings about being abroad and at least some of her reluctance was connected with a sense that she could not perform her duty toward her parents properly. When I was thirteen years old we moved house and went to live in Norfolk. Getting from Norfolk to Northampton would be easier. However, at this juncture, my grandfather died.

After Grandad's death Nanna was invited to give up her house and come to live with us in Norfolk. She said that she would give it a try. She arrived and lived with us for ten days. Then she said that she wanted to go back to her house in Northampton to deal with some business. There was still furniture to be disposed of and there must have been official matters connected with Grandad's death to deal with.

My parents drove her back to Northampton and dropped her off at her old house. She did not want them to stay with her. I can imagine them being anxious, but also wanting her to put her things in order in her own way and, perhaps, hoping that if she did so she would settle better into a new life. I don't think that any of them really knew how to grieve.

So Nanna went back to her own house and it must have brought forward overwhelming feelings. All the associations of her old life with her husband were there. She wanted to be with him. That night she put her head in the oven, turned on the gas, and thereby killed herself.

**My mother must have been devastated**. How she kept me in ignorance of what was going on I do not know. The norm in the family was that children should be "protected". This meant that nothing of any emotional consequence was said in front of me. However, I was not unaffected. I remember my teenage years as one of the most difficult and most gloomy periods of my life.

I speculate that Mother must have felt guilty, inadequate and rejected. I have indirect evidence that all this may also have affected my parent's marriage. After mother died I found love letters from my father to her dated just prior to this incident written during a period when they were separated by his work. He was clearly very much in love with her then. However, I also know from other sources that not long after this he had an affair with a woman that he met at work and there may well have been others.

I ponder on the fact that Mother invited her mother and it ended in tragedy, whereas I invited Mother and it proved a great success. I was lucky. How things can hang by a thread! Here I was sitting at Mother's bedside. She is peaceful. Yet she could have died of choking the night before as a result of me giving her her milk too fast. How would I have felt then? Or, earlier, she could have come to live with us, hated it, and left with a wake of trouble.

It makes one reflect upon the contingency of so many things in life. I have had ups and downs enough. Caroline is my third wife – "Third time lucky," Mother would say. How we like to take the credit when things go right and how sorry we feel for ourselves when they do not. In fact, however, a great deal is just touch and go. Why did Nanna kill herself? Perhaps she felt she was imposing upon my mother. Perhaps she felt that nobody cared about her. Perhaps she simply could not bear the grief. Perhaps she wanted to be with her husband and thought that was the way to achieve it. I will never know. I do know that sometimes I look up into the sky and I see Mother there, and when I do, Nanna is standing behind her.

**The Image of Paradise**
**By early afternoon on Friday** we had had many phone calls and several visitors. We had had another delivery of morphine and joked that we now had enough drugs in the house to run an opium den. Mother had not, in fact, needed any of it. We had piles of absorbent pads for coping with Mother's incontinence. The family doctor had arranged for us to have a supply of oxygen so that we could deal with any further breath-

ing crises ourselves. Various other pieces of equipment had been delivered and explained to us. The community nursing and domiciliary services had proved tremendously helpful. We were being prepared for the weekend when services might be less on tap.

Mother lay with her head inclined as if looking at the window beyond which her beloved garden lay, but she saw nothing now, I think. Sometimes I stood by the window and looked at it for her. There were bees on the sill and I wondered where they had come from. The garden was full of colour at that time of year. The sight of it and the knowledge of her love for it filled me with tenderness. The pathos of impermanence hung in the air.

Caroline and I had lunch together in Mother's sitting room while Jenny sat with Mother. My eyes stung from crying. After lunch I sat with Mother, as I had done now almost continuously for several days, not having been out of her room for more than an hour since she got home from hospital on Tuesday. I now had a sense that she may not still be entirely in her body. She is no longer in communication with us. Perhaps she hovers above us as one reads in accounts of near death experiences. We have run a red cord from Mother's right hand to the Buddha statue on her chest of drawers. Red is the colour of our style of Buddhism, symbolising life, love and compassion. I take out our scriptures and, in a full voice, read the passages about the Pure Land paradise. I hope she can hear. I realize as I read that I personally hope she will go to a land where there is a fine garden. Gardens have been such a central part of her life.

I read:
Millions of miles to the West from here,
There lies a land called Perfect Bliss
Where a Buddha, Amitayus by name
Is even now the Dharma displaying.

Oh Shariputra, why is that land
Given the name of Perfect Bliss?
It is without pain; only pleasure dwells there
That's why they call it Perfect Bliss.

Around the Land of Perfect Bliss
There are seven balustrades
Seven fine nets, seven rows of trees
All of jewels made, sparkling and fine;
That's why they call it Perfect Bliss

There are lakes of seven gems
With water of eightfold merit filled
And beds of golden sand,
To which descend on all four sides
Gold, silver, beryl and crystal stairs.

Pavilions and terraces rise above
Gold, silver, beryl and crystal
White coral, red pearl and agate gleaming;
And in the lakes lotus flowers
Large as chariot wheels
Give forth their splendour

The blue ones radiate light so blue, the yellow yellow,
Red red, white white and
All most exquisite and finely fragrant.

Oh Shariputra, the Land of Bliss
Like that is arrayed
With many good qualities and fine adornments.

There is heavenly music spontaneously played
And all the ground is strewn with gold.
Blossoms fall six times a day
From mandarava, the divinest of flowers

In the morning light, those who live in that land
Collect the blossoms and offerings make
To millions of Buddhas in other regions;

At the lunchtime hour
They have their meal and take a stroll.

Oh Shariputra, the Land of Bliss
Like that is arrayed
With many good qualities and fine adornments.

There are wonderful birds of many colours:
Swans and peacocks, parrots, charis, kalavinkas
And even the bird with double lives.

Six times day and night they sing
Melodious songs of fivefold virtue, fivefold power,
Of the seven factors of spiritual light and of the eightfold path.
Of all the divisions of Dharma they sing.

Entranced by the songs
All the beings of that land
Quickly take refuge in
Buddha, Dharma and Sangha.

Those birds were not born as such

Through karmic retribution
For no evil realms in that land are there.
Not even the names of such realms are found:
How much less the evil realms themselves.

Shariputra, all those birds
Were by Amitayus expressly made
That the voice of Dharma melodiously spread.

When in that land a gentle breeze blows
The precious trees and bejewelled nets
Emit a delicate enrapturing tune
Like an orchestra of myriad parts.
All who hear will naturally conceive
The thought of refuge in Buddha, Dharma and Sangha.

Oh Shariputra, the Land of Bliss
Like that is arrayed
With many good qualities and fine adornments.

So Shariputra, what do you think?
Why is that Buddha called Amitabha?
Why does he have the name Amitayus?
His light is boundless and unimpeded
It spreads over all the lands of ten quarters
Therefore is he called Amitabha.
The lives of that Buddha
And all of his people
Go on forever, endless and boundless
Therefore Amitayus is his name.

He has been a Buddha more than ten kalpas
His disciples, all saints, are beyond calculation.
The great bodhisattvas who dwell in that land
Are also far too numerous to tell.

Oh Shariputra, the Land of Bliss
Like that is arrayed
With many good qualities and fine adornments.

Nobody born there ever falls back
Those in the stage of one more life only
Are immeasurably many
Beyond clear expression.

Shariputra, all who hear
Should long and pray to be born there
To share in the realm of such noble beings
For never by one's own roots of virtue alone
Could one hope to attain such a wonderful world.

**The image of paradise** occupies a central place in our faith, which is, in fact, named for it. We are the Paradise Buddhists. The paradise to come and the paradise we would make here are reflections of one another. That is why Pureland is life affirming and is an engaged Buddhism at the same time as being a fully spiritual religion focussed on the sacred realm beyond. The paradise we hope for reflects the paradisaical vision that great seers of faiths the world over experience in the ecstatic transformation we call spiritual rapture. Spiritual awakening allows the light to come flooding in. Then, for a time, while the access lasts, all around one, the Pure Land paradise extends, as though the sun had tripled its output and everybody in the world had become tender and filled with love – one experiences them so. Such experiences in which one finds asylum from the troubles of the world and experiences its benign dimension completely are rare in a lifetime and many never have such a revelation, or only minor ones where a glimpse is granted rather than an overwhelming flood of experience. The majority simply have faith in those who have done so. Buddhists are those who believe that Siddhartha Gotama was such a one. To have faith in another can be enough. After all, all that the experience itself gives, in the longer term, is certainty of conviction. If one has that, then one has what is needed. One has faith. To live in this world in settled faith is what matters. That is what bears fruit. The Buddha wanted to create a body of such people who could be a leaven in the world, naturally spreading love, compassion, joy and peace; a body of people who live in communion with Nyorai's unimpeded grace.

The most common time for such experiences is during the process of dying. This is because a person is most ripe for it when their attention is not gripped by other attachments and at the death-time a person may let the things of this life fall away. One who goes to their death as blithely as Mother did are in the most likely condition. However, the coming of the light is not something one can force. It is a gift of grace. We can make ourselves ready for it and open, but this does not guarantee anything, for grace is part of the life of the universe, not part of its mechanism. Access sometimes comes to those who seem most unlikely. In fact, the Pure Land paradise is never more than the thinnest of thin veils away from us, whatever our life may have been, and the Buddhas and bodhisattvas do not come into this world principally to point it out to the good and the wise, but to save the mass of humanity lost in complete darkness and delusion.

Of course, modern people are not educated any more to believe in paradises of tranquil ponds and golden sand where all goes well and one is surrounded by unfailing love. But does it not answer to a deep need within us? Does it not speak to something fundamental to what we are? Why do children like to hear such tales? Are they not in touch with a simpler sense of the spirit of life? The longing for a Pure Land is part and parcel of us. If we had no sense of a better place we could not have a sense of how to improve this one and death would occasion only indifference. Amida and the Pure Land are the limit of human experience.

## The Other World is More Real than the Self

**Faith is something inherent in human life**, part of what it is to be a person. What we do with our faith, however, is a matter of the choices we have made, consciously in some cases, but blindly in many. Life is full of so many seductions. When we take stock honestly, we find that we all have faith. We have more faith in some things than others. Those who say, "I do not have faith, I am scientific", for instance, are simply saying that they have faith in science. Even those who think that they do not have faith in anything, may, if they examine the matter, find that they have invested their faith in cynicism, hoping thereby to keep themselves safe. Some have faith in rationality, some in worldly matters, some in relationships. Conversely, there are those who declare a religious faith who, when the matter is laid bare, really have put their faith in self-serving things and worldly principles and merely dressed them up in spiritual language. In matters of faith, things are often not what they seem. However, everybody has their refuge. Buddhism asks us to assess whether the refuges that we hold to are the most noble or reliable. As Buddhists, we seek refuge in Buddha, Dharma and Sangha. As Amidists, we see Buddha, Dharma and Sangha manifest as a Pure Land.

In the midst of life our paradise inspires us to live a better life and to create realms where it is easier to live the spiritual life. Buddhist monasteries and communities are modelled on the Buddhist paradise and Buddhists have been forward in promoting such communities of harmony. A Pure Land is a land where the optimum conditions exist to assist us in living a pure life. Pureland has become the most popular form of Buddhism in the Far East because people realize that they need that kind of help. "Never by one's own roots of virtue alone could one hope to attain such a wonderful land." Not only do we need help, we need to help one another. We need to enter the field of influence of a Pure Land, and when we do, we naturally want to work together to create lands like that. The actual architectural details will vary, of course, but Buddhism aims to bring better worlds into existence before death, after death, and in every conceivable realm. Even the hells, if there be such – and many find them even within this life – must be transformed. Buddhism is a paradise construction company.

There are many who say that the idea of a Pure Land as an external reality is just for naive beginners. When we attain deeper practice we will find or establish the Pure Land within our own mind. Then we can experience the Pure Land all the time. Perhaps they are right, or maybe not. It may be that such a view is not as healthy or as advanced as its proponents believe. Locating everything holy inside the mind has its drawbacks. Buddhism is not just "all in the mind". People believe that by doing so they are being less metaphysical. However, the idea of "inside the mind" is quite a metaphysical idea. In the Buddha's time the mind was not conceived to be a container. Mind did not have content. Mind was more like a sense organ. It perceived or cognised things. The things it perceived were, therefore, all "outside". In its basic structure, Buddhism is a completely extrovert spirituality. The Buddha's stirring ideal does not actually require half a lifetime of navel gazing. It requires the faith to take refuge and go forth in that vision. As we go along, we will, for sure, keep bumping into our own blind passion and ignorance, but, if we are inspired by faith, vision and love, we will quite naturally do something about it. We will experience times of contrition and times of unexpected softening of the heart as we are moved by the afflictions of others and we will become more tender.

The structure of Amidist thought rests upon a paradigm of encounter with what is not self. Spiritual maturity is not seen as lying in the direction of making everything internal and relying only upon oneself. One's own merit is necessarily meagre and one's own spiritual power correspondingly slight. If the Pure Land is not outside of one's self then it is probably not much use to anybody. The products of our own mind are rarely that inspiring.

Also, if one despairs of perceiving the Pure Land outside of oneself then one has really despaired of the spiritual life and fallen into a kind of solipsism. The Pure Land that we should aspire to lies around us, not within us. The idea that "The Kingdom of God is within" may actually be a diminution of the divine not an enhancement of it and the parallel assertion is just as true in Buddhism. The Buddha was enlightened when he saw the morning star. The morning star was outside. He was enlightened when he really saw it. The Pure Land is imminent in the morning star. It is not a projection of mind. It is objective reality stripped of mind and so truly encountered. Mind is what gets in the way, not the source of wisdom. Sometimes this is called the "no-mind" doctrine.

I do not mean by these remarks to give offence to those who think in a different way, merely to make a plea that we not take for granted assumptions that are questionable. We can each have our perspective and they all contribute to meaningful encounter between us. What I do hope to do is to dislodge the kind of complacency that thinks that by locating everything in the mind all problems are solved. Certainly such "innerism" is no more scientific nor any less metaphysical and most cultures have thought otherwise.

Those who have never encountered it do not know the true radiance of this world, that world, or any other world. Those who have known it never forget it. They no longer rely upon self alone. They sense their own fragility and unimportance. They know their inner darkness, but they live in glory. We should restore the ability to talk about such things, for there is nothing better.

## Involved in Something Real

**We were reaching the final scene**. The medical stand-by service had been alerted that Mother would probably die that night. About ten o'clock a doctor called by. We had not met this one before. He was pleasant and spoke at length about how to help dying patients. Most of the methods, however, were, as he said, no longer appropriate since Mother no longer communicated and no longer consumed anything. She did not seem to be in pain. Sometimes she seemed a little disturbed, but we were reluctant to give her morphine. The doctor agreed and suggested aromatherapy – after all, the thing Mother was still doing was breathing and the breath goes straight to the core of life. Her breathing was becoming congested again with fluid, so first we gave her olbas oil. This was immediately effective in clearing her nasal channels. We could see it helping her. Then, once she was breathing more easily, we gave her lavender oil. In each case we put the oil on a cloth close to her face and also sprinkled the oil on the front of her nightdress so that she could breathe it in. Again there was an immediate result. Mother noticeably relaxed. She now seemed very peaceful. An hour later two nurses called and we were able to tell them about this success, which they found interesting, making a note that, no doubt, would be passed on to others in similar situations.

During that period we were all focussed upon Mother. We also, however, had a strong sense of being part of a team that included many people previously unknown to us, each of whom has a role in caring for the sick. The proximity of death created instant bonds. We were able to talk easily to whoever came since we were all engaged in the same drama and there was no ambiguity. Everybody knew that they were involved in something real. Death is so much more real than many of the other things in life. We say that the most important thing in Buddhism is the great matter of birth and death. Under the influence of indigenous Indian religion, some branches of Buddhism tended to become life-denying. They started to see the whole aim of the exercise as being to eliminate birth and death. The goal of the spiritual life became to ensure that one was not reborn in any shape or form and, in the meantime, to live as if already dead so as to cause the minimum likelihood of reactivating this life process. The question became, how to escape from birth and death. What one experiences at the birth-time and the death-time, however, is that these are the times when we feel most alive, most real. Intuitively, one knows that the ideal would be to be able to live like that all the time. The great matter of life and death is not in fact how to escape from birth and death, but how to live as if at the birth-death-time all the time. Spirituality should, therefore, be about converting ordinary life into birth-death-time life. The famous Zen master Dogen therefore said: "If we can find the Buddha within birth and death there is no need to avoid them," and, we can perhaps say that it is in the birth or death time that Nyorai is most likely to find us.

At such times there is a natural friendship. My mother remembered the time of the Second World War as a time of close and important friendships and of great vitality. It is a consideration established by social science that the incidence of depression and suicide declines steeply during wartime and increases during peacetime. Superficially we would think that war is a bad time and when times are bad people should be more depressed. The opposite is the case. The philosopher Jean Paul Sartre who had served in the French resistance during the war later famously wrote: "We were most free when we were most oppressed." During the oppression there was no uncertainty or ambiguity. Life flowed and people were in that flow. The great dilemma that faces the world is not how to escape from birth and death, but how to live with comparable vitality without having to have the stimulus of war or tragedy to force it from us.

One answer to this is that a certain quantity of tragedy and affliction is inevitable. It is part and parcel of being alive. This was the "First Noble Truth" pronounced by the Buddha. If we need affliction in our lives in order to be fully alive, then there is plenty to be going on with. We do not need to create more. However, instead of deeply responding to the affliction that naturally occurs, people try to avoid it and in the process bring down many further tragedies – both the major ones of war, famine and oppression and the everyday ones of bitterness, cynicism and petty greed.

## The Secret of Life

**We felt very close to one another at that time**. Anomadharshi, Jenny and Sujatin, another member of our Order, sat with Mother late into the evening, partly out of a desire to be with her and partly to give Caroline and me a break. At 11pm Caroline and I went to sleep. Caroline woke at 1.30am and it was apparent to her that the important moment was getting close. Jenny went to bed. I was woken and joined them. We sat close to her around the bed holding hands. I sat at Mothers side holding her hand, which was limp in mine. There was an atmosphere of great warmth and love among that little assembly. We chanted. Mother's breathing got weaker little by little. At precisely three o'clock, as we were chanting the Buddha's name, she breathed for the last time. As she stopped I felt a slight squeeze of my hand and then she was gone. Moggi the cat sat on her feet to the last. Outside, the first bird of the morning started its song.

Reality is not answerable to one's personal will. With all my heart, might and being I did not want her to die, yet, she lay there dead before us. She was at peace. She had gone, not by her choice, not by mine, but by the natural process of this universe where we dwell and where we strive to make sense and to tread a meaningful path through life and beyond. That sense and meaning has to accommodate the implacable fact that we live in the presence of power infinitely more formidable than our own.

**I was filled with tenderness**, seeing her lying there, her face now looking somehow like that of a young girl. I also felt huge pride in her. It had been a wonderful death. You cannot know the final score until the game is over, and she had done so well. She had loved steadfastly, lived fully and died consumately. I felt deeply humbled and knew that this event was teaching me, as little else could, all that one needed to know about the secret of life. Above all, I felt grateful to her. It seemed that even her death had been a great gift.

Caroline and I cleaned the body and laid it out on a clean sheet. The lifelessness of the body seemed strange. I felt no reluctance to touch. Somehow something was impressing itself upon me in a way beyond the expressive capacity of words. Outside it was starting to get light. I went out into the garden. As so often over the past week, as soon as I left the room tears welled up in me, my throat straining to accommodate their compelling pressure as sobs poured forth. I made my way out to stand amongst her flowers, her trees, her grass, convulsed with grief.

Caroline followed after a little interlude, saw me standing, half way down the garden engulfed in pain and called me back. I was reluctant to go to her unable to arrest the flow of tears, but she understood and said, "No, no, come... come and look up." Only then did I become aware of the noise all about us, as if a helicopter was coming in to land, a tremendous droning sound. Directly above us, right outside Mother's window, bees in their thousands were swarming in a great spiralling mass, like a small tornado. The air was full of the smell of honey. Over the next half hour we watched spellbound as the bees coagulated into a carpet-like mass on the wall of the house and eventually processed in through a hole to make a new home in the roof of the bay window of her room.

EIGHT

# EPILOGUE

More than a year has passed. Mother was buried at the natural burial ground as she wished. We visit and tend the flowers growing there. The bees continue to reside in her bay window roof. After she died I moved into her room for a while and now a new house resident has taken it over. Living in a community we have quite frequent changes of accommodation as people come and go. There are many comings and goings here as we have projects in Africa and in India and there are invitations from many parts of the world to fulfil.

For ten months I grieved. It seemed as though the feelings were always with me. Then a founder member of the Amida Trust died and I was asked to conduct the funeral. Something changed for me at that event. Being amongst other people who were just starting their grieving and having the responsibility to minister to them, my own process was affected. It was as though I was being told at that point to step aside and make way for others to have their turn.

Since then my mood has lightened. I still weep from time to time when something especially poignant reminds me, but otherwise I am at peace with it. Mother had a good life and a good death. What else could one wish for. I have learnt much.

In regard to my Pureland faith, I feel immensely grateful to it. It gives my life meaning and depth without making impossible demands. I do not feel any pressure to be beyond learning new things, nor do I feel that an unreachable standard is demanded of me. Amida accepts us just as we are. In his absolute grace we are acceptable.

Of course, I am incapable of such a standard myself. I make judgements and choices. I like this and dislike that. I feel joy and grief by turns. I am ordinary. My role as a Buddhist teacher is primarily that of helping others to be aware that, just as they are, they are accepted by the Buddha. By writing this book I hope that I may have encouraged some to overcome the widespread taboos that exist in modern life against thinking in an overtly spiritual way. No doubt most readers will agree with some things I have asserted here and disagree with others. There is nothing strange about that. What is more important than finding total agreement is establishing the legitimacy of discussing matters of the spirit and living within a spiritual framework.

As a spiritual house we have our practices and they are a great support and provide the cohesion for a life in community that in turn provides a basis for work of assistance to many people far and near. I am frequently astonished that so few people can do so much with such scant resources. This is, however, all by the miraculous power of faith.

The other day we visited a Catholic convent, a community of Poor Clares, women who follow the religious path established by St Francis of Assisi and St Clare. We had a most fruitful interchange. It was so interesting to see how people living in religious community had so much in common notwithstanding that they belong to different religions. It made one reflect upon the folly of the divisions that tear our world apart.

There are those who say that only one religion can be right and so one must decide which it is and be willing to fight for one's cause. This does seem a completely misguided approach. The world is full of bombu religions. Some are called religions and some are called secular philosophies, like capitalism or communism. The key to peace lies not in finding which is the one true creed. It lies rather in acknowledging that none are perfect. We long for a better world – for paradise. We long with all the might of our fallible selves. We express that longing in flights of poetry and praise. We worship and we discipline ourselves. We grow in insight sometimes. We may even dream dreams and see visions. But all of this is soon ruined when we fall into the hubris of thinking that we are more than we are.

So my faith, like that of my mother, begins with acknowledgment of human frailty: with the bombu paradigm. This is the real foundation for peace in the world and in the home. Bombu beings need help, so we acknowledge the highest help we can conceive. In Pureland, we call it Amida Nyorai. Nyorai brings hope of paradise – of what we long for. When we have an acknowledgment of our own limited nature and reverence for the highest, then we have in place the framework within which a meaningful spiritual life can unfold. For it to do so there has to be a practice. In Amidism this is the nembutsu – the Buddha prayer. It is a simple utterance that encompasses all the range of feelings that the religious life give birth to: longing, awe, gratitude, grief, fellow-feeling, love, assurance.

I sit on the grass beside Mother's resting place and look out at the setting sun in the West. There are bees here too, buzzing round the bugloss plant on her grave. She has gone on from here on her own Westward journey. I remain, pondering the meaning of things and saying the nembutsu. Namo Amida Bu.

# GLOSSARY

**Abha**. Light. A principal attribute of Amida.

**Abhidharma**. Third section of the Tripitaka (q.v.). Books of Buddhist philosophy, psychology and analysis compiled in the centuries immediately after the death of Shakyamuni (q.v.).

**Ajattashatru**. Son of, assassin of, and successor to Bimbisara (q.v.)

**Alagaddupama** (Pali). The Snake Simile Sutra. A section of the Majjhima Nikaya (q.v.).

**Amida**. The Buddha of infinite light, life and grace. A contraction of amitayus-amitabha. Amita means measureless.

**Amida Order**. Religious order established in UK to propagate Pureland teaching and practice.

**Amida-shu**. Amidaism (q.v.); the religious communion of those who practice Amidist faith

**Amida's vows**. In the Larger Pureland Sutra (q.v.) Dharmakara (q.v.) bodhisattva makes 48 great vows, the fulfilment of which leads to the creation of a Pure Land (q.v.) called Sukhavati (q.v.).

**Amidism**. The Pureland tradition of Buddhism focussed on faith in Amida Buddha.

**Amitabha**. Measureless light. Absolute grace. The Buddha of the West. See: abha.

**Amitayus**. Measureless lifespan. Infinite time. The eternal.

**Ananda**. Cousin and best loved disciple of Shakyamuni Buddha (q.v.). In the Larger Pureland Sutra (q.v.) the main teachings are addressed to Ananda.

**Anatma**. Non-self. Buddhism is the spirituality that focusses upon onself. Grace is other.

**Anitya**. Impermanence.

**Anjin** (J.). Settled faith. Peaceful heart. See also: shinjin.

**Attakanagara** (Pali). A sutra (q.v.) within the Majjhima Nikaya (q.v.).

**Arhat**. A saint. One who has overcome greed, hate and delusion.

**Asava** (Pali). Outflow. Issue, in the spiritual or psychological sense as well as the literal one.

**Avidya**. Non-seeing. Obstinate refusal to appreciate grace. Opposite of vidya (q.v.)

**Awakening**. Spiritual realization. See also, bodhi, shinjin.

**Bardo** (Tib.). Strictly, any phase of the process by which one life succeeds another in the doctrine of rebirth. Commonly, the interlude between death and rebirth.

**Bhakti**. Ecstatic devotion. Loyalty and devotedness.

**Bhikshu**. Buddhist mendicant monk or friar.

**Bhikshuni**. Buddhist nun.

**Bimbisara**. King of Magadha (q.v.), patron of Shakyamuni (q.v.) and husband of Vaidehi (q.v.).

**Bodaishin** (J.). Bodhichitta (q.v.). The faith that results in action to benefit others. See also: shinjin, anjin, shimmitsu.

**Bodhi**. Enlightened vision. Being awake to grace.

**Bodhichitta**. The mind of enlightened vision. The mentality of a bodhisattva (q.v.). Altruism.

**Bodhisattva**. One on the path to full Buddhahood. One who has the courage or spirit (sattva) to live by the paradigm of absolute grace.

**Bombu**, or **bonbu** (J.). Foolish being. The Pureland dosctrine of the fallibility of ordinary humans.

**Bombu paradigm**. The principle that no human artefact or understanding can be faultless, including religion. See also: bombu.

**Bombu shin gyo** (J.). Faith and practice for ordinary people. See also: bombu, shin, gyo.

**Buddha**. One who is awake to Dharma (q.v.). A tathagata (q.v.).

**Buddhakshetra**. Buddha field. The Pure Land (q.v.).

**Buddhanusmriti**. Keeping Buddha in mind. Contemplation of a Buddha, especially Amida. See: nien fo, nembutsu, contemplative nembutsu.

**Ch'an** (Chin.). Chinese Buddhist school that emphasises meditation practice from which the Zen School (q.v.) of Japan derives.

**Chih** (Chin.). Shamatha (q.v.). Stopping, especially letting go of worry and anxiety.

**Chih I**. Chinese Buddhist teacher. Third patriarch of the Tien Tai (q.v.) school. He wrote the Moho Chih Quan (q.v.). He lived 538-597.

**Contemplation Sutra**. One of the three Pureland sutras (q.v.) in which Shakyamuni describes to Ananda (q.v.) and Queen Vaidehi (q.v.) how to visualise a Pure Land (q.v.). The text also describes events surrounding the giving of this teaching and also the categories of persons who enter the Pure Land.

**Contemplative nembutsu**. Meditation on a Buddha, using visualisation or other means. See also: verbal nembutsu.

**Contrition**. Regretful reflection upon one's actions that leads to a softening of heart.

**Dainichi** (J.). Vairochana Buddha (q.v.).

**Dark World**. A domain in which faith is defeated by the three poisons (q.v.). See also: three darknesses.

**Dependent origination**. A key doctrine of Buddhism. All things arise in dependence upon other things. We are dependent and therefore vulnerable and changeable. In particular, ordinary mental states arising from avidya (q.v.) culminate in marana (q.v.). The universal applicability of dependency leads to the doctrine of shunyata (q.v.).

**Deva**. A god. A radiant celestial being.

**Devadatta**. A cousin of Shakyamuni, initially a disciple, who rebelled and tried unsuccessfully to usurp leadership of the Buddhist order.

**Dharma**. Grace. The Buddhist teaching. Reality. Real things. Whatever is other than self.

**Dharmakara**. Name of Amida Buddha during his bodhisattva (q.v.) stage, as recounted in the Larger Pureland Sutra (q.v.).

**Dharmakaya**. The Buddha as pure grace. The unfathomable absolute nature of enlightenment. See also: trikaya.

**Dhyana**. Rapture. State of contemplative absorption.

**Divine Abidings**. See: four immeasurables.

**Dogen**. Pre-eminent Soto Zen Master. He lived 1200-1253.

**Dori** (J.). See: Odori.

**Dukkha**. Bad space. Affliction. Spiritual danger. Grief, lament and despair.

**Eightfold Path**. Right view, right thought, right speech, right action, right livelihood, right effort, right smriti (q.v.), right samadhi (q.v.). See also: four noble truths, marga.

**Ekohotsuganshin** (J.). The mind that willingly transfers merit. One of the sanjin (q.v.). See also: merit transference.

**Enjoyment Body**. See sambhogakaya.

**Faith**. See: anjin, prasada, shinjin.

**Five skandhas**. A schematic analysis of how the ego responds to life. Sometimes called five aggregates of grasping. They are rupa, vedana, samjna, samskara and vijnana (q.v.). The doctrine of skandhas is a subset of the doctrine of dependent origination (see Brazier C. 2001).

**Four Immeasurables**. Four signs of grace. They are: maitri, karuna, mudita and upeksha (q.v.).

**Four Noble Truths**. A basic doctrine common to all schools of Buddhsm. The four are dukkha, samudaya, nirodha, and marga (q.v)

**Gotama**. See: Siddhartha Gotama.

**Grace**. A free gift. Dharma (q.v.). The Light of Amida Buddha (q.v.). The entry of spiritual power into our world. The experience of being received by Buddha. Other power (q.v.). Merit bestowed upon us by Amida.

**Gyo** (J.). Spiritual practice. Each school of Buddhism has its preferred practice(s). Thus nembutsu (q.v.) is the preferred practice of Pureland (q.v.) whereas meditation is the preferred practice of Zen (q.v.).

**Haiku** (J.). An 18 syllable poem.

**Hiei**. Mountain near Kyoto in Japan where the head temples of the Tendai School (q.v.) are found.

**Hijiri** (J.). Mendicant Pureland priests, particularly during the medieval period.

**Honen**. Founder of the first independent Pureland denomination of Buddhism in Japan. He lived 1133-1212. See also: Jodoshu, Shinran.

**Horizontalism**. Spirituality. The domain in which absolute grace prevails and where there is no judgement. The samadhi of equality (q.v.).

**Immeasurables**. See: Four immeasurables.

**Inagaki**. Zuiken Inagaki, a modern Pureland master and poet, lived 1885-1981.

**Indriya**. Power. Faculty.

**Jinshin**. Profound mind. One of the sanjin (q.v.).

**Jiriki** (J.) Self-power. The approach to spirituality in which one attempts to achieve enlightenment or salvation by one's own effort or accomplishment through ethical perfection, mastery of meditation, wisdom or other means. See also: tariki.

**Jiva**. Life.

**Jivana**. Lifeness. The realm of life. See also marana, dependent orignation.

**Jodo** (J.). The Pure Land (q.v.).

**Jodo-shu** (J.). The denomination of Pureland Buddhism established by Honen Shonin (q.v.), or its teaching.

**Jodoshin-shu** (J.). The denomination of Pureland Buddhism established by Shinran Shonin (q.v.), or its teaching.

**Joko** (J.). The light that shines everywhere. Universal grace. Cf. Shinko (q.v.). See also: ko.

**Karma**. The doctrine that one's fate is determined by one's wilful deeds.

**Karuna**. Compassion. The wish that others be relieved of suffering.

One of the four immeasurables (q.v.).

**Kaya**. Body.

**Ko** (J.). Light. See: abha, mugeko, joko, shinko.

**Koan** (J.). Case study. A spiritual exercise used in the Zen School (q.v.).

**Kshetra**. Field. See also Buddhakshetra.

**Kusinagara**. Place of death of Shakyamuni.

**Larger Pureland Sutra**. Also called the Sutra on Amitayus. The most important scripture of the Pureland tradition. In it, Shakyamuni transmits to Ananda the teaching of Amida Buddha's creation of a Pure Land (q.v.) and Amida's vows (q.v.). See also: three Pureland sutras, Dharmakara.

**Light**. Grace. The influence of Amida Buddha and the illumination that he brings into our lives. See: abha.

**Loka**. World.

**Lokavid**. Seer of worlds, i.e. of the sacred realm and the mundane one. An epithet of a Buddha. See also: vidya.

**Lotus Sutra**. A major text of Mahayana Buddhism that includes exposition of the doctrine of upaya (q.v.).

**Magadha**. The largest state in North India at the time of Shakyamuni.

**Mahayana**. The schools of Buddhism that emphasise the bodhisattva ideal.

**Maitri**. Love. Kindness. One of the Four immeasurables (q.v.).

**Majjhima Nikaya** (Pali). Middle Length Discourses. A volume of sutras (q.v.) in the Pali language recording the conversations and lectures of Shakyamuni.

**Manjushri**. A bodhisattva who plays a central role in many Mahayana (q.v.).

**Mara**. Death. The anti-Buddha.

**Marana**. Deathness. The dead world. See also: jivana.

**Marga**. The spiritual path, especially the Eightfold Path (q.v.) that results from faith and grace (q.v.). Fourth of the Four Noble Truths (q.v.).

**Maya**. Shakyamuni's mother. She died when he was seven days old.

**Merit**. Happy mind. Fruit of good action. A putative quantification of such as yet unrealized fruit.

**Merit transference**. The doctrine that merit can and should be transferred to others. When the transferrer is Amida this equates with grace (q.v.). Pureland Buddhists feel free to wish away their own merit because they are in receipt of grace. See also: merit.

**Moho Chih Quan** (Chin.). Work on meditation by Chih I (q.v.). It includes specification on how to do intensive nembutsu retreats.

**Mudita**. Joy at the successes and pleasure of others. Sympathetic rejoicing. One of the four immeasurables (q.v.).

**Mugeko** (J.). Unimpeded light. One of the attributes of Amida.

**Nagarjuna**. Pre-eminent Buddhist philosopher. A spiritual ancestor of the Pureland tradition. He lived approxemately 50-150CE.

**Naikan** (J.). See: nei quan.

**Namandabu** (J.). An alternative form of the nembutsu (q.v.)

**Namo Adida Phat** (VN). Vietnamese form of the nembutsu (q.v.).

**Namo Amida Bu**. The nembutsu (q.v.). Homage to Amida Buddha. I, a foolish being, call out to the Buddha of absolute grace.

**Namo Amitabhaya**. An alternative form of nembutsu (q.v.).

**Namo Omito Fo** (Chin.). Chinese form of nembutsu (q.v.).

**Nei Quan** (Chin.). Introspection, especially an intensive method of life review leading to a catharsis of contrition (q.v.).

**Nembutsu** (J.). The act of calling the Buddha's name. The verbal formulae by which this is done. The most common of these formulae: Namo Amida Bu. See also: contemplative nembutsu, verbal nembutsu.

**Nien** (Chin.). Mindfulness. Smriti (q.v.). See also: nien fo.

**Nien fo** (Chin.). Keeping Buddha in mind. Nembutsu (q.v.). Pureland Buddhist practice.

**Nikaya** (Pali). Buddhist sutras in Pali. See also sutra, Majjhima Nikaya.

**Nirmanakaya**. The transformation body of a Buddha, i.e. the appearance of a Buddha here in this world in concrete action and form. See also: trikaya.

**Nirodha**. Containment or overcoming of uprising passion. The path of faith rather than indulgence. Third of the Four Noble Truths (q.v.).

**Nirvana**. The cessation of worldly or self-centred obsession. The sacred realm. See also: other shore, samsara.

**Noble Truth**. See: Four Noble Truths.

**Non-self**. See: anatma.

**Nyorai** (J.). Thus-come, or, come from thusness. Tathagatha (q.v.).

**Odori** (J.). Dance, especially sacred dance.

**Other Power**. see tariki.

**Other Shore**. Paramita. The domain of grace. The ground upon which Buddhas stand. The goal of the spiritual life.

**Pajapati**. Shakyamuni's aunt and step mother, sister of Maya (q.v.). The first Buddhist nun. Founder and leader of the bhikshuni (q.v.) order.

**Panna-indriya** (Pali). The indriya (q.v.) of prajna (q.v.). Power of wisdom. See also: saddh-indriya

**Paramita**. Other shore (q.v.).

**Prajna**. Wisdom.

**Prasada**. Faith. Clarity. See: shinjin, shradha.

**Poison**. See: three poisons.

**Pure Land**. The realm or field of a Buddha. The domain where a Buddha's influence prevails and optimum conditions exist for spiritual awakening. Each Buddha has a characteristic Pure Land. Generally, in Amidism or Pureland Buddhism, one is referring to the Pure Land of Amida Buddha, the Buddha of absolute grace.

**Pureland**. A synonym for Amidism (q.v.). The broad tendency within

Buddhism that emphasises devotional practice and reliance upon grace.

**Quan**. (Chin.). investigation. Vipashyana (q.v.). See also chih, nien, nei quan.

**Quan Shi Yin** (Chin.). Bodhisattva of compassion. One of the two attendant bodhisattvas who assist Amida Buddha. See also: Tai Shih Chi.

**Queen Vaidehi**. See: Vaidehi.

**Rain of Dharma**. An image from the Lotus Sutra (q.v.) indicating that Dharma falls into the lives of all beings enabling each to grow spiritually according to its nature.

**Rinzai Zen**. A denomination of Zen Buddhism noted particularly for the use of koans (q.v.).

**Rupa**. Appearance. Form. The iconic aspect of things. Things may be seen in one of two aspects. In the first aspect we are concerned with the power that they exercise over us. In the second we are concerned to see them as instances of grace. The first is called rupa, the second dharma (q.v.). First of the five skandhas (q.v.). An icon.

**Saddh-indriya** (Pali). The indriya (q.v.) of shraddha (q.v.). The power of faith.

**Saigyo**. Japanese Pureland monk poet who lived 1118-1190.

**Sambhogakaya**. Enjoyment body of a Buddha. The spirit of Buddha continuing in this world, enjoying access to infinite grace and giving access to those who call upon it. One aspect of the trikaya (q.v.).

**Samadhi**. Concentration. Enlightened vision. Ultimate focus of mind. The heart's desire.

**Samadhi of Equality**. The enlightened vision in which judgments of relative worth fall away. All beings are acceptable in the eyes of Buddha. The rain of Dharma falls on all alike.

**Samjna**. Entrancement. Programmed or unconscious thought or behaviour. Being on autopilot. Third of the five skandhas (q.v.).

**Samsara**. The mundane realm of going round in circles. See also: nirvana.

**Samskara**. Confection. Mental constructs, especially proliferating thoughts and feelings generated by self-concern, self-justification or fear. One of the five skandhas (q.v.)

**Samudaya**. Uprising passion. The second of the Four Noble Truths (q.v.).

**Sange** (J.). Contrition (q.v.).

**Sangha**. The Buddhist order. Sometimes the term only covers monks and nuns, sometimes, especially in Western countries, lay and ordained Buddhists together.

**Sanjin** (J.). Three minds. The qualities with which nembutsu (q.v.) should be practised. They are: shijoshin, jinshin, and ekohotsuganshin.

**Sarana**. Refuge.

**Shakyamuni**. Sage (muni) of the Shakyan people. An epithet of Siddhartha Gotama (q.v.).

**Shamatha**. Meditation that brings tranquility. See also: chih, vipashyana.

**Shan Tao**. Pre-eminent Chinese Pureland master. Lived 613-681.

**Shariputra**. Leading disciples of Shakyamuni and friend of Ananda (q.v.).

**Shijoshin** (J.). Sincerity. One of the sanjin (q.v.).

**Shimmitsu** (J.). Intimacy. Faith that is hidden in one's heart. See also: shinjin, anjin, bodaishin.

**Shin** (J.). (1) Faith. Contraction of shinjin (q.v.). (2) Mind. Heart. See also: bodaishin, sanjin. (3) True. See also: Jodoshin-shu.

**Shinjin** (J.). Faith. Prasada (q.v.). Especially the enlightening experience of the sudden awakening of faith. Religious rapture and conversion. See also: anjin.

**Shinko** (J.). Heart light. Grace that comes to oneself alone. Cf. Joko. See also: ko.

**Shinran**. Disciple of Honen Shonin (q.v.). Teacher to whom the Jodoshin-shu (q.v.) school traces its origins. He lived 1173-1263.

**Shonin** (J.). Saint.

**Shraddha**. Faith. See also: prasada.

**Shunyata**. Emptiness. A central Buddhist doctrine especially associated with Nagarjuna (q.v.), according to which nothing is self sufficiently existent. See also: dependent origination.

**Siddhartha Gotama**. The historical Buddha, founder of the Buddhist religion.

**Sila**. Morality.

**Skandhas**. See: Five skandhas.

**Smaller Pureland Sutra**. Shortest of the three Pureland Sutras (q.v.). It describes the Pure Land (q.v.) of Amida (q.v.) and recounts how all Buddhas praise that land.

**Smriti**. Mindfulness. Keeping in mind. Remembrance, especially of Buddha, Dharma and Sangha. See also: buddhanusmriti.

**Smritimant**. Mindful.

**Soto Zen**. A denomination of Zen Buddhism founded by Dogen (q.v.).

**Stupa**. Burial mound. Stupas were the main focus of early Buddhist devotionalism.

**Sukhavati**. The "sweet realm". The Pure Land (q.v.) of Amida (q.v.).

**Sutra**. Buddhist scripture, especially one recording the words of Shakyamuni Buddha. The word literally means "thread". The sutras are the threads of teaching. See also: Tripitaka.

**Tai Shih Chi** (Chin.). Bodhisattva of creativity. One of the two attendant bodhisattvas who assist Amida Buddha. See also: Quan Shi Yin.

**Tannisho**. A work compiling sayings of Shinran (q.v.), lamenting deviations in doctrine. Much used by Jodoshin-shu Buddhists.

**Tao Cho**. Chinese Pureland Master. Teacher of Shan Tao (q.v.). He lived 562-645.

**Tariki** (J.) Other power. Grace. Amida (q.v.). The doctrine that it is not by one's own power that one attains spiritual enlightenment. See also: jiriki.

**Tathagata**. One who goes to and comes from tathata (q.v.). Bestower of grace.

**Tathata**. Thusness. A synonym of Dharma (q.v.).

**Tendai** (J.). School of Japanese Buddhism, centred on Mount Hiei (q.v.), derived from the Tien Tai School in China. Honen Shonin (q.v.) and Shinran Shonin (q.v.) were both Tendai monks in their early life.

**Theravada**. Way of the elders. The school of Buddhism that predominates in Sri Lanka, Myanmar, Thailand, Laos and Cambodia.

**Three bodies**. See: trikaya.

**Three darknesses**. Distraction, defensiveness and destruction. See also: dukkha, dark world.

**Tien Tai** (Chin.). A mountain in China that gave its name to the school of Buddhism centred there. The Tien Tai School was, for a time, the pre-eminent school of Chinese Buddhism, especially under the influence of its greatest teacher, Chih I (q.v.). Tien Tai practice included both verbal and contemplative nembutsu (q.v.).

**Tree minds**. See: Sanjin.

**Three poisons**. Greed, hate and delusion.

**Three Pureland Sutras**. The most revered scriptures in the Amidist tradition. They are: The Larger Pureland Sutra, the Smalled Pureland Sutra, and the Contemplation Sutra (q.v.).

**Three refuges**. The main focus of devotion in Buddhism. They are: Buddha, Dharma and Sangha (q.v.).

**Three signs**. The doctrinal formula: sarva samskara anitya, sarva samskara dukkha, sarva dharma anatma. It means: all confections are impermanent, all confections are spiritually dangerous, all instances of grace are independent of self. See also: anatma, anitya, dharma, dukkha, samskara.

**Trikaya**. The trinitarian doctrine of Mahayana Buddhism. A Buddha has three bodies or persons called Dharmakaya (q.v.), Sambhogakaya (q.v.) and Nirmanakaya (q.v.). Dharmakaya is beginningless and endless, the Unborn (q.v.). Sambhogakaya begins with the appearance of a Buddha in this world and is potentially endless. Nirmanakaya is the appearance of a Buddha in this world and has a beginning and an end.

**Tripitaka**. Three baskets or collections of Buddhist scripture. They are: sutra, vinaya and abhidharma (q.v.).

**Uji** (J.). For the time being. Title of a text by Dogen (q.v.).

**Unborn**. The eternal. The spiritual. Nirvana (q.v.).

**Upaya**. Skilful or tactful means. Teachings adjusted to the capacity of the listener. All Buddha's actions are upaya. See also: Lotus Sutra.

**Upeksha**. Equanimity. One of the four immeasurables (q.v.).

**Vaidehi**. Queen of Maghada (q.v.) and protagonist of the Contemplation Sutra (q.v.). Although a laywoman she has a vision of Sukhavati (q.v.).

**Vairochana**. A Buddha commonly taken as personifying the Dharmakaya (q.v.) aspect of Buddhahood.

**Vedana**. Reaction to rupa (q.v.). Jumping to conclusions. Superficial knowingness. Second of the five skandhas (q.v.).

**Verbal nembutsu**. Utterance out loud of the name of a Buddha, especially Amida. This practice gradually replaced contemplative nembutsu (q.v.) in the history of Pureland.

**Verticalism**. Worldly thinking in which everything is measured on some scale of relative worth.

**Vidya**. Radiance. Seeing. Being awake to Dharma (q.v.).

**Vijnana**. Mentality, especially the mentality that sees the world from a self-centred perspective. One of the five skandhas (q.v.).

**Vinaya**. Buddhist monastic discipline. Scriptures recording such discipline. A school of Buddhism in which such discipline plays the central role. See also: Tripitaka.

**Vipashyana**. Meditation that brings insight. See also: shamatha, quan.

248

**Vows**. See: Amida's vows.

**Yugen** (J.). A quality of subtle meaning in works of art imparting irony, profundity or bittersweetness.

**Zen** (J.). A group of schools of Buddhism of Buddhism in Japan that emphasise meditation practice. See also Soto Zen, Rinzai Zen.

[1] Batchelor S. (1983) Alone with Others: An existential approach to Buddhism. New York: Grove Press

[2] I owe much of my thinking on the horizontal and vertical to discussions with Japanese friends of whom I would like to particularly acknowledge, in the context, Takemaro Shigeraki sensei.

[3] Women's Royal Air Force

[4] Kidd S.M. (2002) *The Secret Life of Bees*. Viking Press

[5] *Tannisho*, ch II, translated by Kosho Konyo Otani, Tokyo: Honganji International Buddhist Study Center 1991, p.19.

**O books**
O is a symbol of the world, of oneness and unity. In different cultures it also means the "eye", symbolizing knowledge and insight, and in Old English it means "place of love or home". O books explores the many paths of understanding which different traditions have developed down the ages, particularly those today that express respect for the planet and all of life. In philosophy, metaphysics and aesthetics O as zero relates to infinity, indivisibility and fate. In Zero Books we are developing a list of provocative shorter titles that cross different specializations and challenge conventional academic or majority opinion.

For more information on the full list of over 300 titles please visit our website
**www.O-books.net**

**myspiritradio** is an exciting web, internet, podcast and mobile phone global broadcast network for all those interested in teaching and learning in the fields of body, mind, spirit and self development.  Listeners can

hear the show online via computer or mobile phone, and even download their favourite shows to listen to on MP3 players whilst driving, working, or relaxing.

**Feed your mind, change your life with O Books,**
The O Books radio programme carries interviews with most authors, sharing their wisdom on life, the universe and everything...e mail questions and co-create the show with O Books and myspiritradio.

Just visit **www.myspiritradio.com** for more information.

# SOME RECENT O BOOKS

## The Other Buddhism
### Amida comes West
Caroline Brazier

The Pureland schools are the largest Buddhist denominations in Japan, and yet this approach to Buddhism is hardly known in the West. Pureland centres on our relationship with Amida Buddha, the embodiment of measureless love, light and life. It offers a fresh view of spirituality, recognising us in our mundane lives, whilst lifting us into relationship with the eternal. As ordinary people, we cannot fathom our own depths nor can we know the immensity of the universe. We can but stand in awe and reach out to what we intuitively know to be beyond the small orbit of our lives. Pureland is a path of simplicity and beauty, poetry and nature. It is the path of faith.

*In this profound work, Caroline Brazier looks at the apparent opposites of Pure Land Buddhism and psychotherapeutic practice in a deep and unifying manner. Leading us gently but firmly, she shows how the Other-power – which is the essence of the Pure Land (Jodo) Path – can be a vital factor in a full restoration of the harmony of self. The result is not only an essential book for Buddhists, for students of religion, and for therapists of all schools, but for anyone who seeks an improved ability to cope with the stresses of our everyday world.* **Jim Pym**, editor of *Pure Land Notes*, and author of *You Dont Have to Sit on the Floor*.

Caroline Brazier is a practicing psychotherapist , a senior ordained member of the Amida Order, a Pureland Buddhist community and a founder of Amida Trust.

978 1 84694 052 1 **£11.99  $24.95**